ARE WE *IN* TIME?

Northwestern University
Topics in Historical Philosophy

General Editors David Kolb
                 John McCumber

Associate Editor Anthony J. Steinbock

ARE WE *IN* TIME?

And Other Essays on Time and Temporality

Charles M. Sherover

Edited and with a preface by Gregory R. Johnson

Northwestern University Press
Evanston, Illinois

Northwestern University Press
Evanston, Illinois 60208-4210

Printed in the United States of America

10 9 8 7 6 5 4 3 2 1

ISBN 0-8101-1944-7 (cloth)
ISBN 0-8101-1945-5 (paper)

Library of Congress Cataloging-in-Publication Data

Sherover, Charles M.
    Are we in time? : and other essays on time and temporality / Charles M.
Sherover ; Edited and with a preface by Gregory R. Johnson.
        p. cm.
    Includes bibliographical references and index.
    ISBN 0-8101-1944-7 (alk. paper) — ISBN 0-8101-1945-5 (pbk. : alk. paper)
    1. Time. I. Johnson, Gregory R. II. Title.
BD638 .S528 2003
115—dc21
                                                            2002151125

To the memory of Josephine

Contents

Preface

When I first encountered Charles M. Sherover's essays on the philosophy of time, I was impressed that here is a philosopher who takes time seriously. Sherover's tight focus on time is not, however, an example of mere academic overspecialization, for he shows us that by taking time seriously we can discover something essential to almost every question of human concern. Thus Sherover deals with time and cognition, time and morality, time and action, time and physical nature, time and being, time and God, time and freedom, and time and politics. Sherover's essays show the influence of Royce, Heidegger, Kant, Leibniz, and even Rousseau, Hartshorne, and Bergson. But they defy categorization by method or school. Sherover does not believe that a comprehensive definition of time in itself is possible. Nor does he try to reduce the diversity of temporal phenomena to a single, privileged, originary time. Sherover sees all such concerns as merely distractions from taking time seriously.

The essays in this volume are not just about time, they were written "in" time: at different times, for different audiences, at different stages of the development of the author's thinking. Thus it is inevitable that they overlap in some places and diverge in others. They may even contradict one another here and there. However, since all the essays deal with the omnipresence of time and change, it was easy to resist the temptation to edit them into a systematic, timeless whole.

Despite their diversity, the essays in this volume fall into four natural divisions.

Part 1, "First Considerations," offers an overview of the history of thought on time and some essential conceptual distinctions.

The first essay, "The Concept of Time in Western Thought," is based on a lecture delivered at the Smithsonian Institution in Washington, D.C. Here Sherover surveys the history of Western philosophic thought on time from Parmenides and Heraclitus—whose role in giving rise to two divergent strands of thought on time is often overlooked—

to Whitehead and Heidegger, giving pivotal place to Plotinus and Augustine. Sherover also lays out a number of important distinctions, one of the most significant being between the time of nature and the time of man: of causal processes in the physical world on the one hand and of human thinking, planning, and deciding on the other. The temporal flow of natural processes is from the past through the present to the future. The temporal flow of human action moves in the opposite direction, from future to present to past. The temporality of nature is a push from behind into what lies ahead. It is the temporality of causal determinism, causes coming before effects, effects coming after causes in an endless chain. Freedom, according to Sherover, has its own temporality. Human freedom exists insofar as we are presently confronted with different possibilities for temporal development; we can and must decide on which possibilities to make actual and which to discard. Once we decide on a new course of action into the future, it creates a new present that becomes past. This distinctive temporality was first discerned by Plotinus and Augustine.

The second essay, "Talk of Time," clarifies an important distinction in the ways we speak of the relationship of events. We can say that *a* was before *b* and *c* was after *b*. Once such a statement is true, it is always true. It may be a statement about time, but its truth is timeless and unchanging. On the other hand, when we say that an event has not yet happened, but will happen, we are speaking about the future. If the predicted event does indeed happen, it will soon pass from the perceiving person's expectation to his present and then as past reside in his memory. The truth of any statement about such an event changes with time. It is for this reason that statements with fixed dates, which are in a before-and-after ordering, are regarded as objective, while those in which the tense changes with the time of the perceiver are seen as subjective. But the question remains as to which perspective is primary.

Part 2, "A Kantian Rethinking of Some Kant," is a critical appropriation of Kant. Sherover takes Kant seriously, because Kant took time seriously. Kant is the first thinker to recognize that all human experience has a temporal form. Indeed, Sherover thinks of himself as a kind of Kantian. Thus Sherover's critique of Kant is an internal critique, a friendly critique that seeks to expand the Kantian outlook, not replace it.

The third essay, "The Question of Noumenal Time," is an ingenious critique of a central incoherence of Kant's thought. In the *Critique of Pure Reason,* Kant argued that time is the prime form of our sensory outlook and the form of all consciousness. All that we see outside us must appear as both spatial and temporal; all the elements of inner life—our thoughts, recollections, hopes, fears, and joys—must appear to us merely as temporal, as before and after one another in what Locke called the "train of ideas." Since Kant held that free will, the immortal soul, and God lie beyond the limits of possible sense experience, they lie "outside" of time. Yet the free will is somehow supposed to decide, and decision is an action, and actions take time. Eternal life is supposed to be an unending progress toward moral perfection, and progress takes time. God too is supposed to enjoy not a timeless existence, but an unending duration. Kant is careful to speak of duration (*Dauer*) as opposed to time (*Zeit*), but durations take time. Therefore, contrary to his own protestations Kant must presuppose some kind of time beyond the realm of possible human experience. Sherover not only argues that Kant must embrace the idea of noumenal time but also that he can do so without compromising the coherence of the Critical project.

The fourth essay, "Time and Ethics: How Is Morality Possible?" extends the argument of "The Question of Noumenal Time." Sherover argues that Kant's moral philosophy depends on the reality of freedom, and freedom is impossible unless time is real. Then Sherover uses the lens of Heidegger to discover in Kant traces of an understanding of the distinctive temporality of human freedom. Kant did not, however, fully develop these intimations. Nor did he integrate them into his account of human being in *this* world.

The fifth essay, "Experiential Time and the Religious Concern," shows the temporal import of Kant's three central philosophical questions: "What can I know?" "What should I do?" and "What can I hope for?" Sherover uses these three questions to ground his most extensive discussion of theological matters. Like Kant, Sherover argues that belief in God and immortality cannot be established by theoretical reason, but can be established by practical reason and made consistent with theoretical reason. Sherover then argues that if our belief in God is founded on practical reason, then the characteristics we are entitled to attribute to God must be based upon practical reason as well. We must be able to relate to God in the activity of living. Thus he stands with Pascal for a God of living religion, not a God of the theologians. He questions the basis for belief in an infinitely transcendent God who can be spoken of only in negations.[1] God must be close enough for us to worship, intelligible enough for us to understand in positive terms. God must, therefore, be a finite being "in" time who, although very wise, beneficent, and powerful, is neither omniscient nor omnipotent.

Part 3, "Metaphysics—as If Time Matters," is a valuable corrective to the dominant metaphysical tradition that talks about being as if time does not matter. Sherover offers temporal answers to such metaphysical questions as being, internal relations, individuation, mind, free will, and the distinction between potentiality and possibility.

The title essay, "Are We *in* Time?" is an essay in ontology. It asks: "What does it mean to-be?" Sherover's response is: "To-be means to be temporal." From the originary depths of German idealism, Sherover retrieves the basic presumption of the theory of internal relations, i.e., that all things are intrinsically related to each other, but rejects its traditional confinement to the theory of formal logic. Sherover maintains that temporal predicates inhere in the essential definition of each and every thing that exists. Thus the short answer to the essay title's question is a simple "no." We are not in time because time is in us. Sherover sees this suggested by Leibniz's notion that all things are in a continuing dynamic relationship with each other; and Kant seems to have suggested something like this when he said that time is the form of inner sense—and thereby of all consciousness. Like Peirce, Lotze, Bergson, and James, Sherover distrusts all spatial metaphors for time. Like them, he sees time as sui generis. It cannot be defined by differentiation from a higher genus. Time is not a kind of space. Time is time. Although time can be "defined" only tautologically, Sherover believes that the human experience of time can be phenomenologically described in some detail.

The seventh essay, "Perspectivity and the Principle of Continuity," develops several themes of the title essay in relation to the question of individuation: the individuation of spans of time and the individuation of temporal processes. Like Kant, Sherover affirms the Leibnizian principle of continuity. There are no gaps in the processes of nature and mind. Both knower and known are subsumed in the continuity of temporal becoming. The principle of continuity thus bridges the Cartesian duality of mind and nature with which modernity began. Sherover explains how the continuum is cut, how entities and spans of awareness are individuated, in terms of "perspectivity." The continuum is cut by means of individual and social interpretive decisions. These decisions themselves arise out of the continuity of life, whether they be pragmatic responses to the exigencies of life or appropriations, creative or conventional, of one's cultural heritage.

The eighth essay, "*Res Cogitans:* The Time of Mind," is a Heideggerian retrieval of Cartesian dualism. Descartes divided the cosmos into physical and mental substances. Descartes had defined physical substance in essentially spatial terms—as extended—and as subject to deterministic laws of mathematical physics. When it came to mental substance, however, Descartes defined it in essentially negative terms, as what is not physical. The only positive description he offers of mental substance is *res cogitans,* "thinking being." This is Sherover's point of departure for his most detailed phenomenology of the temporality of consciousness. On this basis he questions the meaningfulness of the ideas of timeless consciousness, timeless truth, and timeless being. If physical being is defined spatially and is subject to deterministic laws, thinking being must be understood in temporal terms and as free to choose between different possibilities for development. The phenomenology of the temporality of cognition and freedom is implied by Descartes's introspective method coupled with his belief in the reality of freedom and his dualistic ontology.

The ninth essay, "Toward Experiential Metaphysics: Radical Temporalism," is a programmatic overview of Sherover's philosophical path from the experience of time to the reality of time. After discussing the pervasively temporal nature of cognition, decision, and freedom, Sherover faces the question of whether they are grounded in time, processes, and possibilities that exist objectively, that exist "in themselves" and not merely "for us." As a good Kantian, Sherover rejects the possibility of ever strictly knowing the answer to this question. But as a good Kantian, he is also entitled to speculate, particularly where such questions touch on moral concerns. Thus Sherover argues that possibility, freedom, futurity, and time are necessarily real, insofar as this presupposition best accounts for the nature of our experience of ourselves as knowers but above all as actors.

Part 4, "Time, Freedom, and the Common Good," takes its title from Sherover's treatise on political philosophy. The tenth essay, "The Temporality of the Common Good: Futurity and Freedom," can be regarded as a sketch of that book. Sherover argues that the common good of a society depends upon employing both its freedom and its collective wisdom in assessing the possibilities given to it. These phenomena are intrinsically related to each other. The fulfillment of each involves the other two.

A society is not to be understood spatially, as a collection of contiguous individuals. Our fellow citizens can be far away, and strangers can be in our midst. Individuals belong to a society by sharing a common history. As Royce pointed out, society is based on temporal continuity, not spatial contiguity. Likewise, the relationship of the individual to society cannot be understood spatially, in terms of the relationship of parts to wholes, a metaphor that leads either to an atomistic individualism or a mystical collectivism. Instead, individuality must be understood in temporal terms, as the development of self-consciousness within a developing social context. Such a perspective grants both the developmental priority of the society over the individual (the individual develops in a social context) and the teleological priority of the individual over society (the aim of society is the cultivation of the autonomous and self-actualized individual).

Freedom is futural. Freedom means having real options. Our past—our education, our socialization—can make us freer by providing us with knowledge and skills, augmenting the potentialities that we bring to bear on objective possibilities. Freedom is a precondition for all distinctly human characteristics and activities: rationality, dignity, responsibility, creativity, action, work, and so on. Freedom, therefore, is the highest and the deepest value, because it makes all other values possible. But freedom is always finite. Its exercise is based on objective, enabling social conditions. True freedom exists under law. It is "positive" rather than merely a "negative" liberty. Some social arrangements make us freer than others. Sherover argues that the freest form of society is a representative republic with a market economy moderated by rules that regard the common good as taking priority whenever it may conflict with the unhampered liberties of individual citizens.

In the final essay, "The Process of Polity," Sherover expands upon his temporal account of freedom, offering a concrete definition of positive freedom as one's mastery over one's own time. A free society allows its citizens to make use of their own time. An unfree society monopolizes the citizens' time. Sherover uses this distinction to argue for the superiority of representative republicanism over a direct participatory democracy. Direct democracy, as practiced in ancient Athens, made such demands on the time of citizens that it restricted their freedom. It also restricted the freedom of others, for the time the citizens spent on politics was purchased with the work of slaves. Representative republicanism, by allowing a few accomplished individuals to represent the many in political matters, not only gives the citizens free time, but also undermines the necessity of slavery.

Sherover also shows the dangers of thinking of social time in spatial terms. The idea of "social engineering" rests upon a false "spatial" conception of time. The future is seen as a "place" we are trying to arrive at. The paths by which we arrive are different from the destination. This encourages the idea that ends are independent of means, specifically, that good ends can be pursued by evil means. The future is not, however, a determinate place we can seek out by different routes. The future is a realm of possibilities. Different means will create different ends. In other words, there is a continuity of time—a continuity, not a disjunction, between means and ends. The continuity of time also forecloses both reactionary and revolutionary forms of politics. Time marches on. The reactionary can neither halt nor reverse its flow. The past, like the future, is not a place to which we can return. The past is alive only in the present. Traditions can be honored only by constantly appropriating them in new ways. By the same token, the future is not a different place, but something we create out of the present, just as the present was created in the past. One cannot make a radical break with the past any more than one can outrun one's own shadow.

Gregory R. Johnson
Berkeley, California

Acknowledgments

The following essays come out of classes, as student or teacher, discussions with teachers, students, colleagues, friends, and fellow conferees too numerous to mention. Of all who are entitled to thanks, let me just mention those few with a direct connection to what is in this collection.

To a physicist, Professor Lawrence Fagg, I owe the invitation to deliver the Smithsonian lecture and his kindly retrieving a copy for me when my only copy was lost. He and I met at one of the sessions of the International Society for the Study of Time, an interdisciplinary organization whose meetings invariably produced rare intellectual fare and often inspiration and insights, as developments in one academic field shed light on those in another. The essays of mine that were originally published in one of the volumes entitled *The Study of Time* emerged from papers originally delivered at one of the International Society's sessions. I am deeply indebted to Dr. J. T. Fraser for inducting me into the Society (which he founded) and for the numerous discussions we had over the years. I am grateful to all the publications in which these essays were first published; they are duly credited in the notes for this volume.

I want to express my deep appreciation to Dr. Gregory R. Johnson for his interest and patience in working with me to put together this collection of essays, editing them, and providing the preface and index; without Greg I doubt that I would have been able to complete this collection over the course of a long illness. I am also grateful to Basil Paules, who helped with the original presentation while I was hospitalized. Last but certainly not least, I want to express warm thanks to Susan Harris for her enthusiastic encouragement in initiating this project, and to Susan Betz and Rachel Zonderman for helping us see it through.

Charles M. Sherover
Santa Fe, New Mexico

Part 1

First Considerations

1

The Concept of Time
in Western Thought

The question of time is central to most of our intellectual concerns. But our questions about time are not themselves timeless. The way we think about time comes out of a long temporal development, the historic development of the culture that has nurtured us. For this reason, an overview of the history of the concepts of time is helpful when we try to think through its meaning for us today. Indeed, it was concern with the nature of time and change that first provoked the Western development of rational thinking about the world, the rational thinking out of which came three aspects of Western culture: the reflective tradition of philosophy, the investigative tradition of science, and the political tradition of citizen government. As central as questions of the nature of time and change have continued to be, it is only recently that Western philosophy has taken the fact of time with full seriousness.

Before launching into this review of some prime landmarks along the way, let me ask that one general fact be kept in mind. From time immemorial, the pervasive human encounter with time was gauged not in quantitative but in qualitative terms. Our earliest ancestors gauged the passage of time by their perception of the Sun's movement across the heavens. Differentiation of day from night was marked by the presence or absence of sunlight. Consider what this means: the duration of each day, and of each night, varies with the season. In the Northern Hemisphere, the span of day-time is longer in the summer and shorter in the winter. No two successive days are mathematically identical. When we divide the duration between sunrise and sunset into one set of twelve hours and the duration between sunset and sunrise into another twelve hours, as the ancient Greeks had already done, a day-time hour lasts much longer in summer than the same hour in winter; the durations of day-time and night-time hours continually vary as the seasons change.

For most of recorded history—in ancient Greece and ancient China—the sundial, not the mechanical watch, provided the key to the passing of the hours. If you pace a sundial with a wristwatch it quickly becomes apparent that a sundial reports no two hours of any successive days as mathematically equal. The contemporary tendency to equalize the moments of time as arithmetically equivalent, to quantify time in terms of irreducible moments of equal duration, is of very recent vintage—and raises a host of new questions.

The experience of variable time periods is profoundly authentic and, despite our contemporary dependence on mechanical clocks, still governs our outlook. When we turn from the way we measure the passage of time to the way we actually experience it, we find that our experience of time is still tied to the quality of events. Whether expressed in terms of time or of change, this qualitative kind of experience characterizes "lived time," "felt time," the time of our lives.

Two fundamentally different ways of understanding time were present at the beginning of Western thought. According to the Greeks, time was a cycle and was pictured as moving around the circumference of a circle. By contrast, in the biblical view, time flows in one direction and can be depicted as an arrow. Let us look at each in turn.

Among the early Greeks, there were two opposed schools of thought on the question of time, the Ionians and the Eleatics. Both schools, however, agreed on two basic points. They both agreed that time is experienced as a cycle of change and that any attempt to understand it should be guided by their newborn faith in the power of reason. Beyond that, they were divided. Their principal dispute was whether time is part of the reality of the world or is an illusion. The opposition between the Ionian and Eleatic schools still underlies many contemporary debates—even on issues far removed from this immediate concern. By setting out the issues between them, we gain a key to understanding the issues bequeathed to us, as well as what is behind the differences between Plato and Aristotle, who together finally shaped the form of all subsequent Western thinking. For the sake of brevity, let us contrast the thinking of Heraclitus, who spoke for the Ionians, with that of Parmenides, the foremost thinker of the Eleatic school.

The Ionians—Greeks who settled on what is now the Asian coast of Turkey, centered on the town of Ephesus—took the pervasive experience of continual change as profoundly real. Every particular thing, they noted, is in a continual process of change. All things seem to be changing, even if at what we today call different "rates." But if things change, then we must have a conception of past and future by which to distinguish the stages of change. So, if change is real, then time is also real; we can only talk of one in terms of the other. Only by distinguishing a "before" from an "after" can we note a sequence of change. Time and change then become reciprocal concepts: we only become aware of one by means of the other.

To this first elemental observation they added another: changes do not seem to be haphazard or chaotic. Each changing thing seems to follow orderly sequences of change; if we can understand the reason for these orderly sequences, we can then anticipate the future state of a thing by distinguishing its past from its present state. The world of things, always changing, seems to incorporate rules of regularity: acorns become oak trees which then provide lumber; babies become adults who eventually become corpses. The sequence of change seems to be governed by some principle, law, rule, or guiding force that renders the multiplicity of change in an ordered way of directional development.

Biological development transpires in the natural environment, which itself seems to follow regular patterns of change. Epitomized in the sequence of the seasons, we see that spring follows winter, winter follows fall, fall follows summer, and summer follows spring in an unending pattern without beginning or end. Seeds are planted in spring, grown in summer; their fruit, reaped in fall, tides us over through the sparsity of winter. The cycle of the seasons displays the regularity that governs changing phenomena and the activities humans undertake in response to them. And so Heraclitus urged that there is a kind of rationality—a supreme reason, principle, or Logos—that governs the regularity of the environment and of the patterns of change we experience within it.

If we take the cycle of the seasons as our prototype, as virtually all premodern thinkers did, we note that while the change of seasons is continual, so is the pattern of human responses to them: the farmer's activities are guided by them. The particular generations of farmers continually change, but the patterns of seasonal activity continue without change. Some thinkers apparently took this cycle of the seasons as a prototype and concluded that the regularity of the pattern was more important than the particular farmers and plants abiding by it. The focus of explanation was not, then, on the particular activities that transpired, but on the patterns they exemplified. The burden of explanation was shifted from the particular to the general, from "this farmer" to "any farmer." The pattern, what was common to all farmers, was to be regarded as an explanation and the activity of any particular farmer as merely an example, an instantiation, of the general or universal pattern of activity.

Although particular farmers and plants died and were replaced, the pattern of activity they represented was as unending as the cycle of the seasons. This cycle, whether we look forward or backward, seems to be endless. The cycle of change, whether in nature or in man, appeared to be without beginning or end. Time then appeared to be literally forever—without beginning or end—but governing a cycle of change that, like a circle, has no beginning or end. But "forever" is what we mean by the word "eternity." Out of this elemental experience of time one notion of eternity—of selfsame activity without any progression—soon thrust itself forth. In due course, this cyclical notion of ongoing time was to become Aristotle's notion of eternity, an eternity of endless time, an eternity of time-bound change that conformed to a nontemporal cycle or pattern of sequential development, without temporal beginning or end. The non-changing but ever-recurrent patterns of change were deemed more important than the changing individual persons and things. But, ironically, the question was at least rhetorically raised: what is being accomplished? What is the point of this continuing selfsame pattern of continual change?

Heraclitus, the great pioneer of the notion of an eternal dynamic becoming, sometimes invoked the standard Greek notion of endless cyclical change. But he also seems to have dimly seen that every actor is affected by what he brings to pass, that if time and change are real, then the causes or principles or governing laws of those changes will themselves be modified by the processes they bring about. Taking fire as the symbol of the continuity of change, he at least raised the possibility that even the divine law of change, and therefore the divine itself, must itself somehow change; as he stated it, "God . . . changes like fire when it mingles with the smoke of incense" (Frag. 67). So, we are given the question of whether the Law of Change changes, or to put it into a more modern theistic terminology: if God is the author of all change, is God immune to the processes of time, or does God himself change?

However this may be, the view Heraclitus encapsulated comes to this: change and thereby time are a real aspect of the world we experience and permeate every existent entity; change is not chaotic, but is governed by a Law or Logos which explains the regularity of its patterns. Whether this governing Law or Logos is itself changing was a question that for the most part was waived aside.

The attack on Heraclitean dynamism was soon launched by Greek thinkers who had settled in southern Italy. The Pythagoreans were fascinated, not by the world of change, but by the number system which cannot change. The fathers of mathematics, their focus was not on the changing world but on rational principles that are seen as absolutely changeless. Their successors were the Eleatic philosophers whose prime spokesman, Parmenides, focused not on the continuity of dynamic change that one experiences, but on the presumed regularity of the laws invoked as explanations of those changes. They insisted that these governing laws, such as the laws of arithmetic, cannot change. That is to say, they are immune to time-marked changes; they are literally eternal. Eternal, please note, *not as unendingly time-bound,* but as beyond all time, as immune from all temporal description, devoid of all temporal predicates or location, as absolutely time-*less.* The patterns of change, conceived as changeless governing laws, were seen as providing the complete explanation of the changing details of the world. This very different notion of "eternity," as literally devoid of time, was to become Plato's.

Time and eternity—two seemingly independent but truly reciprocal themes—run through the course of Western philosophic thought. But they are often confused in our language with two radically different sets of meanings. The Heracliteans (and the Aristotelians) hold that time is the reality of the continuity of changing experience, of being, of reality, and that eternity is merely a name for endless time, an endless continuity of the patterns of change. The Parmenideans (and the Platonists) hold that eternity is a changeless reality, the principle of Being itself, the set of unchanging governing Laws or true Ideas which describe the unchanging patterns of change and on which our experience of change depends. In this Platonistic view, the particular changing things we experience are merely how things appear to a misguided time-bound perspective; change is but an illusion of the human outlook, which depends upon literally unchanging laws to explain the continually changing content of what appears before it. The question between them is whether the appearances of change that form our experience are truly real—or are they merely the illusions we accept until we recognize the unchangeability of everything fundamental to the constitution of the universe?

The ongoingness of time and change—whether regarded by Heraclitus as our reality explained by a Logos incarnate within it, or by Parmenides as the pale, disordered reflection of a changeless eternal Being—was still regarded as essentially cyclical. For both, the patterns of change were ongoing; the patterns themselves were explanatory and the particularities of change—which farmer is sowing which particular seeds of wheat—were what needed explanation. For both, even as they directed their focus to contrary ends of this spectrum—even as Heraclitus seemed to suggest that the explanation was immanent in the world, and Parmenides that it was somehow transcendent above the world—time was not conceived as developmental or as evolutionary, but as essentially repetitive in nature, an "eternal return of the same," as Nietzsche was to come to describe it.

Yet, as we have seen, in Heraclitus' notion of an immanent Logos there seemed implicit some notion of developmental change. For it was one of his disciples, Anaxagoras, the first of the "pre-Socratics" to venture forth onto the streets of Athens, who transformed it into a developmental temporal metaphysic, implicitly accepting the biblical notion of a directional time that was not cyclical but developmental. For Anaxagoras speculated that if there were a supreme Mind (Nous) to set experiential reality into motion, then the consequence is a continually unidirectional developing universe. Even if all might have been set at the beginning, change would be endemic to reality and the continuity of developmental novelty would pervade the content of all subsequent experience. So before the entrance of biblical thought into the Western intellectual development, the question of whether time itself was cyclical or developmental had already been introduced, even if that question was immediately set aside.

However this might have been developed, Anaxagoras, albeit on other grounds, was subjected to a bitter condemnation by Socrates, and the course of Western philosophic thought on time was set. Plato took up the Parmenidean vision of a timeless eternity governing the world of change. Time was to be understood in Plato's classic phrase as but "the moving image of eternity," a rational principle introduced into the physical world to govern the direction of change. And all temporal events were to be explained as examples, instantiations, or copies of the eternal Ideas or laws of Being that timelessly constitute ultimate Reality and timelessly govern a derivative world of change. No thing or process is to be explained in its own terms; each changing thing is to be explained only as an incarnation or example of nontemporal, timeless, eternal laws.

It was not long before Aristotle wondered how we could explain the changing by means of the changeless, the temporal by means of the nontemporal; but he seems finally to have accepted the inherent cyclicity of all change, the view that the temporal course of experience is truly modeled on the cycle of the seasons in which patterns of activity continually recur without substantive qualitative change. His departure from Platonic atemporalism seems in the end to have been, despite his taking the historicity and particularity of actual experience more seriously, to look for recurrent explanatory patterns over longer stretches of experienced time.

What then is time itself? In the end, Aristotle described time as nothing in itself, but merely the way we "measure motion," the way we "measure the difference between before and after," that is, reduce our descriptions of motions to statements of the sequence of change. But some of his side comments suggest that he thought time to be somehow not only more personal but also more cosmic than this.

Whatever other issues may have been raised, whatever differences these two views present, they all shared one common perspective: time is to be seen as the form or structure of the processes that constitute the physical world in which we live and of which we are a part. They generally agreed that time was cyclical—that the future would resemble the past. They disagreed on whether change was to be explained by transcendent nontemporal Laws or Ideas, or whether the principles of change were somehow incarnate within the processes of changing things themselves.

But however explained, time and change were described as referring to things that could be observed; time was *not* taken as referring to our own experiences of those things. In terms of English grammar, the Greek descriptions were third-person statements: statements about what "it" or "they" or "those things" are doing. The next stage in the development of our temporal outlook was to transpose this question of time into the first-person voice of "I" or "we," into the center of personal experience.

Plotinus, the greatest philosopher the Roman Empire produced, died five hundred years after Aristotle. An avowed pagan, he nevertheless had a decisive influence on the Christian introduction of Scripture into the developing Western world. He claimed to be a Platonist and like Plato regarded the universe as essentially a spiritual harmony. Time, he held in Platonic fashion, was but a second-order reality. But even so, it provides the core of every living being. "Time," he said, "is contained in the differentiation of Life." If time is the mark of any living being, then he asked, "Would it, then, not be sound to define Time as the Life of the Soul in movement as it passes from one stage of act or experience to another?" Clearly attacking Aristotle's reduction of time to merely the way in which the changes we perceive are measured, he proposed the alternative—in accord with our everyday use of chronological instruments—that time is not our way of measuring motion or change but rather is a higher order of reality that is itself measured by observable motion or change.[1] Time is the condition of change and thus has a kind of ultimate reality that supervenes over any particular motion or change that transpires within it. Time is not only the form or nature of the world which encompasses continual change. Time also functions within every living being. "Time," he said, "is in every Soul . . . present in like form in all."

And that is why Time can never be broken apart" into the diverse moments that constitute its being.[2] For, note, we do not experience the time of our lives as merely a sequence of moments we mark on a clock; we each regard our own lives as a continuity of coming out of a past and facing a future which we necessarily take as open to our own decisions.

In contrast to the Greek focus on time and change as merely the form of the processes of physical nature, Plotinus pointed out that all living beings experience their own experiences in temporal terms. Plotinus, then, was the first to internalize the question of time.

This internalization, or personalization of time, was quickly developed by Saint Augustine. A convert to Christianity, perhaps the most influential of the Church Fathers, and in many ways the father of "the West," he anguished over the nature not only of time itself but also of our temporal experience of it. In grappling with his quandary, he brought to bear not only the whole of the biblical inheritance which enunciates a chronologically progressive concept of time, but also the philosophy of Plotinus.

At least two factors in the biblical account of the Creation required a new look at the question of time: the first is the biblical postulation of chronological time as opposed to the Greek notion of cyclical time; the second is the temporal nature of the requirement for continuing moral decision. From the opening lines of Genesis to the last lines of Revelation, time is presented as unidirectional, as sequential; time is represented not by the cycle of the seasons but by an arrow that moves in one direction and cannot retreat. On this account, no event can ever be literally repeated; every new moment builds on what went before; the time of things continues from an unrepeatable past into a future that is, at least to us, new and thereby presently unknowable. From Augustine's thesis of chronological time follows a consequence of crucial importance to him: because what-will-be has never been experienced, the future is beyond present knowledge. Yet we are required by the necessity of making decisions to proceed into it. Thus we can only proceed to create the future not with knowledge but with faith.

What specifically seems to have prompted Augustine's anguish over the question of time was the biblical account of the Creation which suggests that time cannot be unending or eternal. God is supposed to have created time along with the physical world and man, and to have used time in this process of construction; the biblical account of the Creation is numbered into seven sequential days. This account quickly leads to the perplexity: "What was God doing *before* he made heaven and earth?" If time is not unending but was created, how can we understand the notion of a "first day"? For what was before it? How can we abjure an unending past, a time before time itself came into being? Or a last day, a day after which nothing occurs!

Augustine's anguish over this question led him to pen one of the most poignant passages in the literature of time, and a question that still perplexes us:

> What then is time? I know what it is if no one asks me what it is; but if I want to explain it to someone who has asked me, I find that I do not know. Nevertheless, I can confidently assert that I know this: that if nothing passed away there would be no past time, and if nothing were coming there would be no future time, and if nothing were now there would be no present time.
>
> But in what sense can we say that those two times, the past and the future exist, when the past no longer is and the future is not yet? Yet if the present were always present and did not go by into the past, it would not be time at all, but [let me add, a Platonistic] eternity. If, therefore, the present (if it is to be time at all) only comes into existence because it is in transition toward the past, how can we say that even the present is? For the cause of its being is that it shall cease to be. So that it appears that we cannot truly say that time exists except in the sense it is tending toward nonexistence.[3]

Assuming the premise of chronological time, at least two crucial queries emerge: first, the ultimate bafflement before the nature of what time itself might be; and second, the way in which our temporal experience meets the pervasively chronological time of the processes of the physical world. Let us look at each in turn.

First, the personal quandary: "I have," Augustine says, "been spilled and scattered among times whose order I do not know." Time emerges as the great mystery, a great mystery that encompasses the nature of the divine creation, the physical world, and even more so, the nature of the self-conscious human being. For even if time forms the processes of physical nature, it also functions at the heart of every human life. Time may indeed be the form of the world in which our experiences are had. But perhaps more profoundly, time is in us—it forms the lives we live and the ways we live them. Time is at the heart of the inmost experiences we have. Time is inseparable from the "I" that every living being feels himself to be. As such, time is at the heart of each person's own reality, the one reality each of us most intimately knows.

With Augustine, we may then reiterate the query: What, then, is time? With Augustine, this is no longer a question merely about the nature of the enveloping cosmos. With Augustine, the question of time is a question about our own being, about the individual selves we experience ourselves to be. It is a question, not only of the external reality within which we experience our own being; it is also a question of the ways in which our own personal experiences are temporally organized: *how we experience our own experiences of self and of world.*

The question of time—no longer cyclical but chronological—has thus been first internalized, and then universalized to include all that is. The nature of time comes into our own time as the core question of every experience we claim to have, of every thing we claim to know. Whether we are dealing with the nature of nature or the nature of the individual self who experiences aspects of nature, the question of the nature of time emerges at the core of every question we can ask.

But a second and perhaps more subtle question is embodied in Augustine's famous passage: How is the temporal structure of human experience itself formed? In answer to this question, Augustine suggested a revolutionary thesis: within the framework of the human outlook, the future comes before the past, and the past is thereby younger than the future. What is must have first been future before it becomes present and only later does it become past. Let me repeat one sentence, and please note the direction of temporal passage: "If, therefore, the present (if it is to be time at all) only comes into existence because it is in transition toward the past, how can we say that even the present *is?*"

We generally speak of the changing process of things as emerging out of the past, entering the present, and then marching on into the future; time, as an arrow, seems to go forward. Augustine did not question this, but in the passage in question, he suggested an additional dimension to temporal experience. When we speak not of what we experience but of our experiencing itself, time does not seem to be what propels us forward; rather, time comes *at us* from ahead; the time of life, Augustine suggested, is like swimming or sailing upstream *against* the current. It is the oncoming current that makes us exert ourselves as we swim or sail into it. If the water were placid, no special direction would be required. If we were merely wafted along with the flow of the stream, no special effort or decision would be required.

But the experience of lived time is that we are continually required to make decisions; indeed, we are compelled to make them—just because the decision not to decide is itself a decision. Think back to any decision you have made, no matter how trivial or profound. The decision was about the future. It projected a future possible situation which did not then exist or a hoped-for future that was threatened unless you acted; once the decision to pursue the selected course was made, that quandary about a future state was resolved by your decision which brought to pass a situation that became actual in the present, and is remembered now as being past. Your decision to leave a room is a commitment to a future time when you will be somewhere else; once you have acted on that decision to leave, your exiting will become your present, and then in turn will be a past event in your life. The direction of decisional development is from a future perceived as possible to a present state that is actual to a past that is remembered.

Temporal experience, then, has two faces that are as integral to it as the two sides of one coin. Existent entities, including ourselves, seem to come out of the past into the present in which we face a presently nonexistent state which we call the future. But it is the openness of the future that forces us to decide what to do about the alternatives we now see as presented. As we look at the objects of experience, we see a progression from past to present to future. But our decisional outlook first looks ahead to what is not yet and then acts to bring it into present actuality and then into the past of recorded fact. To comprehend the complexity of human temporal experience, then, we must come to terms with two opposite forms of temporal flow: (1) the temporal flow of process—from the past through the present into the future, and (2) the flow that animates our decisions from the future through the present into the past.

The implications of this insight are pervasive and have only recently provoked serious thought. This insight brings the pragmatism of the classic American philosophers—Peirce, James, Royce, and Dewey—into communion with the development of European phenomenology and existentialism, which only emerged after the impact of pragmatic thought had been taken up by Continental thinkers. Both have effectively taken up this Augustinian insight: the time of things and the time of human decision flow in opposite directions. Within the human outlook they come together in what we call the living present. On the common ground of this perspective on time, both schools of thought have effectively called into question the legitimacy of efficient causality as the sole mode of rational explanation and have found a ground for the justification of the thesis of human freedom.

However this contemporary development may be resolved, it remains that Saint Augustine had enlarged the question of time to include not only the time of natural processes that we seek to understand, but also the temporal nature of the human understanding itself. The two seem quite distinct from each other, although they need to function in some sort of harmony if the human understanding is to understand itself as well as the processes of those things it seeks to control or direct.

The addition of one new and central question to these others helped initiate the rise of modern thought. In sharp contrast to the others, it arose not out of any attempt to understand nature or man, but as the theoretical

justification of the central technological failure of one of the most crucial inventions in all of human history. I speak, of course, of the invention in thirteenth- and fourteenth-century Germany of the mechanical
clock.

The story of the attempt to replace the sundial with a machine that
can tell time both day and night is a fascinating one. Most narratives lose
themselves in the intricacies of levers and escapements and other ingenious mechanical contrivances. But when we look beyond the technolo-
gist's fascination with its mechanisms, we are tempted to say that no
invention since the wheel has had such a pervasive impact on all subsequent history, and for at least three distinct reasons. (1) It laid the
ground for the Industrial Revolution and all subsequent technology by
requiring a systematic evaluation of different metals for different functions and by initiating the principle of assembly-line production from
standardized parts made by specialized craftsmen, thereby giving rise to
the factory system of industrial production. (2) It broke the hold of feu-
dal values on the new urban centers by governing town life by the intrusive chimes of town hall and cathedral clocks in place of the quiet
rhythm of solar time and thus opened the way for the rise of modern science and philosophy and the revival of civil government which came to
flourish in clock-governed commercial towns. (3) It provided a means of
measuring space precisely in terms of elapsed time—remember Plotinus' argument against Aristotle, that it is time that enables us to measure
change or spatial motion—making possible navigation beyond the sight
of land and thereby enabling the great explorations which opened the
parochial view of a rather closed European world to the globe.

But the mechanical clock had one central technological failure—
which, in its way, was to crown its success. In a pre-computer age, it could
not be made to report the changing duration of each hour in each day
in accordance with the passing of the seasons. Much of early clock-
making was consumed by attempts to do precisely that. Finally, in their
confession of technological failure before the complexities involved, the
clock-makers provided an instrument that ignored the difference between winter and summer days by reporting each hour as composed of
sixty *evenly paced* minutes, each of which was composed of sixty *evenly
paced* seconds. The grudging acceptance of a clock incapable of replicat-
ing the varied time of the sundial changed all inherited temporal parameters. The measurement of time was reduced to arithmetic and was
regarded as infinitely divisible. In the face of all history—reaching back
to ancient China as well as ancient Greece—the mechanical clock proclaimed a new notion of time, an invariable sequence of evenly paced
moments. Clock-time, no longer able to report natural processes as they

were experienced, was now to be used to measure the natural processes themselves as well as the time that humans lived within them. And a new metaphor came upon the scene. The time that had been seen as flowing—flowing as irregularly as any mountain stream—was now made audible in the steady tick-tock of the pendulum. And the new tick-tock time, because it was mathematically describable, came to be regarded as more "objective" than the subjective evaluations of the temporal qualities of experienced events.

It was not long before Descartes, generally regarded as the father of modern thought, took this new notion as axiomatic. Time, now describable in mathematically equal units, was subsumed to geometry. And the spatially drawn line, which can be readily divided into equal distances, became the standard way to represent the passage of time. Just as each segment of a divided line can be considered independently of the rest of the line, Descartes reasoned that each discernible moment stands alone, as an ultimate instant of the cosmic process. The reality of the world was now to be seen as a series of discernible moments, each infinitely divisible and as such each separately sovereign. The durations of any particular thing or process were to be measured against a clock, which imposed a standard and unvarying metric on all that it was called to measure. It would not be long before Sir Isaac Newton took up this new notion and proclaimed that "Absolute, true and mathematical time, of itself, and from its own nature, flows equably without relation" to anything else—and within its encompassing frame, all particular things are to be located.[4] Mathematical time, according to which each transpired moment is arithmetically the equivalent of any other, represents the most creative acceptance of a technological failure; it thenceforth provided the paradigm for the study of physical nature and physical processes.

But how does this all bear on the time of man, that is, not the new mathematical formulation of time which men use for the study of nature, but the notion of time that forms the structure of human living? To face this new question, we must turn to a quick survey of modern temporal thought.

The development of modern philosophy can be seen, in part, as an attempt to reconcile this new notion of an essentially quantitative time to time as we experience it. Descartes had set the stage by completely accepting an arithmetic momentary time, which the new physics quickly adopted. The attempt to square quantitative clock-time with qualitatively felt-time went through three stages.

First, Leibniz, the generally acknowledged genius of the German Enlightenment, quickly repudiated this spatialization of ultimate time.

Time, he insisted, cannot be reduced to an infinite series of points or moments on a line. Time itself is the pure continuity of development—of nature as of man. The particular moments which we use to measure cosmic time are but our own ways of coming to terms with it; they denote an often useful way of talking about it. But time as such is experienced in the continuity of life and development. The life of each one of us is only understood as the continuity of temporal or biographical development. Time is experienced as a continuity of individual development within which past, present, and future appear as the structure of our outlook onto what can be regarded as settled and what is still open for decision.

Second, Kant took up this distinction of time, on the one hand, as the chronology of process which proceeds from the past to the future, and on the other, as a way of making conscious decisions. As a mathematical mode of temporal measurement, the notion of time is merely directed to understanding the observed processes of nature in order to use and direct them. Time, mathematically understood as a series of numerable moments, is but an interpretive artifice to bring physical nature into our own cognitive grasp. By projecting a notion of mathematical time onto nature as it appears to us, we tie it to a notion of efficient causality—that the past produces the future—and then deduce scientific laws by means of which we can understand and interpret the processes of change that seem to describe the natural world so that we can conform to its requirements as we function within it.

But to understand our own selves, Kant urged that we recognize that we are living durational beings who continually experience the need to make responsible decisions; this decision-making capacity is our freedom, which takes us beyond clock-time and the notion of causal determinism bound up with it. We need to understand ourselves as reaching out to a future only dimly perceived while we use our knowledge of past and present causal processes in the physical world around us to anticipate their outcomes, allowing us to inject our own decisions into them and utilize them for our own purposes. Mathematical or quantitative time is not then to be seen as ultimate; it is but a useful artifice—and whether it ultimately describes the nature of the real universe as such, we are in no position to know. But to conduct our own lives as decisional beings, we find it necessary to presume, beyond any possible proof, a kind of ultimate time that sustains our decision-making capacity and our ability to project our own willful decisions onto a future which is beyond all possible human knowledge.

Finally, Fichte and Hegel took Kant's distinction, in their own peculiar ways, to suggest that human time is tied not to physics but to history. History, they maintained, reveals the onward push of human freedom beyond any clock-time descriptions, however useful they may be. What was taken out of Kant was a new crucial divide: one between the onward thrust of natural development, to be explained by the human cognitive understanding in terms of the determinism of strictly efficacious causality, explaining present happenings in terms of causes in the past—and the nature of human decisional freedom in the outlook of practical reason that always looks into the future, and cannot be authentically described by reducing the present to the past.

The question of time had now been tied to the question of freedom and determinism in nature and in man; it had also been tied to questions of the meaning and direction of history. The common scientific understanding of nature is of a process within which each stage is determined by the preceding stage. If we take this literally, then any present is already determined by what has come before. In a determinist system, the present is completely reducible to the past—in which case, the processes of time-bound change really add nothing except a "working-out" of what was already decided in principle. To push it to the limit, the entire future development of nature was determined at the outset, be it by the "big bang" or God's act of creation. Whatever transpires is to be understood as the inevitable outcome of the preceding stage. The present is reduced to the past. And whatever occurs is the inevitable outcome of what took place before.

The crucial breakthroughs in the contemporary discussion of time took place in France, Germany, and the United States at the turn of the twentieth century and in communication with each other.

In France, Henri Bergson, in a landmark essay translated as *Time and Free Will*, initiated the rise of European phenomenology, out of which the existentialist preoccupation with time and individuality arises. He marked out the crucial distinction between the world that is experienced and the ways in which we each experience our own unique experiences of it. He pointed out that we describe the time of world processes in essentially spatial, i.e., mathematically describable, terms, as a sequence of numerable moments. Our clocks do not really report time, but rather the position of the Earth in its journey around the Sun. Because traditional clocks report, not time, but changing celestial geography, time is thought to be truly measurable, like any spatial entity. But what is not measured or measurable is the felt duration, the experienced quality of our own experiences. One's experiences of a leisurely chess game or an exciting concert, of a relaxing picnic with family and friends or the excitement of a football game, of standing in line for a bureaucratic function or experiencing the thrill of winning a race—these cannot be described as they are actually experienced by means of the number of clock-time moments they consumed. To tell me how many measurable minutes were involved says nothing to me about my experiencing of the experience itself. My experience is qualitative, and to tell me that it required a greater or lesser number of measurable moments to transpire is really extraneous to the authentic experience itself.

This Bergsonian insight was carried forth first by Husserl, who tried to subject it to the outlook of a mathematical understanding, and then by Heidegger, who tried to come to terms, in a systematic way, with the crucially temporal quality of all human experience. Taking up Kant's distinction between that understanding which seeks a theoretical explanation for what transpires and the perspective of a forward-looking human reason which finds itself continuously compelled to make decisions by the temporal surge into which we swim, Heidegger urged that the crucial element of the human perspective is one that looks forward to the practical effects of selected actions: they are bound—not to the slavery of pervasive causal explanations of the present in terms of the past—but to a liberating understanding of what the present permits in terms of the possibilities it now sees before it. Our perception of ever-new possibilities is like a new mound of clay the sculptor transforms into the statue he envisions and anticipates. The future, then, is not "some thing" waiting for us to enter into it; the future, like a work of art, is to be created by our evaluative freedom.

Such varied thinkers as Berdyaev, Sartre, Marcel, Ortega, and Merleau-Ponty have all focused their attention on the magnetic attraction of perceived possibility that draws our own activities forward. However else they may disagree, they seem united on this one central perspective: the continuing creation of a future is the task that is always presently in our hands. We learn from the past what we can. Our own present free activities are creating, from out of diverse possibilities, the future we shall bring to pass. The future is to be created, not merely caused by an inexorable development from a past that determines the future—in which case, all decisional experience is but an illusion reducible to role-acting. What will be is as yet inherently unknown and unknowable just because the actuality into which the future will develop depends upon the decisions of freely oriented persons who are somehow able to select, by default or by design, the futures that will be theirs.

And in ways more focused on method than on metaphysics, American pragmatists took the opening invitation of futurity with complete seriousness. Effectively presuming that the time of the world was not reducible to a mathematical enumeration of recorded moments which could report the future as an accomplished fact along a line of projected inevitable development, they asserted that, within the human perspective, the future appears open to our own decisions. Charles Peirce and William James, the two fathers of the pragmatic thesis, took up Emerson's clarion call: "Honor truth by its use!" Truth must make a difference. The future is to be rendered by the ways in which we take up and utilize those truths which have already been established. But their meaning for us consists in the options they present, how they may instruct and guide us. Every truth presents an option as to its future course of development. And the difference is yet subject to what we do about it. The difference is to be rendered by how human judgmental freedom uses it.

Those who are concerned with the cosmic reach of our existentially temporal situation can opt for either one of two governing outlooks. Those who are convinced that nature is all and that there is nothing beyond it are compelled to come to terms with the time of nature; they must face the question of how to reconcile inexorable natural development out of the past with the forward-looking stance of the human participants within its processes, which so often redirects those natural processes. Those who have accepted the theist commitment and are convinced that God governs not only the world of nature but also the world of men, are compelled to come to terms with the ultimate reach of the question of the meaning of existential time; they must face the question of how God could be God were he unaffected by the course of temporal development. They must also face the additional question of the proverbial problem of the question of evil—for if God is indeed immune to the course of temporal challenge and change, how can God be exempted from responsibility for all the evil that transpires within the world? Although the naturalist can take evil as incarnate in the ways of things and talk about a principle of being beyond good and evil, the theist cannot opt for this course, for tragedy and trial are inherent aspects of the human condition, and if one believes in an ultimate purpose and rationality that render the patterns of continuing change meaningful, then one must be able to explain how these fit into any rationally acceptable divine plan, unless one grants that God is also affected by time and is thereby a finite being. It seems that the "process" metaphysics of Alfred North Whitehead and his American student Charles Hartshorne grapples most fundamentally with the systematic relationships of the temporality of man, nature, and God himself. It was Whitehead's ambition to tie the temporality of man and nature into one grand metaphysical system. He was followed in this by Hartshorne, who focused his attention on religious questions.

Have we not reached a description of our present situation? Don't we agree that, within the constraints of nature's temporal development, it is now incumbent upon ourselves to make innumerable decisions that will effectively help to form the future that will be ours? In personal terms, as each lives one's own life? In social terms, as each feeds one's own perspectives into the social consensus that drives our society forward? On both levels, and both together, we look ahead, invoke what aspects of the past seem relevant to making definitive decisions about what we think should be.

We act as free beings—or as beings who find that we must act as if we are free to make the decisions we are all continually called upon to make. We take a moral responsibility for the decisions we do make and expect to be held accountable for them. We act now, in a living present. As individuals and as citizens, we face the future, which is not yet, but to some extent in our hands right now. We know that we cannot control the future. But we do act on the principle that we are each presently creating aspects of the future that actually shall be. And we do indeed find ourselves acting—just because the oncomingness of time forces decision.

The questions of time and freedom tie into all of our current social concerns. For if time, in any meaningful sense, is the form, nature, or structure of human existence, then it must have something to say to the politically organized societies within which we find our individual being. The nature of human time, then, becomes a core question of all social and political questions, and lies at the core of all justifications of a civil society. So we must start to think through the ways human time bears on the nature of a free society. This import of existential time to the time of human political existence has rarely been thought through. It is a task to which we need repair.

When all questions are stated and answered, do these last not lay out in starkest terms the meaning of time for us? Time is inseparable from the freedom we each experience in the core of our being. Time and freedom, we have been traditionally told, are conjoined in each individual experience that is lived out within the context of an immense physical context. But we find our own selves only as members of a sociopolitical organization that also seems to be temporally structured.

On each and every level—as individuals, citizens, and inhabitants of the physical universe—we find ourselves functioning in temporal terms. Somehow, we can come to terms with and even explain just how time functions within nature, within the various strata of human life. We can come to understand how temporal processes function. To neglect doing so is to leave us bereft of any understanding of the prime dimension or formative force in life. But when we turn to the grander question of just *what is* the time that forms these temporal perspectives and processes, we find ourselves joining Augustine's classic plaint: "We know what we mean by time when no one asks us; but when we have to explain it to ourselves or others, we only know that we do not know." Temporality forms the being that each one of us is. It appears to us in diverse and often contradictory ways. We do know that the temporality of our being somehow reaches out to and brings into us an encompassing time that lies beyond the limits of any human understanding.

2

Talk of Time

An early discovery one makes when learning French or German is the need to explicate diverse temporal meanings that are left unvoiced in English. *Zeit* and *temps* translate only some uses of the English "time." Conceptually distinct words such as *mal* and *fois*, *Uhr* and *heure, Takt, mesure, époque* are but a few of the words needed to translate various meanings all expressed by the English word "time." This one inherently ambiguous word covers a multitude of uses which can, necessarily depending on context, refer to an epoch, a punctually discerned moment, a general duration, a specific time period, a calculation, a repetition, a unique event. Usually appearing as a noun, "time" can also be used as an adjective and as a verb—in each case with a multitude of possible meanings.

The compounding of widely diverse meanings into one word accentuates the ambiguity of meaning focused in this one word; this conceptual confusion is true not only of the word "time" but of other time-referential words as well. The confounding of meanings in language only encourages a confounding of meanings in thought, which is shaped by the language in terms of which it proceeds and is expressed. Our talk of time, as our other talk, generally claims reference to a world somehow independent of our speech about it; yet our thinking is shaped by the grammar and vocabulary we use for our own thought processes and for their communication to others as to ourselves. We need, then, to clarify some of the many ambiguities which our manner of speaking builds into our thinking.

First, perhaps, we need to make a crucial distinction between two modes of temporal discourse. We generally sequence two distinct events in terms of "before" and "after" when we are speaking of the events themselves. But when we speak in terms of our experiential perspectives of them we use the terms "present" and "past" and "future." A descriptive statement in terms of "before-and-after" is, once true, always true. But the truth of a descriptive statement in terms of "past" or "'present" or "future" depends for its truth upon the time of its utterance. So far the turn-of-the-century philosopher John McTaggart has pointed us. Thus, to say that the American Revolution was before the French Revolution is to describe an unalterable fact; such a statement's truth does not change with the passage of time, and will retain its truth a thousand years hence. But descriptive statements concerning those two revolutions were true only in the future tense when spoken by their prophets and are today true only in the past tense as spoken by their historians. The truth of each statement thus depends on the tense of the pronouncement, just as a statement by any participant would necessitate a shift from "future" to "present" to "past" to maintain its truth.

Not only is the first kind of statement timeless while the truth of the second is dependent upon the temporal relation of the speaker to the described event, but the first is clearly quantifiable while the quantifiability of the second is at least questionable. The interim between a "before" and an "after" can be clearly stated in terms of some metric—hours, days, years. And this measured interim can be verified independently of the person making the assertion, by measuring the "distance" between the so-called terminal points in terms of some standard reference.

But tensed statements cannot avoid their personal experiential reference, and the boundaries of present with past or with future cannot readily be identified. Statements about wholly completed events or those not yet immediately imminent present no special problem regarding their "placement" in terms of a "before-and-after" dating. But the extension of the experiential present is clearly ambiguous. Just when does the present emerge from the future or pass into the past? As William James pointed out, "Say 'now' and it was even while you say it." The present, understood as a precise point in time, is a non-existent but ever-moving boundary between an artificially segmented continuity between past and future. As James was quick to note, neither time nor our experiencing itself is experienced in this way.

Our experiencing is a continuity of temporal "flow." We often take notice of how the clock marks periods along the way, but few of us are likely to claim that each discernible "moment" has anything more than a fictional quality to it, a fictional quality that is useful when we seek to correlate one experience with another, but intrinsically not true to the experiencing itself. When we use words such as "now" or "present," we do not generally mean anything fleetingly momentary. We do mean an experiential spread of time that indeed contains sequence within it. Locutions such as "the present age" and "the present moment," or "now is the

time to do x" indicate the range of possible temporal spread. Philosophers as various as James and Bergson, pragmatists like Dewey, and phenomenologists like Husserl and Heidegger have pointed up the import
and complexity of what Whitehead had termed the "ill-defined" present
within which "the past and the future meet and mingle."

Our speech generally suggests that time is some peculiar kind of
line analogous to a geometric connection between two physical points.
But what these near-contemporary thinkers have effectively joined to
urge is that the time frame of our experiencing is a moving present field
of focus, not a discernible fictional point; it expands or contracts in
scope as the attention and reference of meaning expands or contracts.
Depending upon the speaker's intention, "the present" might mean
"the twenty-first century," "the modern era," "the current semester," "the
short meeting I am attending," or "this precise instant" which a digital
watch claims to report. However widely or narrowly the net of meaning
is cast, any lived present includes the merging of future and of past
within its scope; the borders are not only constantly changing in any
clock-time sense, they also merge almost indiscernibly into that which
was present but is no longer and that which is not yet present. The word
"present" is thus a dynamic term of reference which, when authentically
used, should be seen as continually reminding us of the essential temporal quality of living experience.

In English, Spanish, and Chinese, unlike many other languages, we
are readily able to give direct expression to the time-consuming quality
of the "present" by using the present progressive tense. To say "I am eat-
ing" or "I am thinking" forces our attention upon the use of time as the
simple present "I eat" or "I think" does not. Indeed, the decision to
translate Descartes's *je pense* or Kant's *ich denke* into English as either "I
think" or "I am thinking" carries quite different temporal connotations
and leads to radically divergent interpretations of their work. The former can be treated as a logical or trans-temporal term, but the latter
brings the essential time-binding nature of process to the fore.

Thus, for example, the cliché "this point in time" is seriously misleading in philosophic import. It presumes a spacelike timeline of precisely determinable sequential moments marked off by a super-celestial
clock ticking away in august transcendent splendor. What was meant was
a decisional present situation that was to be correlated with other unfolding events regarded as germane. What was meant was essentially referential to individual perspectival judgments on problematic events.

This is to suggest that our temporal references are originally perspectival and relational. Although we may translate into the "objective"
order of measurable "before and after" sequential intervals, the experi-

ence from which such statements arise is the living present of individual discernment in which what was first future melds into the present field of focus and indiscernibly becomes the experience that was but is no longer except as brought back into the present as recalled memory. The "before-and-after" sequence can be usefully painted as a series of metaphorically distinguishable moments. But the living present in which all experiences are to be had is not authentically representable as a series at all. For the experienced present, wide or narrow in focus, is a synthetic whole, a *Gestalt,* in which the present of perception, the present of anticipation, and the present of recollection are experienced together in an organically inseparable unity. And such experiential presents are not temporally neutral. Kant had already anticipated much current study of time-experiencing phenomena when he pointed out in his *Anthropology:*

> Men are more interested in having foresight than any other power, because it is the necessary condition of all practical activity and of the ends to which we direct the use of our powers. . . . We look back on the past (remember) only so that we can foresee the future by it; and as a rule we look around us in the standpoint of the present, in order to decide on something or prepare ourselves for it.

Our perspectives, like the judgments and assessments we build into them, are essentially future-oriented. We recollect what seems pertinent to the problem at hand. If rational activity may be described as goal-oriented behavior, then our rational perspectives on what transpires before us are largely in terms of questions concerning what should be or needs to be done. Past experience is brought into the moving present as it seems relevant to the discerned problematic. Perception is not passively neutral but actively interpretive—and it is for this reason that witnesses to the same incident so often honestly disagree.

This consideration should act as a warning against taking too literally our usual tendency to talk about the temporal aegis of events in spacelike terms. One outcome of this tendency is to speak of events as though they come out of the past, coming into the present and veering off into the vague future. But experientially events come to us out of a more or less ambiguous future, pass into a defining present, and pass on into a definitive and unalterable past. In many fundamental ways, time experience is very different from that of space. We can see for miles but only directly experience the content of a few seconds at a time. We can return to the same landscape many times but cannot actually revisit any particular period of time. Space has an essentially static quality which is radically discordant from the dynamism of time. We cannot experience the sight of a landscape without "taking time" to do so; but we can close our eyes and imagine or think without concurrent spatial perception. Our dreaming, and our thinking, are temporal and time-consuming events which do not necessarily involve spatiality. The process of being conscious, as the process of thinking, takes time, is essentially temporal in form, and is always constituted as a moving field of present focus or attention.

This suggests that the experiencing of time is a pervasive characteristic of all the experiences we have. Indeed, it can be argued that this fact but betokens the reality that our thinking is essentially concerned with the temporal and with the manifestations of time relations in specific situations. This pervasiveness of the temporal should be reflected in the way in which we talk about it. In this regard, our English language both helps and hinders. It provides us with the progressive present tense which, in its essentially time-binding function, is the one verb form which authentically expresses the way in which we do experience our experiencing itself. Language seems to center on static nouns instead of time-centered verbs. We seem to presume, when we name a thing and then apply a verb to it, that the named thing remains constant and is untouched by the action, and the time of the action, attributed to it.

And yet, without a verb, the word that announces the activity, we cannot have a sentence. But we can have a sentence by using a form of the verb itself as the grammatical subject. We can speak meaningfully of actions without supposedly static things, but we cannot speak meaningfully of static things without verbs. This brief consideration should indicate that the verb—the action-word, being-word, time-word—is the keystone of any statement. The point is not a new one. Aristotle had already pointed to it when he noted that although a noun "has no reference to time . . . a verb is that which, in addition to its proper meaning, carries with it the notion of time" (16a19–20, 16b6–7). We need then remember, when examining our use of language, that to separate the notion from its time is to abstract the tense from the verb; doing so yields no concrete description of a real event, but only an abstraction. For no activity, in its individuating concreteness, can be truthfully known or truthfully described when sundered from the "when" of its being or its being known.

Facing the ambiguities about expressing the temporal that is built into our language, we need to be alerted to them whenever we talk about time, our experience of time, and the time of our experiencings. For waking or sleeping, our thinking and dreaming are always in the form of time which the experiential present provides. When we express these thoughts, we are talking of what is experienced as temporal and even our talking about it takes time. Time relations are then intrinsically involved in all of our thinking and thereby in all of the things that we think about insofar as we are able to think them; time relations are also intrinsically and obviously involved in all of the time-consuming problems we feel called upon to resolve.

If time is the form of all existence at least insofar as we can think about it, then the time relations that are manifested in the particular things and tasks of concern we think about provide the unifying content of all of our thinking as well. A careful and authentic use of descriptive language will then explicate the fact that we can only think about the world, or about the events being discussed within the world, in temporal terms; concernful use of language then requires that the time predicates and time references we use be handled with exceeding care. For, if the forms of time mold all our thinking, the forms of time mold our picture of the world and our ways of being within it as well. All of our talk about our experiences is, then, talk of a world seen and thought of in terms of time; our authentically descriptive talk is, then, descriptive of our temporal experiencing; authentically experiential descriptive talk is talk of time.

Part 2

A Kantian Rethinking
of Some Kant

3

The Question of Noumenal Time

In posing the question of "noumenal time," I mean to pose the question of whether time is really real, whether time has any being aside from the human outlook. And I mean to pose this question from within a generally Kantian perspective.

Raising this question of temporal realism enables us to make some existential sense of what Kant was about and what he saw himself as doing; we may then develop a new comprehension of the synoptic unity of the critical enterprise, its essential thrust, historic significance, and enduring import. By reopening the Kantian perspective in this way, we may hopefully see some old ambiguities resolved while others are perhaps newly opened. Just because of the central import of the notion of time in Kant's work, we may expect that suggesting the thesis of an ultimate temporal realism may have far-reaching implications for variances from common readings of key texts—thus forcing to the forefront issues which have possibly been shunted aside for too long. In this brief compass, I can only suggest the reach of what is involved in thinking through the problematic being offered. This overview of what a more extended argument would offer is not only crucial to keeping its constituent elements in focus; it is, perhaps, also necessary to provoke serious consideration of the question itself.

The question of "noumenal time" obviously arises from Kant's fundamental thesis that time is but a subjective form of human apprehension. Time, we are told again and again, in different ways, "is nothing but the form of inner sense [*Anschauung* < = > looking out], that is of the intuition of ourselves and of our inner state." It is thus "the formal a priori condition of all appearances whatsoever." The universal form of all awarenesses, whether of external and spatial, or of internal objects of attention, "Time is therefore a purely subjective condition of our (human) intuition . . . and in itself apart from the subject is nothing."[1] Time's objective reality, then, is only as the fundamental form of representation. In itself it is an *Unding*, a "non-entity."[2] As the fundamental form of all our apprehensions, we may justifiably claim time to be a property of objects only insofar as they are in relationship to us as perceiving subjects. But this is to say that the ascription of time to objects as they may be in themselves, aside from our apprehensions of them, is illegitimate and illusionary. If we think of the noumenal not merely as the intelligible but also as the independently and ultimately real, we are then bound to wonder whether time, or something like it, has any meaning, any intelligibility, any reality aside from the human perspective, aside from our own way of representing experiential objects to ourselves.

Kant's central thesis, pursuit of which sets out the structure of the First *Critique*, is quite clear: time is the fundamental form of human apprehension. Any object of which we may be aware can only be represented in consciousness in the temporal form of all human thinking. All ideas, as Locke had already pointed out, must be susceptible of sequential ordering and therefore be thought in temporal sequence—before some and after others. For any idea, any representation to enter into human awareness, it must be in the temporal order of human thinking. This much Kant's "Aesthetic" maintained.

The "Aesthetic" thus set the problematic for the "Analytic" which follows directly from it: if human cognition depends upon the union of the reports of sensibility, which are in the form of time, and of interpretive conceptual thought, then the concepts entering into that cognition must be able to do so in temporal form. It is just because of this need for temporal conceptualization, in order to come to terms with the particularity of our time-ordered representations, that Kant argued the cognitive inadequacy of the traditional logic and the need for a new transcendental logic. And this new logic of cognitive concept-formation, he explicitly argued, is structured out of the four discernible ways in which time may be conceptually understood. Argued in the "Schematism" and the balance of the "Analytic of Principles," it was thus made clear that the categories (or pure concepts) of the understanding are but the principles of human knowledge as abstracted from their essential temporalizing predicates, while the cognitive principles are only equivalent to the categories as transmuted by the temporalizing predicates of the schematic system. If time is the form of all of our apprehensions of objects as they appear to us, Kant argued, it must also be the form, and the limitation of applicability, of those interpretive concepts in terms of which we are able to understand them.

The "Dialectic" follows from this as its obverse: those objects of thought which cannot be ultimately represented in temporal form cannot be apprehended in the form of time, cannot be subjected to the interpretive understanding by temporal principles of knowledge, and thus cannot be cognized by us. The scope of empirical knowledge, then, is limited to those objects which can appear and be understood in terms of temporally formed concepts. Apart from such temporalization, the categories, which generally designate the logical structure of our empirical concepts, "can find no objects, and so can acquire no meaning which might yield knowledge of some object."[3]

Of the many questions which might be raised at this point, two are fundamental to my inquiry; disparate as they first appear to be, they are really complementary and demand that we focus on each in turn.

1. Did Kant *really* believe that time is *merely* subjective? That time predicates are inherently meaningless except as characterizations of the human mode of apprehending and understanding objects?

To accept the answer of the "Aesthetic" in literal seriousness is to propound a profoundly existential conundrum: can we bring ourselves to believe that physical objects, appearing *to us* under the form of time, are really exempt from any meaning of temporal predicates? Can we really believe that our own selves, abiding through experiential changes, are not subject to time predicates of continuity, growth, and qualitative change? Can we make moral judgments, apply the categorical imperative in daily situations, engage our moral reasoning, without regarding time considerations with profoundly moral seriousness? Can we explain, if not the principle of the moral law, at least the principles of its applications, without invoking some notion of moral judgments as being affected by the time-order of sensible objects, without invoking some conception of my moral self as indeed affected by its own moral experiences, its successes, failures, frustrations, and triumphs and their sequential relationships to each other?

Can I really read Kant on the three encompassing questions of all concern: what can I know?, what should I do?, what may I hope for?—without being aware of their temporal dimensions? Can I read Kant's discussions—of the temporal distinctions grounding the "Analogies" of possible experience, of the pros and cons of the "Third Antinomy" grounding the possibility of morality, of his reflections on morality, religion, politics, and history—and still substitute for each use of the word "time" its definition in the "Aesthetic"—"nothing but the form of inner sense"—and still make any sense out of what he is trying to say?

If Kant's writings on diverse topics are to be meaningful, it is apparent that he must have understood "time" in a sense more independently objective than is suggested by this initial definition out of the "Aesthetic." For "time" seems to function in his writings as something more than a merely subjective form of cognitive apprehension. It seems to be taken as something to which the adjectives "objective" or "real" may be legitimately applied. It seems tied in with the notion of the structure of objectivity itself. Did Kant *really* believe that time *is merely* subjective? Might it not be that definitions such as this in the "Aesthetic" are to be taken, not in the ontologically descriptive terms in which he offered them, but as either propaedeutic or metaphoric in import, as of regulative value?

2. Why, then, did Kant place that absolute priority on time rather than space in our cognitive ordering? Why is the whole theory of knowledge of physical objects enunciated in the "Analytic" worked out in terms of the *temporalization* of otherwise empty categorial constructs?

Kant's theory of knowledge, it seems clear, is advanced as a theory of knowledge, not of persons, but of things. Of things that are essentially denominated in spatial terms. Indeed, in the "Aesthetic," Kant made his concern with spatial entities abundantly clear: he speaks there of "space, to which our chief attention will therefore be directed in this enquiry."[4]

Knowledge of a person involves that of the noumenal self, moral conscience, the experience of freedom, the principle of autonomy, the transcendental ego, the transcendental unity of apperception, the meaning of spontaneity, the self-imposition of a responsibility to a moral commandment, and the objective limitations of the possibilities of legitimate claims to knowledge, obligation, and expectation or hope. Such knowledge does not seem to require essential spatialization; such knowledge is not of physical things appearing in spatial form.

The cognitive principles are concerned with representations of the appearances of physical entities, entities which are apprehended in external sense. Indeed, this seems to be the "message" of the "Analytic": concern is with knowledge of objects to which spatial predicates are to be applied. And it is for this reason that we are continually confronted by the *duality* of the presentational requirement: cognition is only possible with regard to objects that can appear in the forms of time *and* of space. Which is to say that knowledge is directed to objects that are taken as having extension and are also representable in the time form of human awareness.

This duality—of the spatiality of outer sense and the time of human consciousness—seems to have been Kant's prime reason for limiting possible knowledge of objects to those which can simultaneously appear to us in *both* forms. Obviously, we can have time-ordered conceptions of the self, of God, of freedom, of noumenal realities, of transcendental subjects and objects—but we cannot represent them as appearing under the rubric of spatiality; hence they are beyond the bounds of possible cognitive experience. This seems to have been the crux of the defense against charges of a Berkeleyan subjective idealism. And it is easy to see that such a defense is consonant with the central argument of the First *Critique*—as long as we recognize the fundamental import of spatiality in the definition of the objects of possible knowledge, an import that is often hidden behind Kant's focus on cognitive structuring entirely in terms of time acceptable to inner sense.

My second question, then, comes to this: if our knowledge—as distinct from convictions, beliefs, hopes, and faith—is to be of entities appearing to outer sense, entities subject to the legitimate use of space predicates, why did Kant place this absolute priority on time as the *one* pervasive principle of our cognitive processes? Epistemologically, why did he feel it necessary to reduce or subordinate space to time? Why are spatial entities to be understood solely in terms of *time*-formed principles?

In seeking out some answer to these two queries, I think our first requirement is to set aside any lingering tendencies to read Kant as some peculiar German kind of Berkeleyan phenomenalist. The word "appearance," Kant made it quite clear, refers to real appearing, not to illusion.[5] As he forthrightly stated at the outset, "though we cannot *know* these objects as things-in-themselves, we must yet be in a position to *think* them as things-in-themselves; otherwise we should be landed in the absurd conclusion that there can be appearance without anything that appears."[6]

Appearances to my consciousness, as my representations of them, attest to the scope of my finite human cognitive perspectives onto a world which I inhabit but which spreads beyond my view and, even within my field of vision, is not wholly open to my cognitive capacities. That there must be real being which does not or cannot appear to my finite cognitive capability is indicated by Kant in that same passage where he already points us to the promise of practical reason to extend my insight, if not my understanding, beyond those aspects of objects which I am able to cognize.[7]

The frequent attempts to dismiss Kant's insistence on the requisite for real being that appears to us in only limited guises seem to beg the entire question in at least one of two ways.

1. The charge that Kant is merely providing the comic outcome of a superseded subject-predicate logic ignores Kant's fundamental disavowal of the cognitive capacity of any formal logic. Indeed, the whole of the "Analytic" is devoted to developing a transcendental logic as "a logic of truth" because a formal logic will not do, will not serve as a vehicle for cognitive discovery.[8]

2. The presumption that there can be nothing behind or beyond the appearance itself already presumes a very narrow kind of sense-empiricism which has yet to come to terms with Kant's opening statement: "though all our knowledge begins with experience, it does not follow that it all arises out of experience."[9]

It seems clear that Kant's ontological presumption is that the world in which we are is constituted by objects which appear to human consciousness as presentations of things only insofar as they may be recognized and cognized by the limited capacities we bring to our attempt to comprehend them. The subjective forms of intuitive receptivity, like the interpretive categories of our understanding, refer to a real world of objects, a world not depending upon our perceiving in order to suffer its state of existing.

Kant did not see himself as doing empirical psychology; that he had left to John Locke, the "celebrated physiologist of the human understanding," from whom he seems to have learned much, and from whom he seems to have taken his notion of time as the form of inner sense. Kant was not doing psychology; he claimed to be doing metaphysics. As W. H. Walsh has pointed out, his work sought "to recommend a certain set of metaphysical *convictions,* if not exactly a certain set of metaphysical truths."[10] He presumed something of the nature of man and of the world in order to tell us of ways in which man could deal with different aspects of his world.

It is quite clear that Kant's conception of possible cognition involved a cognitive relationship with a real world, that his theory of knowledge is primarily object-oriented. As he had said, "All our cognition has a *twofold* relation, *first* to the object, second to the subject. In the former respect it is related to *presentation,* in the latter to *consciousness,* the general condition of all cognition in general [for us]."[11] It seems clear that what is presumed is, first, a world that I am experiencing in my own essentially limited way, and second, my own self as experiencing subject; the entire transcendental "machinery" is concerned to relate the second to the first.

It is wise, I think, not only to listen when a philosopher tells us what he is *presuming* or thinks he is doing; it is also well to pay some heed to any admonitions he may offer us as to how we may proceed to expand "the horizon of our cognitions."[12] Condemning "material" ignorance, that is, ignorance of the historical, he has warned against that "self-victimization" (only too current today) practiced by "the philosopher [who foolishly] believes that history is dispensable to him." Deriding the "historically ignorant [who] are commonly the teachers of reason," he has told us that philosophy, as "the science of the tools of learning," be-

longs to "historical knowledge."[13] Kant, himself the author of several essays pointing to a philosophy of historical development, had urged, in
introducing his lectures on logic, that we begin to take history seriously
as intrinsic to the discipline of philosophy itself.

If we are to understand what Kant was doing, it would then seem
appropriate to try to see him in historical perspective. In order to develop responses to my two queries—did Kant really believe that time is
merely subjective? Why did he rest his whole theory of knowledge of spatial objects on time-ordered principles?—we ought to start by repairing
to some philosophic history.

We do not have far to go. At least as an heuristic device, I suggest the
imaginative experiment of thinking of Kant as seeking to carry forward
to completion the Cartesian program. Doing so requires us to use that
imaginative capacity, of which both Descartes and Kant made much, in
trying to look at some Cartesianisms from a Kantian perspective.

Kant's dissatisfaction with the cognitive competence of the inherited logic has already been noted. We now need but recall Descartes's
own repeated call for a logic, for a system of reason, which could lead,
not to conceptual confirmation of already established truths, but to new
cognitive discovery. Is this not the rationale of Kant's new transcendental logic? Any glance through Kantian texts will remind us of his recurrent homage to the Cartesian criterion of "clear and distinct ideas." A
comparison of Descartes's "Sixth Meditation" with Kant's "Transcendental Deduction" presents a somewhat similar doctrine of imagination as
central to the theory of cognition. Although Kant's ontologization of
many Cartesian entities is radically altered, their *functional* similarity is
quite startling: consider, in the light of Kant's cognitive synthesis of sensibility and thought, the Cartesian doctrine of the

> passive faculty of perception, that is, of receiving and recognizing the ideas
> of sensible things . . . [which] would be useless to me if there were not . . .
> another active faculty capable of forming and producing these ideas.[14]

Consider how the end of the "Fifth Meditation" together with the beginning of the "Sixth" must have struck the Kant whose first two cognitive
principles were described as mathematical and who lodged the a priori
science of mathematics within the scope of inner sense:

> And now . . . I have the means of acquiring a perfect knowledge of an in-
> finitude of things [including] those which pertain to corporeal nature in
> *so far as it is the object of pure mathematics.*

> Nothing further remains but to inquire *whether material things exist in so far as they are considered as the objects of pure mathematics. . . .*[15]

We can almost sniff out the intimations of the Copernican revolution. The limitation of possible knowledge of the sensory world of material objects in space by the limited a priori powers of intellection did not start with Kant; such *limited* knowledge of physical nature is all that Descartes had hoped to achieve. Lest there be much doubt about the doctrinal affinity of the two on this one point—which may be more crucial to Kant than to Descartes—let us look at the "Sixth Meditation":

> Hence we must allow that corporeal things exist. However, *they are perhaps not exactly what we perceive by the senses* . . . ; but we must at least admit that all things which I conceive in them clearly and distinctly, that is to say *all things which,* speaking generally, *are comprehended in the object of pure mathematics,* are truly to be recognized as external objects.[16]

These objects were described by Descartes as material or corporeal things, as bodies, as objects of perception to which predications of extension and quantitative determination were to be applied. This world of extended things, appropriately described in terms of "primary qualities," comprised the objects which, Kant maintained, could only be apprehended, could only enter into possible experience, in the forms of space *and* time. For his own very good reasons, Kant added the crucial connective with time to the import of spatial extension; but doing so in no way augmented the denotational field. The possible population of Descartes's world of extended bodies and Kant's world of objects in space-and-time would seem to be pretty much the same.

Kant did, indeed, appear to work from the Leibnizian priority of the temporal, but in doing so he seems to have carried forward an essentially spatial view of time. In the First *Critique,* time is usually described as a line of the sequence of before-and-after; it is used as the measure of change in respect of the before-and-after; it is then an internally grounded version of Aristotle's concept of time—which has always served the concern of the physical scientist to chart the measure of motion in space. Kant certainly carried forward Aristotle's intimation—that time, as such, is in the mind of the measurer; Locke had explained that time is the train of ideas in consciousness, and Kant apparently translated this to mean that time is the form of inner sense.

But after this is done, and without denigrating the import of all that has been done, it is clear that Kant's quantitatively spatialized time serves pretty much the same discriminations as Descartes's notion of spatial extension. For Kant's distinction between the phenomenal and the nonphenomenal closely parallels the Cartesian distinction between the extended physical and the nonextended mental. The *ich denke*, as the cogito, is not to be described in spatial predicates. But the Kantian *ich denke* is effectively restricted in its cognitive employment to that world which Descartes had described as extended and which, in Kantian terms, appears in the form of outer sense.

Kant's conjunction of space and time, in characterizing the reach of possible experience, indeed goes far to ground that experience—but the effective scope of its empirical cognitive claims has been severely restricted. Kant has effectively used the import of time to restrict cognitive claims to the spatial world. The function of time is to provide explanation of how and why our cognitive claims about that spatial world are to be structured and thereby substantiated. Kant has suggested no example of empirical knowledge dependent on inner sense alone.[17] Functionally, the conjunction of inner sense with outer is not to expand the area of possible cognition; it is to restrict the competence of *inner to outer* and to explain how it is possible for consciousness, not subject to spatial predicates, to attain knowledge of entities justifiably describable by spatial predicates. By this device, Kant claimed to provide a set of time-structuring principles upon which, or through which, all knowledge of a spatial world is to be had.

But we then must ask again: why are purely temporal principles requisite for the understanding of a world appearing to us in the form of space? Why should a cognitive structure composed solely of time-concepts necessarily refer to, and be restricted in its proper employment, to the content of outer sense or spatial apprehension?

Crucial to a response to such questions is the fact that Kant seems to have taken Descartes's distinction between two different concepts of time as fundamental. This distinction, anticipating Newton's between "absolute" and "relative" time, seems to have served Kant as his initial fundamental metaphysical divide. We can see this by considering Descartes's Fifty-seventh Principle. It is entitled: "That there are attributes which pertain to the things to which they are attributed, and that there are other attributes which depend upon our thinking." It reads:

Of these qualities or attributes, there are some which are in things themselves, and others which are only in our thinking. Thus *time*, for example, *which we distinguish from duration* taken in general, and which we say is the number of motion, *is nothing other than a certain manner in which we think about that duration*. . . . But, in order to comprehend the duration of all things under the same measure, we ordinarily make use of the

> duration of certain regular motions which form the days and the years, and having thus compared it, we call it time; although in effect *what we name in this way* is nothing, over and above the true duration of things, *except a manner of thinking.*[18]

Time and duration: one the human perspective, the other a reference to the reality of the world. Only one aspect of this Cartesian Principle was questioned by Kant. For Kant's crucial move was to question the legitimacy of attributing predicates to things outside of the human perspective on them; Kant's restriction of this Cartesian Principle was against the legitimacy of any claim that the competence of the perspective of human time pertains to the structure of duration itself.

All of our cognitive statements, Kant insisted, are within that more restricted sphere, the time-structured "manner of our thinking" about the durational reality of things appearing to us. Our thinking, he insisted, is of real appearances, appearances of a real world insofar as *we* are able to think about them. Time, as the form of inner sense, as the "manner of our thinking," is essentially referential to a world of durational reality independently objective beyond the ken of the human potentiality for experiencing or comprehending it.

Lest there be doubt about this, we should proceed to two brief arguments which sustain the point. Aside from their brevity, they have the virtue of being drawn out of the discussions of practical reason which, be it never forgotten, Kant had insisted from the outset always points beyond those limits inherent in the constitutive structure of any merely cognitive claims.

1. In the Second *Critique,* Kant very clearly used the term "time [*Zeit*]" when discussing the frame or intellectual structure of knowledge of appearances, when discussing the phenomenal realm; but when he referred to noumenal realities, he used the term "duration [*Dauer*]."

He speaks, of course, of man as an end-in-himself and not just a means to an end, a distinction which itself involves temporal predicates. The postulate of immortality is explicitly grounded as coming "out of the practical necessary condition of the adequacy of duration for the complete fulfillment of the moral law." It is because of this that "practical reason, through the postulate of adequacy with the moral law in the highest good as the whole end of practical reason, gives to the [individual] soul its *requisite duration.*"[19] Pointing out the thesis that practical reason's postulates should not be transformed into theories of cognitive reason, he discusses the "knowledge of God" which comes out of practical reason and cites attributes including the divine understanding, will, independence, and "the transcendental predicates, as e.g., the immense magnitude of existence [*Existenz*], *i.e.*, *duration*, which however does not occur in time although time is the only possible means available to us to represent this existent [*Dasein*] as that immense magnitude to us."[20]

The same word, *Unendliche*, variously translatable as "unending," "eternal," "infinite," is used to describe both God and the immortality of the human soul. God is identified as "*der Unendliche*, to whom the time-condition is nothing"; the hope for immortality is described as an "unending, ongoing and continuing duration [*Unendliche, gehenden Fort-dauer*]"; it is hoped that my immortal "duration should be endless [*dass meine Dauer endlos sei*]"; and we are assured that the reality of morality requires the postulate of "a *blessed* future" which "as *holiness* is an Idea which only can be contained in an unending progress," a formulation surely reading temporal spread into a postulated durational reality.[21]

In Kant's book on religion, in support of such formulations, we are told that immortality is to be conceived as "an immeasurable future . . . [which] we call *eternity*." And also that any such "future times" as "in our earthly life . . . [are] ever only a *becoming*."[22]

It would seem clear, from these citations, that Kant's conception of noumenal reality—certainly on the level of God's existence and that of the human soul—is to be described in the essentially human time-predication of duration or lastingness. The meaning of the word "eternity," be it noted, is *not* that of timelessness but of endlessness or lastingness and is seen as being dynamic in character. Whether such dynamicism is intrinsic to ultimate duration itself or is merely a metaphoric kind of projection from within the human outlook is certainly not made clear. But what seems to have been explicitly declared is the presumption that we can only think properly of those levels of noumenal being involving the concepts of God and immortality in terms of predicates that are, in the human perspective, essentially akin to the form of time.

2. As we all know, Kant clearly regarded the reality of God and immortality as necessary postulates of rational faith, not of scientific understanding; they are regarded as necessary insofar as conviction as to their objective reality emerges from the axiomatic nature of the moral law. In sharpest contrast to this derivative necessity, Kant urged that the idea of freedom does not emerge from but grounds the moral law and practical reason. The objective reality of freedom can then be asserted without question or caution. As Kant clearly said, "One cannot provide nor prove objective reality for any idea but for the idea of freedom and this is because freedom is the condition of the moral law whose reality is an axiom."[23]

And morality itself—in its essential preoccupation with formulating the "should" (in which it serves as the self-determining "lawgiver") instead of with the descriptive "is" which is the referent of cognitive understanding—is but the epitome or absolute of the whole of practical reason. Practical reason itself is not separate from, but encompasses within its scope, that theoretical or cognitive reason whose functioning and limited competence much of the First *Critique* was concerned to elucidate. That the understanding is encompassed within and subservient to the unity of practical reason, Kant emphatically reiterated: "Only if pure reason in itself can be and really is practical, as the consciousness of the moral law shows it to be, is it certainly always one and the same reason which judges a priori according to principles be it for theoretical or practical purposes."[24] Indeed, all reasoning "gravitates ultimately toward the *practical;* and in this tendency . . . consists the practical value of our cognition."[25]

It would then seem apparent that some kind of temporal realism must be presupposed. Nothing is instantaneous and even light takes time to travel. Reasoning, which at least for us, takes time, veers toward and is ultimately identical with the practical, with the objectively real exercise of freedom. This exercise of freedom itself consists in autonomous deliberation about ends and means, the discrimination of alternative possibilities, the self-imposition of a determination as a commandment, the consequent commitment of the self to a specific course of action and to the process of fulfilling that commitment. Freedom, then, like the individual self who exercises it, requires the reality of the spread of time and the *continuity* of temporal experience.[26]

This argument essentially seems reducible to a simple Barbara syllogism: If the objective reality of freedom requires the objective reality of time, and if practical reason requires the objective reality of freedom, then practical reason requires the objective reality of time. And, further, if practical reason and cognitive reason are functionally identical, then if practical reason demands the objective reality of time, cognitive reason must also.

Yet all this seems somewhat discordant with so many readings of the First *Critique.* Is it conceivable that Kant had either abandoned or neglected Descartes's time-duration distinction in the First *Critique?* That he only reverted to it as he turned his attention from concern with physical entities to concern with God and nonphenomenal realities—not, indeed, to ground knowledge of the things of the world but to ground our powers of self-determination in dealing with them?

Yet it is entirely appropriate that Kant, contending that only practical reason, in exercising the reality of freedom, points us beyond phenomenality—which confines the finite legitimacy of cognitive reasoning—should have faced the question of noumenal time only in that *Critique* concerned to elucidate the noumenal fact of freedom.[27] But one should still inquire as to whether any expression of this conviction of durational reality is to be found in the First *Critique*. Short of an exhaustive examination of the various time references throughout the First *Critique*, the most obvious place to look for some clarification is the section on the "Analogies of Experience"—just because he was there concerned to establish the necessary thesis that all appearances must be connected together in *one* time system.

Indeed, N. K. Smith's translation (upon which most of us have been raised) assures us that Kant had sought to derive the notion of "substance" from that of "duration," that "The three modes of time are duration, succession, and co-existence."[28] If this statement may stand, it would seem to belie some force of what I have argued, for it suggests that "duration" is but one aspect of time rather than time being a particular kind of human perspective on ultimate duration (or absolute time).

The translation appears to be seriously misleading. Kant's word (in the sentence quoted) is not "duration [*Dauer*]," not even "permanence [*Beständigkeit*]" (which Meikeljohn and Müller use), but "persistence" or "perseverance," the proper equivalents of the German *Beharrlichkeit*, which Smith occasionally translates as "duration," but almost always in a form of the word "permanent." Thus, for example, the title of the "First Analogy," which Smith renders as the "Principle of Permanence (of Substance)," was entitled by Kant "Grundsatz der Beharrlichkeit (der Substanz)." The usual word for "permanence" is *Beständigkeit*, which Kant did *not* use. Kant did use throughout various forms of the verb *beharren*, which means "to persist in a state and represents the persistence as active, as an expression of will."[29] Yet every use of the word "permanent" in Smith's text claims to be a rendering of Kant's use of a form of *beharren*.

If one pays heed to the force of Kant's chosen term, it is clear that a radical correction of translation is mandated. Indeed, when one substitutes, for each use of the word "permanent" in the English translation, the more literal translation of "persistence" or "perseverance," many problematic discussions concerning the "permanent in time" or the reconciliation of the static to the temporal lose their point of reference. The text becomes alive with a dynamic quality suggesting something analogous either to Spinoza's *conatus* or Leibniz's *vis viva*.

Smith's translation distorts Kant's conception of dynamism and time and possibly reflects, as H. J. Paton obliquely suggested, a fundamental misunderstanding of it.[30] Not only is the usual word for "permanent" completely absent from Kant's discussion of the "First Analogy"; the word for "duration [*Dauer*]" appears only once, in a sentence whose

English version should read, "Through the persistent alone does successive existence in different parts of the time-series obtain an immense magnitude which one calls duration."[31]

Indeed, the *temporal* force of Kant's notion of substance becomes somewhat clear in two literally translated passages:

> a. In all appearances, therefore, persistence is the object itself, i.e., the substance (phenomenon); all, however, that changes or can change belongs only to the manner by which this substance or these substances exist and therewith to their determinations.

> b. We can, therefore, give to an appearance the name substance because we presume its existence in all time, but this is not well expressed by the word persistence [*Beharrlichkeit*] for this word directs itself to the future. However, the inner necessity to persist is inseparably bound with the necessity to have always been, and the expression may therefore remain.[32]

The essentially dynamic tension of perduring is quite clear. If then one persists in using the word "permanence," it must clearly be done in a trans-temporal sense, abjuring any static meaning, and be understood as the continuing presence of striving or persisting in being.[33]

Is there any fairly direct evidence here of Kant's conviction of some kind of completely objective and ultimate time-order beyond the bounds of human apprehension? Several passages could be cited, but perhaps the most direct to this point is an explicit explanation in the discussion of the "Second Analogy"; for Kant there points out that we must seek efficacious causal relations in the sequential order of appearances just because "absolute time [*die absolute Zeit*] . . . *is* no object of perception."[34] In a way reminiscent of Socrates' contention in the *Phaedo* that our lack of ability to have direct apprehension of truth condemns us to a conceptual way of understanding that is second best, so much of Kant's argumentation here rests on the unknowability of the *real* time order.

If the argument is thus clear, then why did Kant build that rigid wall of separation between the time of cognitive reasoning which deals with phenomenal appearings, and the denial of this "dimension" to that noumenal realm which includes the reality of freedom? The question becomes crucial as we begin to see Kant referring to some kind of absolute durational reality which is beyond the phenomenal, inaccessible to the cognitive understanding, yet undergirding both as it suggests a real world order.

If my suggestion of the Cartesian inspiration of Kant's thinking about time-and-duration has any validity, we can begin to find the answer here. Time, we were told, is the human manner or mode of thinking about aspects of durational reality. But the *kind of thinking* that Descartes essentially had in mind, and the kind of thinking which Kant's interest in physics had to pick up, is quantitative thinking about changes of state or location of spatially extended objects.

This is that mode of time which is the measure of motion and is primarily concerned with the relation of before-and-after in terms of momentary points which themselves have no lastingness or real duration. Curiously enough, Descartes took such momentary points as having some kind of ontological, and not merely regulative, reality.[35] Kant, weaned on Leibnizian notions of dynamism and continuity, seemed to regard them, as perhaps we still do, as arbitrary but useful points on a fictional line. Tying this notion of linear time into the determinism which the notion of efficient causality requires, Kant quickly saw that this notion of time, intrinsic to scientific cognitivity, forecloses the possibility of freedom and the meaning of the human self who cannot be reduced, in his temporal functioning of planning, anticipating, and remembering, to a series of points on a spatially conceived line.

This meant closing off the notions of freedom and self from a concept of time into which the notions of (1) linearity, (2) quantitative designation, and (3) deterministic causal condition had been built. Eschewing such descriptions and working with a traditional table of definition by dichotomous division, Kant saw that he had no choice but to place whatever kind of temporality he saw in freedom and in self, whether human or divine, into that other column of a definitional table which would then be headed "non-time." In doing this, he seems to have followed the intimation of Infinite Quality in the "Table of Judgments" or Limited Reality in the "Table of the Categories." What was obviously *not* subject to sequential description in these three aforementioned ways, was then placed in that broad area of "non-time." Insofar as the restricted notion of time-outlook is the area within which the phenomenal is to be known, that broader and more fundamental area, the noumenal, was then freed of any need for such a restrictive straitjacket kind of time designation.

Now, if the noumenal on its highest level, as for God, is somehow durational and if even the phenomenal order somehow reflects an order of absolute time or durational reality, it must be clear that Kant was *not* denying *every kind* of time-description to freedom and to self. He was only denying *that kind* of spatializing linear temporality of postulated moments used for quantitative description which serves physicists and other clock-watchers as indexes of true duration.

If, however, we begin to discriminate the possible kinds of time-description which Kant declined to place under the narrow requirements of scientifically utilitarian time-description, it should be clear that we must place under this heading of "non-time" a number of different time concepts or formulations that do not fall under the very restrictive notion to which the term "time" has been allocated. We are certainly not limited, as the only alternative (or complement) of mathematical time, to the notion of timelessness, a notion which Kant does not seem to have taken seriously on any ontological level. Kant's very insistent denial of time predicates to freedom, self, and noumenal entities was not a mono-lithic denial of all kinds of temporal descriptions; it was merely the de-nial of the legitimacy of attributing any applicability of the particular kind of time-concept, which has been useful in the natural sciences, to objects that are not describable in spatial predicates. It is a confinement of the legitimate applicability of a quantifiable, determinist time to the world of spatially apprehended entities, to the world describable in terms of spatial extension. It does not foreclose the legitimacy of using other kinds of time predicates for other possible kinds of existences.

It thus would seem that Kant was working with the conviction of some kind of ultimately objective real referent of the temporal predications spelled out in the cognitive principles that was not itself subject to that predication.

If the considerations leading us this far are essentially fair, then several consequents begin to emerge.

The first comes out of the suggestion that Kant seems to have been working with the Cartesian distinction between durational reality and time as the form or mode of the calculating human perspective on it. If this be so, then it would seem that Kant has taken what is implicit in that distinction with the fullest seriousness. He seems to be utilizing the ancient thesis that knowledge must somehow resemble that which is to be known while giving development to the Leibnizian thesis that all apprehension is perspectively defined. If the reality of the world, and of the things in it, are basically grounded in some kind of durational reality, then our modes of knowledge adequate to it must have some kind of essential perspectival reference to durational structures. Our time, therefore, may be understood as a finite form of the human outlook permitting limited aspects of durational reality to be apprehended by us. The argument of the "Analytic" proceeds on the premise that our conceptual understanding works within what the form of temporal apprehension provides. If our finite time is the form in which our apprehension of durationally structured entities is made possible, it takes no great stretch of imagination to see how the particular objects of apprehension should require temporalized principles of knowledge to provide our cognitions of the real durational world appearing to us in the form or "translation" of spatial embodiments. If the Cartesian distinction between time and duration is taken as an accurate metaphysical description, it would seem that something like Kant's temporally structured cognitive principles are but a consequent.

We may then view the cognitive situation from the other, the perspectival side, from the side of the knower's concepts rather than from that which is to be known. The thesis emerging would then assert that Kant's conception of conceptual validity was essentially intentional: a concept, to be meaningful, must have some object of reference which it seeks to describe. Empty empirical concepts are concepts without perceptual reference; they are then meaningless.[36] In order to propose meaning, an empirical concept must refer to some kind of specific thing reported by sensibility in the intuitional forms of space and time. Meaningfulness is, then, concomitant with ostensiveness; it has a denotation. But this criterion for meaningfulness was *not* limited to empirical concepts. The categories, as pure concepts of the understanding, Kant insisted, "can find no object, and so can acquire no meaning which might yield an act of knowing of some object. . . . The categories, therefore, without schemata [i.e., without reference to the forms of time experience] are merely functions of the understanding for concepts; and represent no object."[37]

Kant believed, as already noted, that he was doing, not psychology, but metaphysics; on a metaphysical plane, this discussion would take us into that most obscure of Kantian doctrines, the doctrine of the necessary postulation of the necessity of the transcendental object. I have elsewhere argued that the transcendental object must be equated with time itself.[38] I would still maintain that argument while pointing out one essential ambiguity it contains, namely, the question of just how the reality of the transcendental object, taken as given, is to be related to the reality of the noumenal.

The problem of just how they are to be related was raised by Kant himself in the chapter on "Phenomena and Noumena," where we are told that the "concept of appearances, as limited by the Transcendental Aesthetic, already of itself establishes the objective reality of the *noumena*. . . . " He then proposed the necessity of the transcendental object as requisite for all understanding of sensibility; and then proceeded to insist, without explanation, on a distinction of a fundamental kind between the transcendental object and noumenal being.[39]

Paton indicated the depth of the posed problem when, after a valiant attempt, he said, "I do not know what this means."[40] But the problematic posed by the question of the relationship of the transcendental object to noumenal reality cannot be lightly brushed aside. The question of their relationship is central to any definitive statement concerning the kind of world in which Kant believed our experiences transpire. We might accept the distinction and develop it or we might work to join them together. However that necessary inquiry be pursued, it would seem clear that the transcendental object, like objectivity in general, is the necessary referent of the transcendental structuring of our empirical knowings. This is to say that, however its ontological status is finally understood, it is the ultimate reference of temporally formed principles of knowledge just as noumenal reality has been seen as embodying durational being.

One consequence, then, of this whole discussion is the obligation to take the Kantian doctrine of the transcendental object with a seriousness that has rarely been accorded to it; doing so would mean facing the Kantian presumption, buried in the categorial deduction, that the presuppositions of transcendental object and transcendental subject are *equally* foundational to the theory of knowledge which stretches *between them* like the span of a suspension bridge between its two supporting towers.

We are likewise compelled to face the relationship between any meaningful concept of transcendental objectivity and noumenal reality; if they are not to be regarded as identical, or as two aspects of the same ultimate X, what could Kant have possibly meant by them? On the premise that any viable theory of knowledge presupposes some notion of what is involved in the object of knowledge, what is here being suggested is the thesis that Kant's epistemology structured by temporally constituted principles entails the belief that the world of noumenal reality is somehow constituted, even if metaphorically, in complementary terms.

If this be so, then the breach between cognitive reasoning and the "non-time" of moral reason can be quickly healed. If moral reason were really as remote from *all* kinds of temporal considerations as some of Kant's texts *seem* to suggest, it is incomprehensible how moral reason could function, could enter into the time world, or have any existential meaning whatsoever. Clearly requisite to permitting moral, or more generally practical, reason to function—in the time-spread of inner thinking as in the world of sensory experiences—is the requirement to take time seriously as more encompassing than the quantifiable causal time frame of phenomenal sequentiality. On the premise that Kant's concern with moral reason was not only genuine but also fundamental, it is necessary to take the applicability of *some kinds* of time predicates as valid in a far wider range of application than the very restricted notion of linear time, as the form of inner sense, would permit.

What seems strange is that Kant never fully formulated or developed several divergent notions of time that he himself used; quite distinct from the moment-counting time of the quantitative outlook used to describe the appearances of spatially framed physical objects, they are not commensurate with his own restrictive and troublesome language.

One need only turn, for example, to the "Preview of the Deduction of the Categories," where he deliberately turned his attention from the things of the world as experienc*ed* by us to the human experienc*ing* process itself. In these passages, we find him dealing with time experience, not in the object-oriented terms of before-and-after, but in terms of past-and-present-and-futural anticipation. Apparently pressed by other questions of concern, he does not seem to have focused on any problems of translation between the two. He was, however, quite aware of the wide range of experiential relations legitimately describable in some kind of time terminology. He was also explicitly aware of some of the difficulties inherent in achieving a comprehensive description of the differing ways in which he found time to be involved in divergent facets of human experiencing.[41]

In the *Anthropology*, for example, he picked up the human experiencing of temporal modes in a passage which cuts deep to the levels of Kant's temporal insights and also suggests the lines of a time-oriented defense of his insistence of the primacy of practical reason:

> Men are more interested in having foresight than any other power, because it is the necessary condition of all practical activity and of the ends to which we direct the use of our powers. Any desire includes a (doubtful or certain) foresight of what we can do by our powers. We look back on the past (remember) only so that we can foresee the future by it; and as a rule we look around us in the standpoint of the present, in order to decide on something or prepare ourselves for it.
>
> Empirical foresight is *anticipation of similar cases* (*exspectatio casuum, similium*) and requires no rational knowledge of causes and effects. . . . [42]

At least three discernible kinds of time description have now been identified in Kant's work. The first two I have traced from Descartes; they are (1) the quantifiable time frame which Kant identified as the source of arithmetic, the time of the physicist who seeks to understand that reality which appears insofar as it can be described in those primary qualities

Descartes had identified as such; and (2) that ultimate durational reality or world-time which does indeed appear in finite ways to our finite capabilities to apprehend and comprehend it but which, because it is outside of our perceptive capacity, is not subject to the possibility of cognitive description.

But (3) Kant had already seen that there must be a third mode of time description—not the time of the things appearing to us as objects of systematic cognition, but the temporal human perspective within which they appear and within which cognitions are sought; for objects appear to us in our anticipations, memories, plans, and recollections and it is only within this nonquantifiable range of temporal experiencing that the attempt for systematic and mathematical cognitive description may arise. It would seem then that as we are able, by acts of practical reason, to project these anticipations and desires out onto a world appearing as spatialized thingness, we are able to read them off in quantifiable references and relations. Thus, the quantifiable clock-and-calendar time arising from time-as-the-form-of-inner-sense would appear to be essentially derivative from the practical cast of human thinking; it would then incorporate spatializing predicates for utilitarian application in an order designed—for some reason beyond our possible ken—in primarily spatial terms.

However such a further development might be, the essential point from which we must start, if we are to start from the Kantian accomplishment, is this underlying presumption or working conviction that our modes of operating in the world in which we find ourselves and our modes of cognitively focusing on certain aspects of that world in rigorous terms must reflect something of the nature of that world which is to be known.

Kant had described himself as something of a Leibnizian, and I would like to suggest that the Leibnizian metaphor, in this instance, is clarificatory: If every percipient indeed reflects the universe from his own peculiar point of view, the better part of wisdom is neither to mistake the reflection for that which is being reflected nor to assume that the reflection is self-sustaining. Although the reflection is, within the capabilities of the mirror and its limited range of outlook, reporting what appears before it, the mirror may neither claim to see the entire object nor to expect that the structuring of the reflection is anything more than analogous to the structuring of the appearing object. What the mirror does provide is an image of the surface aspect of what is before it in accord with its own capabilities for accurately or distortingly "perceiving" and "reflecting." But however distorted, that reflection cannot be wholly disparate from the surface of what appears before it and indeed must be, regardless of inherent perspectival distortions the mirror itself provides, analogous to it. Had Kant further pursued his own transcendental investigation of time and of the durational reality he supposed it reflected, it would appear that he would have found this consideration illustrative.

It seems clear that Kant's conception of the world in which knowledge is to be had and moral and other practical decisions are to be made and used and applied is a world that, in principle, is subject to some kind of time predication by us on the highest level of its being. Could it not be then for this reason that it appears to us, in its various guises, and is always to be understood by us, in the form of a temporal perspective?

4

Time and Ethics:
How Is Morality Possible?

It has frequently been remarked that Immanuel Kant brought the concept of time into the forefront of philosophic discussion, that much of our preoccupation with time stems from his work. But it is too often forgotten that he had carefully and painstakingly restricted the dimensions of time to the cognitive functioning of the human understanding, that he had denied time's applicability to the human self in its exercise of that moral freedom which he regarded as the secured foundation of moral reason.

That he bifurcated the human self and its experience between the temporal and the nontemporal raised serious questions concerning the unity of experience and Kant's new Critical philosophy. That he denied temporality to moral reason effectively attacked the foundations of the moral philosophy and its experiential preeminence he was concerned to ground. That he felt it necessary to propound such perplexities points to the decisive import of the particular concept of time which he inherited and, in turn, passed on to us.

Concerned to validate the new science, Kant argued that our knowledge of the objects constituting natural phenomena—our perceptual experiences and theoretical reason's interpretive understanding of them—are completely structured in temporal terms. Our sense experiences and the principles in terms of which they are to be understood are both grounded, he argued, in the pervasiveness of the form of time which takes in every act of cognitive consciousness. This is to say that what he regarded as the root concepts of scientific explanation—quantifiability, substantiality, causality, interaction, necessary connection—were all ostensibly grounded in the form of time which structures human cognitive experience.[1]

But Kant was even more concerned to secure the foundations of morality. Doing so necessitated defending the possibility of moral responsibility, individual conscience, the autonomy of the self, and a normative ethic. Each of these constituents of morality is itself grounded in the moral freedom of practical reason. The importance Kant attached to moral reason is indicated by the fact that he believed it to be here and here alone, not in the exercise of theoretical or scientific reason, that one could rise above the confines of phenomenality and catch a glimpse into noumenal or ultimate reality itself.

Ironically, he found it necessary to sequester this whole area of practical reason from the domain of time. Having demonstrated the pervasiveness of time in the functioning of cognitive reason, which had hitherto been associated with the timeless, he found himself impelled to deny the temporality of moral conscience and practical reason in order to save the integrity of the autonomous self and the essential freedom which grounded them. Although the painstaking dissection of theoretical reason was explicitly undertaken to safeguard faith in our own freedom and moral responsibility, the only way Kant saw himself able to do so was to foreclose the temporality of practical reason. One consequence was the unresolved bifurcation of Kant's Critical philosophy—an inability to reconcile and unify these two aspects of the human self, an inability to reconcile cognitive and moral experience. Of at least equal consequence is the fact that this detemporalization of a normative ethic, of freedom, of practical reason, rendered Kant's moral philosophy inoperable in his own terms.

Yet, on the face of it, this seems somewhat absurd. Any consideration of practical reason, of moral conscience, responsibility, or decision, points to its temporal field. Morality arises, Kant had argued, from the distinction between inclination and obligation. Focused in the question "What should I do?", moral judgment looks from a present situation which poses a problem to the possibility of a resolution of that problem. Whether one proposes a teleological ethic of utilitarian means to chosen ends or a deontological ethic in which we seek supervening standards of right and wrong, it seems apparent that a temporally defined situation, a projection of moral possibilities into an as-yet undetermined future, and a foreseeable spread of time for requisite activity are all integral to any meaningful notion of moral responsibility and moral freedom.

Having perceived the centrality and fundamentality of time in cognitive experience, Kant seemingly felt it necessary to foreclose its applicability to areas of deeper concern. The concept of time with which he worked was intrinsically connected with the necessary determinism of the physical world and thereby would have subverted the whole of practical reason. To save the moral self, moral conscience, and moral freedom and responsibility (as well as the transcendental ego which underlies cognitive reason), he thus had to foreclose them from subjection to the only concept of time he really knew, the time of linear sequence.

He thus felt impelled to bifurcate human reason into the theoretical and the practical, one essentially to be described in time predicates and the other in their denial. Yet something is seriously wrong, for Kant himself insisted on their ultimate unity: "if pure reason of itself can be and really is practical as the consciousness of the moral law shows it to be, it is only one and the same reason which judges apriori by principles, whether for theoretical or for practical purposes."[2] Indeed, Kant did not merely see them as unified; he insisted that in the distinction, practical reason had complete priority; it had "primacy . . . [just] because every interest is ultimately practical, even that of speculative reason being only conditional and reaching perfection only in practical use."[3] Yet Kant could not show in his own terms just how theoretical or speculative reason served practical interests, because he could not show how a nontemporal reasoning could enter the sequential time of phenomenal events, in which moral reason must be applied.[4]

In a very real sense, Kant's discussion of time mixed two variant concepts of sequential time. When describing our observations of the phenomenal world which we seek to understand, Kant apparently accepted, without modification, that concept of time inherited from Aristotle, which seems to be used by all scientific observers of natural phenomena—time as the numbering of the motion of objects in space in terms of before-and-after. But "motion in space" refers to external phenomena and not necessarily to mental activity.[5] Consequently, when Kant introspectively observed the dynamic content of consciousness, he seems to have used Locke's notion of primary time as the "train of ideas" in consciousness. Indeed, this seems to be the working notion of time enunciated by Kant in the opening pages of the *Critique of Pure Reason*. His essential argument for the fundamentality of the form of time in cognitive consciousness, in fact, seems to be precisely this—that every idea, regardless of its content or reference, is seen in consciousness to be in a sequence of ideas, before some, after others.

Aristotle's and Locke's notions of time—one referring to the external world and the other to internal consciousness—have this in common: they are descriptions of observed sequences from the point of view of an observer supposedly external to them. Looking into a series of events, I see the present scene emerge from that prior to it and in turn give way to a succeeding one. If, as a disinterested and extraneous observer, I am asked to explain what is now before me, I do so in terms of an earlier scene. My explanation, in terms of what I regard as an efficient causal sequence, finds the explanation of the present scene in one that occurred earlier and is no longer. My explanatory scheme is essentially chronological and the present is explained in terms of the past. Insofar as the past is over and done with and thereby unchangeable, we can see why this kind of explanation so easily suggests some kind of determinism. For explanation is in terms of what is not now controllable and the farther back we regress in the causal sequence, the more remote from controllability it appears to be.[6] If every event is then observed in a sequence of before-and-after, no event contains its own explanation; each event is seen as arising from some other event chronologically prior to it, and external from its present. Once we apply some standard metric to this observational field, we are able to quantify and thereby objectively describe the sequence of a train of events, as well as their durational spread, as they appear in the observational field—in a numbered sequence of before-and-after.

For any such explanatory schema, chronology becomes crucial. The later is explained in terms of the earlier; the present, as the product of the past which is beyond control, is thereby rendered determinate. All is then to be explained in the beginning, in a first cause or earlier state: "the future," as Leibniz had once suggested, "is to be read in the past."[7] And if there is an ultimate past beyond which we cannot go, it must contain, in embryo, the entire future which is destined to emerge out of it. Causal explanations in terms of prior states are expressed in statements of if-then relationships, which are statements of causal sequences structured in terms of before-and-after. Such causal explanations of the present in terms of earlier states external to what is being explained are necessary to any kind of predictability. Such explanations arise out of that kind of disinterested observation which is crucial to scientific inquiry; they record observed sequences without reference to the particularity of the observer. They do not really offer any explanation of the reported sequence itself, but merely attribute efficacious necessity to selected chronology.

Kant was, of course, concerned to validate the new science of his time. Indeed, if one prime aim of the *Critique of Pure Reason* was to establish the necessary universality of the principle that "every event has a[n] efficient] cause," it is little wonder that Kant perceived the fundamental import of sequential time to the explanatory scheme of a mechanistic science. For the notions of efficient causation and predictability depend upon linear time, time plotted along the figure of a line in which the later is explained by the earlier. Kant's validation of the new science was, then, a validation of the fundamental import of sequential or linear time in phenomena as they appear to us; it was equally a validation of sequential determinism in the world of observable phenomena. Determination of an object, in terms of the cognitive principles, means determination in a quantifiable causal-time sequence, in which what is "after" is explained as the measured result of what came "before."

If universalized, this identification of explanation, causal sequence, and time sequence, while facilitating predictability with regard to natural phenomena, effectively forecloses the possibility of morality. For morality—under which we include the notions of conscience, responsibility, and decision—follows directly, as Kant claimed, from freedom which it immediately presupposes.[8]

Yet, Kant was so impressed with the import of causality for explanation that he repeatedly identified freedom as a kind of causality.[9] And causal explanation was so identified with chronological explanation of the present in terms of the past that we find him treating free acts of judgment and decision as nontemporal (because not determined), but yet somehow temporally prior conditions, along the analogy of an earlier mechanistic cause, for our deliberate entry into the time-world in order to act within it. The determined causality of the phenomenal order is describable in time predicates; somehow, noumenal freedom is able to provide a causal impetus into the time-world and is a kind of cause which must be prior to the sensible effects which flow from its entrance into the world of sequential time.[10] Yet it is conceived as nontemporal and time predicates are not applicable to it. We must presuppose it in order to understand our experience of our own moral activity, but we cannot understand it or explain it. To be free is to be "independent of determination by causes in the sensible world" which appear in the form of linear time.[11] Somehow, in a way that can be experienced but cannot be explained, freedom means an ability to be an original center of causation, an ability to initiate a causal sequence in the phenomenal sensible world of determined sequential order so as to manipulate or redirect it as the judgment of practical reason demands. But practical moral reason, somehow able to enter and redirect linear sequences, must somehow be outside of time and therefore must somehow be atemporal.

The ironic outcome is that Kant, setting out to reconcile the determinism he considered necessary to scientific explanation of natural phenomena with the freedom that is requisite to moral responsibility, was so bound up by the notion of linear time that he had to detemporalize practical moral reason and morality—leaving the relation of the practical to the world of experience and action unexplained and inexplicable but somehow ultimately real. Somehow they are related—because we experience them as related—but we cannot understand how.

As with freedom and moral practical reason, so with the individual self that exercises freedom while examining conscience and making moral judgments, decisions, and action-commitments—we can have no explanation or understanding just because explanation and understanding are tied to efficient linear causality and thereby to linear time. But explanation in terms of such reduction of present to past cannot explain any act of freedom. Although Kant had identified freedom under the rubric of causality, he saw that it must be somehow exempt from the only concept of time he seems to have used, time as a linear series in which the present arises out of the past and in turn produces the future.

Perhaps one reason for the very strange, detemporalized ontological setting in which he placed freedom, moral reason, and the "real" self, all of which seem to require a permeating temporality, is precisely this insight: linear time and linear causality go hand in hand to deny the autonomy of the self and the reality of that freedom which he was concerned to defend and establish.

Freedom meant, for Kant, self-determination, not determination by an earlier state of an external reality. Freedom as freedom is not reducible to a past state or a mechanistic cause-and-effect relationship between two independent entities or events. Freedom as freedom is not a predetermined reaction to an earlier or external stimulus, but the open option of choosing one's own responses to it. Freedom is characteristic—not of the things we apprehend as phenomenal appearances—but of persons who are centers of experience, who are experiencing selves. This is to say that the linear time of what is observed is not necessarily the time of the observing, that the time frame in terms of which we describe what is experienced is not necessarily the time frame of the experiencing itself.

All of our thoughts may, indeed, be observed to be in some kind of a linear sequence—after some and before others; our thoughts or ideas, as looked at externally as objects of observation, are indeed in that kind of "train of ideas" which Kant seems to have borrowed from Locke. As such we may plot them along a line and number their order. But the import of a thought is not necessarily to be assessed by its sequential location; the import of a thought may more likely be found in its content, in what it is about, in that relationship in which it is found, in that to which it refers. The meaning and significance of a thought may be found, not by observing and numbering it as a point on a line, but by entering into it and looking out on the world, so to speak, from it. The meaning or significance of a thought may be found in the thinking itself, in the way it purports to relate itself to the world, in its intentional involvement. The meaning of a thought may best be assessed, not in terms of an external observation of it, but in terms of the monadological model wherein each act of thinking represents my way of reflecting my dynamic relationship with an aspect of my world from my peculiar point of view.

When we examine the content of our own thoughts, we find that they are primarily referent not to a sequential location in a "train of ideas" but to other ideas and to objects which are in a dynamic, shifting, and overlapping perspective of present and past and future. The content of my present state of awareness is not merely a sensory observation of the actuality of the objects before me; it also includes my anticipations and recollections which are essentially conceptual in character. As Kant himself realized when he turned his explicit attention, however briefly, to the temporal cast of our experiencing, as distinguished from the objects that are experienced, our most rudimentary awareness of a present apprehension is tied up in a synthesis that has melded into one cohesive judgment the presentness of sense-experience, the presence of the past that memory provides, and the presence of the future that conceptual anticipation presents. Our experiencing is not a linear sequence but is a moving synthesis of past and future in a dynamic present that cannot be reduced to a point on a line.[12]

What Kant seems to have discerned but failed to develop is just this: an act of experiencing is not the product of the past. It is an undertaking in a present that brings pastness as selective memory into it, and brings futurity as conceptual anticipation into it as well. The shift here is decisively from the past to the synthesized present *as the focus of explanation* of whatever it is that is happening. The balance of this essay effectively welcomes this shift as proceeding in the right direction and, for all practical purposes, criticizes him for not having gone far enough. In any event, what Kant seems to have suggested here is that the perception of a train of events does not simply arise, or get reflected, in a parallel train of ideas, but is a structured interpretation arising out of a perception that is always a dynamic intellectual synthesis.

Indeed, a Lockean "train of ideas"—just because it is the result of an analytic examination and not immediately experiential—is really pre-Critical in that it ignores Kant's own Critical (or Copernican) revolution, which insisted on the primacy of the structuring of our experiencing *and not* on the objects ostensibly observed by a passive receptor mind which did not contribute its own interpretive structures to the awareness of those appearing objects. The perception of a train of events in a numerable sequence of before-and-after is an activity of a constructed present which itself includes, internal to it, discriminated aspects of future and of past. The experiencing of time and of temporal passage is structured in dynamic temporal synthesizing which makes the frame of present-and-past-and-future (and not that of before-and-after) the fundamental time perspective of the experiencing self. The import of this point in Kant is suggested by the fact that it appears in that part of the First *Critique* where Kant was concerned to establish the fundamental possibility of cognition itself in the integration of sense experience and conceptualization.[13] Unfortunately, Kant did not pursue or develop this insight. Quickly reverting to a traditional, pre-Critical, object-oriented focus on the static before-and-after sequence of observed things, he foreclosed the possibility of the unity of the Critical philosophy as he left it and thereby the validation of the possibility of morality he had hoped to establish.

Yet, if we examine an act of moral or practical reason—which Kant regarded as of greater philosophic import than scientific understanding— we can see that recognition of its temporal constitution saves it from the ironies that are generated by the essentially pre-Critical identification of temporal experience as linear, and thereby as efficaciously causal sequence. We should also see that a fully Critical examination of time— from the viewpoint of the experiencer—points to the mode of unification of practical and theoretical reason in accord with Kant's own intimations and hopes.

Although this essay argues its thesis in terms of moral reason—just because it presents the temporal argument most clearly and succinctly— the argument can be generalized: the time of mental activity, including cognitive activity, is discerned, not in the externality of observation, but in the internality of involvement.[14] Mental activity is not geared to the past but to the future; understanding and explanation depend, not on actual states in the past, but on the projection of future possibilities which are brought back in constituting the meaning of the present. If, indeed, it will be agreed that anticipatory projection and not causal determinism is the key to the understanding of the experiential present, then Kant's thesis concerning the priority of practical reason starts to make sense, and finds confirmation precisely in that existential temporalization which he intimated but apparently never grasped.[15]

If, then, we turn to the experience of moral reason, as the clearest example of mental activity for this purpose, we find that we can discern two theoretically separable "moments" in its analysis. In any situation that can be dubbed a moral one, we can discern the "moment" of judgment, and the "moment" of decision to act. Ideally, each should be looked at in turn; but the essential points can be made by focusing particularly on the temporal frame incorporated into the second. Take any specific moral judgment you have ever made. It was not made in a vacuum. It was made in a particular situation which posed a moral dilemma, a situation which posed a disagreeable prospect and was seen as urging interference to change its apparent course, or a situation which posed an attractive prospect and was seen as inviting action to assure its actualization or fulfillment. Facing alternative pressures, desires, values, or demands, the dilemma was focused in the question "what should I do?" It could not be resolved in terms of desires alone because each one of several conflicting desires merely had set out a claim, and each one of these conflicting claims had to be adjudicated. Rational judgment faces such a conflict of desires by asking "which one should I honor?" "which one should I ignore, sublimate, or suppress?" When I want, or feel called upon, to do three conflicting things and can only do one, which one should I do? Unless I am to be the slave of every passing inclination or external prod, I must judge and decide. If I *am to make a choice,* I have no choice except to invoke the requirement of the "should": what should I do in this particular situation?

By raising the question of the "should" or the "ought," I have radically transformed that situation from a mere happening or flow of events in which there is an observable conflict of desires into a determinate situation which demands rational evaluation and deliberate interference. I have transformed it from an observable event which I can dispassionately witness, behaviorally describe, or study—into a moral situation to which I call myself to prescribe a solution, a solution which looks beyond the present to a future resolution, a future resolution whose possibility gives meaning to the determinate situation to which I prescribe it. In seeking an "ought," I am not only prescribing to the situation in which I find myself; I am prescribing to myself what I ought to do about it. I am anticipating the possibility of resolution and my participation in effecting that resolution. I am no longer a passive observer of a scene external to me: I have made myself part of the situation, defined the situation in terms of the "should" I give to myself, and thereby I have made it also part of me. And I have presumed not only my temporal continuity but also my ability to synthesize the modes of time by joining that situation and myself together under the aegis of the future-referring "should."

How do I form my moral judgment? How can I determine what ought to be done in this situation? Even the most teleological ethic cannot avoid the question. For it must ask (1) which goal or value should be sought, and (2) which means to that goal or value-actualization should be pursued. No method of resolving the question of a moral dilemma can escape the mantle of some future-referring "should."

I need some criterion by which to determine what I ought to do in this, my situation. Moral philosophers have argued various and conflicting proposals about such a criterion. For our present purposes we need merely note that advocates of a teleological ethic, such as Aristotle and Mill, have generally argued that present action should be guided by the anticipation of the realization of certain values and an intelligent choice of means for attaining them. One of Kant's prime reasons for rejecting such an approach is that the future is not ours to see with certainty, that one needs to have a standard of judgment that does not depend either on a prophetic ability or on the contingencies of the particularity of the occasion. He thus proposed what is generally termed a formal ethic focused on the principle of the categorical imperative.

To discuss Kant's reasons for a deontological ethic—an ethic of self-imposed obligation instead of one of prudential advantage—would take us far afield. For the present purpose we need only note two aspects of it: (1) as a completely a priori system of moral decision, it depends, not on sense-experience which he tied to linear time and causal sequence, but on pure conceptualization which he tied to anticipation; and (2) although he argued that the criteria of right and wrong could not be found in a means-end discrimination, he did urge imaginative anticipation of certain kinds of possible consequences for the values grounding the decision as a test for the morality of a contemplated action. This is to say that although Kant did not consider temporal modes or predicates in his moral philosophy, the only one that could be imported without distorting his prime moral theses is that mode of futurity which, I am urging, must be the prime temporal cast of practical reason.

One might conceivably resolve the question of the "should" by the route of a teleological ethic of means-to-end, or by Kant's route of the formal ethic of a priori moral reason. One might conceivably argue that moral judgment is essentially not temporal because it is an appeal to an ideal, transcendent, and timeless standard. However one chooses to resolve the question of moral judgment, it is clear that each route in some way leaves the final judgment—and the decision to act on the judgment—to what we call individual moral conscience.

Moral reason's call of conscience stands in marked contrast to all other forms of reason, and this uniqueness suggests why Kant had insisted on its preeminence. Alone, it turns my focus from the world to myself so that I may function with deliberateness in the world. It calls me from a preoccupation with outward things to the reality of my own being—so that I may utilize things rather than be utilized by them. In contrast to cognitive reasoning, which focuses attention on the things it studies, moral reason, in the call of conscience, calls me back to me, to what Kant had called my noumenal self, my essential reality. In contrast to aesthetic enjoyment, which focuses on the things it contemplates, the call of conscience calls me back into my own reality. It asks me, not about the things in the world, but what *I* should do with them. It asks me, not about other people, but about *my* responsibilities for them. It forces me back into a radical self-awareness, for in facing the question "what should *I* do?" I am facing my innermost being, my own values, my own commitments, my own essential temporal finitude, my own ability to synthesize the modes of finite time, my own ability to control my state of being in the world of other people and of things. It calls me back to myself, not in terms of the past or the immediate present, but in terms of the proximate future, of how my world and I should relate to each other in the next few minutes, hours, days, or years ahead. It calls me back to myself as a decider with a capacity for effecting relationships in the world. In the most literal sense, it calls me to reform and reorient that aspect of the world's development over which I am able to exercise influence and control. It arises out of a present situation which I see, interpret, and understand in terms of moral possibilities. It calls me to decide which of these alternative possibilities *I should* select to become actual. It calls me from my usual focus on things in the world to a focus on my own self, so that I may act decisively in my world of other people and of things. It reveals to me the reality of my own being and continuity in time, the values to which I am truly loyal, the possibilities which are genuinely mine, the limitations which I must accept, the limitations which I freely choose. In facing the question "what should I do about this situation?" I am facing no external scene but my own involvement; I am facing, in my own conscience, my own self in its existential reality as being time-bound and time-binding.

But the call to conscience is not only a call to judgment; it is an imperative for deliberative action. It is an imperative to moral action, to acting *because* my moral judgment demands it. What does this action involve? When I act in a deliberate way, I look ahead, anticipate certain possibilities for development, and delineate the present situation in terms of them. Action means that I determine myself in a commitment to a course of activity, I foreclose other possibilities, values, and desires as distractions to be avoided. I block out, as it were, a portion of the future and commit it to the action to which I have pledged myself to hold. The resolution of the situation which I command myself to pursue involves, then, my own resolute action. I project myself into the situation in terms of the resolution that I see it as demanding. I seize the possibility on which I have determined. I assess what it is factually possible for me to do; I commit myself to a course of action by anticipating a sequence lying ahead of me and resolving my present understanding of my present situation and my course of action in terms of this anticipation.

That all deliberate action is to be described in terms of such anticipatory resoluteness is clearly apparent. Deliberate action can be imposed externally by, say, an employer or a military commander. The peculiar nature of the moral action lies in the call of conscience which initial anticipation initiates: within the realm of what it is factually possible for me to do, is there one course of action which I *should* do, not as a matter of prudence but of obligation to my own self? The call of conscience arises out of the question of the "should" and joins the resoluteness of action in the self-imposition of the "should." Anticipation, as such, is then not an intellectual act of contemplation of an object but an existentially involved reading of my present situation in terms of the possibilities for me which I see suggested in it.

It is in terms of anticipatory resoluteness that my own essential temporality is most clearly revealed to me. In the commitment to resolute action, as emphasized in the imposition-submission of the I "should," I see that I am, in essence, a temporal being. My temporality is revealed in the necessity of making a moral choice: I cannot do everything that I want to do; I do not even have the time to do everything that I feel I ought to do. My temporality is most dramatically apparent in those cases in which I cannot "take time" to decide—but must act at once. I cannot even repeat an action, for any act is irrevocable; once done, it cannot be undone. Any action or inaction contributes to the development of my situation, as of myself, and cannot be turned back. I may, indeed, conclude that my first decision was wrong, that I should try again. But I cannot try again. The original situation has been altered by my first, if mistaken, decision. I now face a new situation created out of my first attempt to act. Indeed, I may try to redeem it by a new, second decision. But this second decision must apply to the new situation which I have helped to create, not to the old one. Each judgment, each decision, each act is an unalterable historic fact of possibility-actualization which may, perhaps, be superseded but cannot be undone, repeated, or replaced.

It is not merely that the situation, the decision, the act is each "in time" as in some sort of neutral container. Time is also in them. Time gives them their reality as their transience and their irreversibility. Time defines that they are and how they are—as time defines my own reality and my involvement with the situation with which I am concerned, whose requirements I judge as demanding that I impose an obligation on my self. The urgency and pressing nature of my moral dilemma then points out its structuring in temporal terms, as my response to it is structured in temporal terms. My moral judgments and moral decisions, then, are judgments and decisions about how I should structure those aspects of temporal existence with which I, as a temporal being, become involved. My moral judgments and decisions are not merely judgments and decisions about approvable acts; moral reason's questions are one and all ontological—about how I should structure the time of my experience.

How can I do this? When I resolutely undertake a course of action in order to resolve a present situation, I reach into the future for an as-yet unrealized possibility and guide my present action in terms of it. I bring it back, so to speak, into the present and read the present situation in terms of its lack of this future possibility—which I resolve to correct. I invoke memory for precedents to guide me in the evaluation of this particular possibility and its attainment. But my evaluation of my present situation, which calls me to act, is in terms of what ought to be in it that could be in it which I can place into it. That aspect of my past experience which I call into the present is precisely that memory selection which seems pertinent to the task lying ahead of me. I then see this situation as my own involvement in terms of a future which is not-yet, but which I bring into the present, and a past which is no-longer, but which I bring into the present. The present situation is, then, no point on a line of before-and-after sequences. It is not the click of a full second, not the "specious present" of some ten or twelve seconds. It is a *spread* of time, as I perceive and understand it, which takes my perspective of future and selected recall of the relevant past into constituting what I take to be the present situation.

When I discern a conflict of desires or values in the situation in which I am, I invoke a call to conscience and ask myself what I should do; I am invoking the mantle of the future-referring "should" as a key to the meaning of the present situation and of my involvement in it. I may, indeed, compare it to similar experiences in the past, but the key to similarity is the call of selected moral possibility.

In each stage of decision, my orientation is toward what is not the case that can be the case if I seek to make it come into being. My orientation is not to the past, which I cannot remake, but to that aspect of the future which lies within my grasp. In a very real sense, then, I am reading my present situation in terms of what is not-yet but truly might-be. I am reading it in terms of possibility for development which I take as genuine. I am reading my present situation as one whose being is not framed by the ticking seconds of a clock which gives notice of passing moments in a spatial idiom. I read the situation as a being who is able to transcend the limits of the immediate present: I can run ahead of myself into a future which is not-yet actual, and bring back a possibility which determines the meaning of the situation to me now, together with the nature of what I am to do about it. I am reading my present situation, not as an instance of atomically independent momentary actuality, but as a dynamic time-consuming synthesis of the specific possibilities of the future which I read into it, and the heritage of the past futures which brought it to its present state.

The situation as such is defined by me as standing out from its background of other happenings and events in terms of the future-pointing possibilities which I see it as suggesting. The problematic which the situation poses to me is the alternate course of possibility development in terms of which I define it as a situation. The resolution of the problem which defines the situation as my situation is undertaken by me in terms of the possibility which I grasp in my moment of vision into a not-yet future which I bring back into the living present.

Moral reason is then fundamental, as Kant saw it to be; but not because of a necessary presupposition that our moral selves are timeless. Moral reason is fundamental just because of our temporal nature. We are not each imprisoned in a series of atomic actual moments measurable by a clock. We are temporal beings just because of our need for temporal continuity, just because we are able to transcend an actual present and reconstitute it in terms of future possibilities that beckon us onward. We are able to structure present activity in a temporal field in terms of a selected future which we bring back to throw meaning on what is now present. We are able to take the immediate presentation and synthesize it with future possibility and selected recollection into a meaningful spread of temporal experience. We are able to read our interpretive canons, structured by the future possibilities brought back or retrieved for use in the present; such retrieved futures reveal certain lacks which we obligate ourselves to realize. We are able to structure our own selves in terms of the self-imposition and self-acceptance of the "should," which charges us to redirect the flow of events by integrating new possibility into the structure of the actual. We are, in short, able to impose moral obligations just because we are able to bring future possibilities into the present as a spur to new activity leading us onward.

Practical reason does not only depend, as Kant seemed to think, upon the distinction between inclination and duty, between sensibility and reason. Practical reason does depend upon our ability to transcend momentary time, select a future, invoke a past, and synthesize them into the intelligible reality of the living present. Moral obligation depends upon our capacity to read the present in terms of what it yet can be and let the synthesis of the three modes of experiential time draw that constituted present into a future that will, in turn, continue to look beyond itself. Man is a being endowed with reason; this means that he can look beyond himself, because he is not enslaved by the actual, because he can actualize those possibilities he has made his own. Man has moral reason, which traditionally has been called practical reason, just because he has a temporal or time-forming perspective, not merely in terms of his cognition as Kant had argued, but in terms of his whole being, because he can deal with what is possible, because he can act today by determining himself in the light of those possibilities which he chooses for his tomorrow.

In this description of the actual functioning of moral reason, I have obviously followed or worked from Heidegger's analyses in a general way. If this kind of description has any validity, it suggests that a projective concept of time saves the coherence of Kant's ethics and the unity of the Critical system from the disintegration to which Kant's own notion of the primacy of linear time had condemned them. This projective description of experiential temporality functions in terms of a priority of the future instead of the present or the past. It sees the focus of explanation of human practical reason to lie primarily in its view of its future rather than its inheritance from the past or the immediacy of the present. Whatever the situation in which we find ourselves, whatever the dilemma which we see posed for us, we read it in terms of what can be done about it, in terms of the possibilities which we see it as offering, in terms of the "where do we go from here?" But this is to see the meaning of the present primarily in terms of future-referring possibilities which we project ahead and retrieve in order to discern the meaning of the present. This is to see the explanation of our own actions not as blindly determined but as necessarily posing options, requiring decisions, always with a reference, not to that which came before, but to that which may come after, always with reference to a future which gives meaning to the present act.

To take a projective notion of time as primary is to give a priority to our experience as *we experience* it, to the way in which we experience time, use time, incorporate time into our living. It is to be loyal to the authenticity of our own experience, which we experience by looking ahead and constituting the meaning of the present in the light of the envisaged future. It is to take the Kantian distinction between persons and things seriously by giving our personal experience of time priority over the time of the things that are the objects of experience. This means that our time is essentially cast in terms of moral reason's self-direction rather than in terms of the sequential time we cast over the things we observe—just because things are seen by us primarily in terms of the meanings and the needs we see them as offering in response to the demands we make on them.

We do, indeed, take the Locke-Kant notion of a "train of ideas" in consciousness as an observable datum of our mental activity—provided, of course, that it is taken as a flow of interlocking ideas and not as truly separable, distinguishable, and thereby numerable units. But their content, in terms of which we look out onto the world, is primarily referential to projecting possibilities of the future into what is given in the present as the source of its significance. The content of our ideas is primarily referential to possibilities for action, to alternatives for action, to the questions "what can I . . . ?" and "what should I . . . ?" do about the situation in which I find myself.

But this is to explain my actions as I perform them, rather than in terms of a past state which has yielded the present. It is to explain my actions in terms of my vision of the future seen as coming toward me, which I accept as genuine or desirable, and in the light of which I mold my present activity. This is to say that explanation in terms of futural possibility is explanation in full accord with the Leibnizian principle of sufficient reason, reason sufficient to explain my activity and to comprehend it, in its own integrity. This invocation of a principle of sufficient reason that is not reducible to efficient causality, resists the intellectual temptation to import an intellectual interpretive framework about inanimate things and impose it on my living experience as I experience it.

Projective temporality not only enables me to explain my present action in terms commensurate with my experience of it; it provides a temporal frame for the possibility of the freedom which marks my experiencing and is requisite for morality; it permits an account of the self in terms of that autonomy which Kant invoked but could not really explain.

Indeed, projective temporality permits that unification of theoretical and practical reason which Kant had sought but could not really achieve. For if both theoretical and practical reason are, as Kant urged, but two aspects of the same reason, and if the practical side is the motive side, we can then see that the primacy of projective time, which grounds practical reason, permits or demands theoretical study of the phenomena of nature in terms of quantifiable and linear time-constructs—for this theoretical activity always involves practical involvement and is undertaken to serve envisaged possibilities of future realization.

This essay has been concerned to show that Heidegger's general notion of fundamental temporality as projective futural-possibility retrieving

activity is the one temporal perspective that can ground morality together with the notions of freedom and responsibility inherent in it. It
also saves Kant's Critical philosophy from the many crucial gaps he had
struggled but failed to overcome.

Although this has its own importance, I suggest it as an instance of
a more general proposal: that the concept of time is crucial to any systematic philosophy regardless of the role it is alleged to play in it. As a
hypothesis, this essay urges that an examination of the particular concept of time involved can conceivably serve either to subvert or to reconstruct the system which it effectively grounds. This is to say that the
concept of time is not an incidental ingredient of a philosophic system
but its ground concept, no matter how disguised its fundamental role
may be—as, for example, in Kant, where it was explicitly restricted to the
functioning of theoretical reason in the understanding of the objects
constituting natural phenomena, without any explicit examination of
the inherited notion of time that was invoked in order to see how it itself
was experientially grounded or what it did or did not inherently involve.

5

Experiential Time
and the Religious Concern

n the midst of crisis Augustine propounded the famous question which
compels us to face the central dilemma of any attempt to comprehend
the human situation in the world. "What, then, is time?" he asked.
"Who can find a quick and easy answer to that question?" Time is central
for each of us. Its presence pervades and structures every process in
which we engage, everything we can know. It bounds every activity of life
and indeed life itself. Yet we usually discuss important issues of life and
thought without even noting their intrinsic temporality.

We do not hesitate to use temporal terms; we freely employ the
tenses of our language. We read of our history, plan or bemoan our future. We take time and its meanings for granted. We may regard it as a
burden or as a source of hope, but we know that we cannot avoid its inexorable sway. Yet we cannot define the word "time." "What, then, is
time?" Augustine asked. "I know what it is if no one asks me what it is;
but if I want to explain it to someone who has asked me, I find that I do
not know."[1] Time pervades everything we think and do; yet just what it
is, how it is, remains a mystery, the mystery of ultimate reality, the mystery of being itself.

What then is time? I believe Augustine was correct: we are not
equipped to answer this question. But I think we can fruitfully explore a
related question: how does time appear to work in the temporal structure of human experience, in animating our fundamental concerns and
the meanings we find in life?

A straight line does not always define the shortest journey. Rather
than seeking to see time, or the world, as each might be in itself, we
might better try to make sense of our pervasively temporal experience,

of our temporal ways of dealing with the world in which we find ourselves. Rather than trying to see over the horizon, I invite a look at the way in which the horizon of the human outlook is itself formed. By making some sense of the pervasive temporality animating us, we might be better equipped to face the fundamental concerns which propose the specific questions we seek to answer, the specific deeds we seek to do.

If every hope and thought and fear is temporally structured, to ask about the structure of human temporality is to ask about the relation of experiential time to our deepest religious concerns. A religion, a religious outlook, Paul Tillich pointed out, is not simply a matter of theological doctrines—often resultant from abstruse disputations long forgotten and often mouthed without being understood.[2] Whether the religion be sacerdotal or secular, spiritual or materialist, based on revelation or inspiration, a religious outlook is a particular response to the fundamental concerns of human beings as they wend their ways through their world. The doctrines of any particular religious tradition are answers offered to the basic questions men ask. To face the facts of experiential time, then, is to face the fundamental concerns that are expressed in whatever religious tradition we choose to adhere to.

These fundamental concerns, Immanuel Kant had already suggested, are but three in number and each, let me suggest, is concerned with the meaning of temporal experience. As Kant summed up the matter: "All the interests of my reason, speculative as well as practical, combine in the three following questions: (1) What can I know? (2) What ought I to do? (3) What may I hope?"[3]

The first asks about the capability of systematic inquiry, of science, in trying to understand the physical environment and the possibilities it offers; it depends upon the temporal structure of finite human reason. The second asks about moral obligation and moral knowledge; it depends upon the temporal structure of freedom and its responsible use. The third asks about immortality; looking beyond human time, it depends upon a conception of the governance of the world, the possibility and the nature of God.

These three fundamental questions are *the* three questions of man's religious concerns, the ground questions concerning the human place in the world, human capability, human destiny. They are each asked from *within* the temporal constitution of the human outlook and are each concerned with the meaning of experiential time.

Some radical implications ensue from an explicit understanding of the human way of being temporal and responding to these three questions. However, it is first necessary to unveil some salient features of the temporal logic which Kant exposed as incarnate in human experience.

Then we can turn to the temporal nature of the three concerns that mold the time of human experience.

Experiential Temporality

Our ordinary ways of talking about the things and events of our experience provide a clue to the structure of our experiential time.

When we describe the sequence of two events, we say that the first came before the second, the second after the first—and we describe the temporal "distance" between them by dating them. The American Revolution came before the French; the French Revolution started fourteen years after the American began. Such statements present unalterable facts that do not change with the passage of time. Once true, always true—even a thousand years hence. And it does not matter whether we measure the temporal distance between them from the "before" or from the "after"; in whichever way we go the answer remains the same.

There are three remarkable things about this: (1) the remarkable lack of change, for, if time and change betoken each other, it seems odd that a true statement about time and change can be both timeless and changeless, that a statement about dynamic change can freeze time and change into a timeless truth; (2) the remarkable disregard of direction, for, if time and change move from the earlier to the later, if time is unidirectional, it seems odd that a true statement about time and change can be equally true regardless of whether we go forward or backward; and (3) the remarkable disregard of the "between," for our concern with an event is what is transpiring, but a terminal dating ignores what is transpiring and only marks its outer limits, the "point" before which and that after which it is no longer in existence.

Fortunately we have a radically different way of speaking that is much truer to the way in which we experience events. We describe an event as past or present or future. The truth of a statement, when expressed in this way, changes radically with the tense, acknowledges the unidirectionality of time and the continuity of process. Statements about the French and the American revolutions are true only in the past tense when spoken by their historians and in the future tense when spoken by their prophets. Statements made in terms of past or present or future thus depend for their truth upon the temporal perspective of the speaker; the same statement may be true in one tense and false in another.

In common parlance we may be tempted to say that statements made in terms of before and after are more "objective" just because they focus on the objects being discussed regardless of the "who" of the speaker. Their truth claims can be tested without reference to the speaker or the "when" of their utterance—but being at least one step removed from the concrete dynamic of temporal experiencing, they are more abstract; they also depend upon having first been experienced in some person's past or present or future stance.

All observations, to which reports of objects observed must ultimately be traced, originate in the outlook of a particular person in a particular temporal situation and must originally be reported in the time tenses of his language. Suppose a packet is now falling; two minutes ago it was not falling; two minutes hence it will not be falling. Change the time of each statement and its truth changes. Tensed reports reflect the essential dynamic quality of concrete experiencing; to test the truth of such a statement one must know the "when" of its being spoken.

Any concrete experience is a tensed experience. It arises in the moving outlook of an individual who is experiencing his own experiential activity as a moving present that does not stand still. Only after I seek to objectify the description of my experience can I sever my description from my experience out of which it arose, translate the continuity into supposed points of beginning and end that are marked by a metric which measures off the between, the extent of the occurrence; I do this, if I wish, by a set of numbers which I can diagram as two points on a line. But when I render my observation in terms of a numbered sequence between T1 and T2, I use a spatialized abstraction that detemporalizes the crucial temporality of my experience. Useful as this may be, it is not experientially true just because it is not true to the dynamic nature of my experiencing observation itself.

All experiencing transpires in a dynamic field of movement within a moving present. Yet somehow we often tend to diagram this too as a line on which we can plot the precise point of the present "now" with past and future on either side. This practice does not accord in any authentic way with the way in which experiencing transpires. A now point on a diagrammatic line represents no extent of time but an artificial boundary, instituted for a purpose, between two allegedly independent parts of the continuity of time, as the precisely marked boundary, say, between the past and the present. Experientially this is fiction. As William James noted, "Say 'now' and it *was* even while you say it."[4] We experience neither perceptual objects nor our own selves as moving from one sovereign moment to the next. Rather, we experience our selves and events in an ambiguously delineated present without sharp boundaries between what was and what is not yet. As Alfred North Whitehead pointed out, we are living in a moving "ill-defined present in which past and future meet and mingle."[5] The experiential present is not a point but a field, a field of perceptual and rational activity in which what-is is continually running off into what has been and is being continually refreshed by what is not yet but is coming to be. The continuity of experiencing depends, then, on the continuity of futurity entering into the dynamic present and being transformed by it.

In the dynamic of actual experiencing, past and future are not evenly balanced by a mythic midpoint we call the present. They are radically different in kind. For one, the past is determinate, unchangeable, and without options. What has been has been; it cannot be changed, although our understandings of it may yet change; it cannot be repeated or undone; it is not subject to choice, experiment, decision. It has become determinate, though not always determinable, fact. It can be investigated; it cannot be altered.

By contrast, the future presents itself to us as a range of often-conflicting possibilities. We have certain expectations, but they have yet to be confirmed. We may mark out areas within which choice and decision may be selective, single out some possibilities for actualization in a future-present and other possibilities for oblivion. We conduct experiments to see what can be reasonably expected henceforth. We make decisions as to how we want to shape what is not yet but may be. We act as if we are free beings who can, by virtue of our choices, responses, and decisions, indeed determine which possible future will be realized and which not. If there is any efficacy to human activity, it is directed only to what is not yet but yet may be. Human experiencing activity is oriented not to the past but to the future. We seek to preserve the continuity of what is deemed good and terminate what is deemed bad. We may seek either continuance or change. But all deliberate activity is necessarily directed only to what is not yet, in the hope or expectation that we may mold its transformation into an actual present that will yet be.

This activity of always facing the future constitutes the field of present activity, whether on a trivial or a sophisticated level. Even a rudimentary perceptual act is already selective and thereby future-oriented. I cannot possibly report all the myriad detail appearing before me. In any perceptual act some features of the landscape, some aspect of my room, will stand out from their background and attract attention. Like a focused camera that centers the entire scene on some element of it, my perception responds to some aspect of the presentation before me, selects some aspect of it for focus, as expressive of my present state, what I want, what I need, what interests or excites me, even if not consciously manifest. I walk into someone's living room and immediately notice a chair in which I want to sit, the bar which promises refreshment, a painting that delights the eye—and I see the room as centered on that object of focus. The object of my focus serves some instrumental need I bring with me. Any focused glance is constituted by some possibility which I see it as suggesting to me.

Any act of thought is likewise goal-oriented. It concerns a problem to be solved, a task to be done, a joy to be had, an end to be attained, a dilemma to be resolved, a decision to be made. Any acts of living, as Plotinus suggested long ago, are but a "continuous process of acquisition; eliminate futurity, therefore, [and] at once they lose their being."[6]

I do not believe that perceiving and thinking are truly separable, but however that may be, we find that any conscious present is structured in terms of what is not yet but conceivably may be. The presence of memory does not belie this. I cannot possibly remember everything that has happened. I could not possibly recall it in any present time. I do remember, seek to recall to present mind, those aspects of past experience which seem germane to the task at hand. We build the lessons of past experience, whether as conscious thoughts or habits of thought, into the present, focused, directed activity.

If the prospect of futurity is what pulls us onward, if particular remembrances are brought into the present because they are needed for the present uncompleted task, then the three phases of experiential time are organized in the present under the tow of the future. If futurity presents itself in terms of possibilities which are built into present activity so that they may be actualized, we can say that the present is constituted as a future-retrieving activity, as bringing conceived possibilities from a conceived future into the present so that they can be used again in carrying the present forward.

If this sketch of the way the present is constituted holds, if the present itself has no sharp boundaries but indiscernibly passes into what is not yet actual and what is already done, then experiential time cannot be conceived as strictly linear. It cannot be authentically diagrammed as a line; it cannot be reduced to spatial representation; it cannot be reduced to nontemporal points without duration; it cannot be described without regard to whether we start from the before or the after. Because it retrieves futurity as reasonable anticipation, because it retrieves memory as instrumental to the task at hand, it is essentially unidirectional. Human activity might be likened, perhaps, to the activity of a shallow brook, not one which flows straight and direct but one which eddies, gurgles, and curls back on itself around rocks and stones while it is continually wending its way downstream. To treat of human experiential time authentically, then, is to recognize its continual forward thrust, from a determinate past into an unresolved future.

However one resolves the speculative question of the nature, extent, and degree of human freedom, human activity is experienced as free; if this freedom is an illusion, so is the free argument of the determinist who belittles its reality. Human freedom is manifested in the selectivity of focus which guides it, the acknowledgment of specific problematics for attention, the evaluation of evidence, the decision concerning possibilities for actualization, the resolve to act, the honoring of our habits or our resolutions to reform them. But this is to say that deliberate behavior is goal-oriented in every aspect of its being; this, in at least the Greek sense of the term, is the mark of rationality. To be goal-oriented is to be future-oriented and to build the commitment to the goal into the structure of present activity.

This then is a sketch of the phenomenological analysis of human temporality.[7] In many ways, we might note in passing, it is very close to that developed by American pragmatism. With it in mind we can now turn to see the implications it suggests for each of the three fundamental concerns underlying human questioning that, taken together, constitute a person's religious outlook.

"What Can I Know?"

Much of modern intellectual history has been seen as a war between science and religion, as though each was monolithic and as though their interests and concerns were antithetical. This view represents a misunderstanding of both and does a disservice to each. No one will deny the conflicts between the world picture of the inherited theology and those of the newly emerging sciences. But just as organized religion gives rise to perspectival doctrinal formulations which change with the passage of time, so the sciences have announced doctrinal formulations that have changed even more radically.

The doctrinal dispute focused on the work of Galileo and Darwin. We may rightly condemn the Catholic Church for the persecution of the Catholic Galileo; but we have no right to condemn its concern for what he had to say. We may rightly condemn the general Protestant reception of the teaching of the Protestant Darwin, but we can only applaud the legitimacy of the interest. In due course the theologies were redrawn to accommodate the doctrines once opposed; more rapidly, interestingly enough, with regard to the second, which struck perhaps more deeply into emotional issues.

One problem seems to be not with organized religion or organized science but with the recurrent attempts of well-meaning people to try to freeze a particular expression of historically developing human thought into an allegedly eternal dogmatic statement. To do so is to belie the essential historicality of all human activity and to transgress on the authenticity of those commitments from which any particular doctrine of belief emerges.

If religion is the human voicing of ultimate human concerns, it needs to be concerned with the nature of the physical world in which men find themselves and spend the days of their lives, raise their questions, and seek out meaningful answers. From the beginning religious concern has been manifested in seeking to comprehend man's place in nature, nature's effect on man, and the history they share. We might note, as but one example, that the opening text of the Book of Genesis presents no call to worship, no admonition, no ethical injunction but rather a purported history of how the physical world, as men knew it, came to be.

The natural sciences first arose in ancient Greece as the work of philosophers who did not believe in any temporal beginning but who did have an unproven faith in the power of human reason to penetrate the secrets of natural phenomena. They did not ask about origins as much as about the continuity of change in the physical world. These sciences historically developed by using the developing methods of human reasoning that philosophic thought provided equally for science, for theology, and for other expressive forms of human questioning activity.

It is perhaps ironical, but the two traditions, supposedly separate and antithetical, have flourished only in common dependence. Unto the present day the legacy of Greek philosophy and science has prospered only in those places where the inheritors of biblical religion made themselves regnant. Largely in the inheritance of the Roman Empire—which venerated Greece while persecuting the heirs of the new biblical religion—and only after the religionists had declared and taken Rome as their own did the sciences begin to flourish to the point where their technological achievements threaten or promise a revolution in the affairs of men beyond any fantasy of early prophets.

Perhaps it seems strange that the sciences developed only in Christendom; but the fact is that modern science is uniquely the product of one Christian civilization. Just why this is so can be debated, but that it is so cannot be lightly dismissed. The way to the rise of modern science was cleared by Thomas Aquinas, whose theology gave a new dignity to human reason. Modern science was itself developed by religious men who set themselves the task of comprehending the complexities of the Creator's creation. Conceived in piety, awe, and wonder from within a theological commitment by Copernicus, Kepler, and Galileo, its methods were refined by René Descartes, Gottfried Leibniz, and Kant by reaching back to Augustine's Christianized Platonism. Their common stance was perhaps best exemplified by Isaac Newton, who insisted that his theological writings were more important than his *Optics*. Whether then or now, the scientific endeavor is a systematic investigation of physical nature which seeks to unveil sequential connections in natural phenomena and to develop techniques for control and redirection of these temporal ties in accord with human needs. By unveiling and enhancing man's possible interaction with the phenomena that constitute the physical environment, scientific activity is thus serving, whether explicated or not, an essentially religious concern.

For this kind of activity its methods were designed and validated; for this its competence has been established. We can then see the activity of science as itself arising out of the larger context of human questioning, as a method of meeting one of these prime concerns of human questioning of human nature, context, and destiny.

But some apostles of the scientific experience, sustained by an enthusiasm that scientific method cannot justify, seek to universalize its authority by usurping all other areas of human concern and foreclosing the truth of any but its own current conclusions. This is not science but scientism, a new and competing theology. Scientism cannot explain the activity of science; it uses a methodology validated only to address physical nature in order to respond to very different concerns. As such, as Kant for one already warned, it thus becomes a new and uncritical dogmatism which reaches beyond its own finite competence and ends by confounding itself.

The reason for this is not far to find. Scientific activity is an activity of men and is rooted in the nature of human time. As such it is but one expression of the human way of being, the human way of thinking, and of expressing the human temporal outlook.

Science does not present a new revelation of transcendent origin. It is a human activity arising out of the outlook of this historic culture. It uses a man-made methodology, which has a history of its own that is still going on. It uses a man-made logic by which to reason and to validate its thinking, and that logic is itself historically developed and still controversial. It has proceeded, as Thomas S. Kuhn for one has pointed out, by a succession of hypothetical and conflicting paradigms, metaphysical assumptions, and discordant explanations in a history of intellectual revolutions and regroupings.[8] Its doctrinal history is not that of the progressive unfolding of a panoramic vision but rather more like political history in twistings, turnings, repudiations, and new beginnings. In even its purest sense, it has been dependent on new technologies, the accident of invention, the politics of financial support, and the interests of both economic and military need. The history of its doctrines is but part of the broader expanse of human social historical development.

The cognitive force of its doctrines, however validated, should not be read for more than they are. The laws of nature the sciences announce are not necessarily the laws of nature as such; they are but the currently successful rules by which men are able to correlate selected phenomena; they are explanatory statements of a finite human outlook, express the human point of view, and are, in each case, the answers secured to questions asked. Human science cannot be a godlike observation of nature as a whole just because its questions and its activities are always within the whole of nature. Scientific probing and questioning is always in specific terms and always from a human perspective within the capabilities of individual human thinking. Just as the sciences have historically provided diverse explanations for the same kind of phenomena, it is conceivable that another creature, thinking in a different way, would ask different questions from those we ask, organize its probing and questioning by different categories than those we use, and emerge with explanatory answers different from those which, at any particular time, serve to satisfy us. Human science, in its cognitive reach, is limited at the outset to the ways in which humans are able to look at the physical world about them, the ways in which that world may appear to the peculiarities of human vision. The activity of science then, as the doctrines that ensue, is a human activity defined in its capabilities and limitations by the human way of temporal thinking as well as by the historical cultural matrix in which it happens to be functioning.

The individual human scientist is a human being who works within a community of other similarly dedicated human beings. Leaving aside the specific animating motives for the individual investigator (which, I suspect, are primarily aesthetic), we may still expect to find at least three personal qualities in any serious investigator: existential commitment, meaningful freedom, and moral reason. These are each manifestations of experiential time.

The individual investigator commits himself to a certain way of thinking; he must, by an exercise of subjective will, determine to bracket the subjectivity of his individual wants. He must aim at objectivity, dispassionate judgment, disregard of purely personal perspective; he must restrict himself in the kinds of questions he allows himself to ask and the kinds of answers he will accept. By seeking repeatability in experimentation, mathematical description in formulation, and public accessibility to data, the individual scientist, in a real sense, makes an existential commitment to sublimate his individuality. And, in reducing temporal description to the measured temporal distance between a before and an after, he has necessarily used his own temporal perspective to deal with time in abstract, spatialized, nonperspectival terms.

To achieve even these abstract time statements he necessarily utilizes the structure of human temporality. He considers possibilities before him in formulating his project; he asks questions, retrieves information from past work or from his colleagues guided by a judgment of purposive relevance. The structure of his investigatory activity is itself a paradigm of the existential nature of experiential time at work, for his present is defined for him as a spread of time, a field of present, in which futurity enters to direct, attract, pull onward, and to do so by injecting a vision of alternate possibility for him to choose. And his own past enters into his present activity not as a mechanistically conceived causality but as lessons to be retrieved, skills that have been mastered, a legacy to be used in selective form in the light of where he sees himself headed.

The effective depersonalization that the scientist requires is a highly personal kind of commitment, a deliberate willful decision about how to utilize his time. In order to do this he cannot be an automaton; he necessarily exercises his capacity to focus, to decide, to commit himself to act in the specific way the scientific endeavor demands, the instances when it shall be pursued, the instances—such as his continuing personal life—when it shall be put aside. He must be able to evaluate his own skills in manipulating his equipment, control his time allocations, build or re-form habits of work and thought, subject himself to the discipline he accepts in order to realize the goals he sets. And he does all this within a time frame explicitly defined by futurity, for his criterion of predictability brings the possible future into his existentially committed present.

The scientist as scientist demonstrates the ability to utilize practical reasoning. He chooses proximate goals as means to longer-range goals and he chooses the means along the way. He demonstrates the ability to make discriminations of what he regards as good and bad, right and wrong, and to adapt his own conduct in the light of these value assessments.

Scientific activity is not, as the cliché phrases it, "value free." Without the ability and commitment to continuing value judgments of a procedural kind, without a commitment to the value of truth itself, science could not be. Scientific activity, then, depends on the moral reasoning of the scientist, who necessarily adapts standards of moral reasoning for application within the particular context of his concern.

Scientific activity is directed in a secular way to the ultimate concern defining the religious outlook—the understanding of the sequential connections within the world in which we find ourselves and the possibilities they offer. Scientific activity proceeds by employing the structured, value-laden, temporal outlook of human beings. It points beyond itself, in its own activity, to human moral reason in at least two ways. The first I have mentioned—the necessity for employing moral value-judgmental criteria of good and bad, right and wrong, in defining methods and focusing on goals.

But it does so in another way as well. The results of scientific investigation continually lead to new practical employments in reshaping and guiding everyday life. The technological revolutions, which scientific achievements made possible and which in turn have fed into redirecting scientific studies, have continual repercussions for all other human activities. Contemporary science, for one, presents human society with new opportunities and dilemmas which can be settled only in terms of moral judgments and the sorting out of moral values. The discrimination among them—the possibility of being accepted or avoided—is dependent on moral reason, which indeed needs the knowledge of what it can do in order to make responsible decisions about what it ought to do.

Scientific activity rests upon the activity of moral practical reason and feeds back into it new problems for resolution. We are thus led to the second of the ultimate concerns, that of moral obligation and the responsible use of freedom.

"What Should I Do?"

The quest for knowledge, as we have seen, depends on (1) an active personal involvement with tools and equipment in the environment, (2) our ability to seize possibilities we see being offered in terms of goals we seek to achieve, (3) moral fidelity to standards of truth and integrity of method, and (4) recognition that no solution is final, that each solution achieved creates new problems for resolution. Just so, moral reason, in its explicit exercise, finds itself in situations that are temporally structured, involves us with the world of other persons and of things that are temporally operative, and reaches beyond its own questionings, in which new problems are continually being exchanged for settled ones.

Moral reason arises out of problematic situations. It arises out of value conflicts, conflicts between alternate desires and alternate goals. As long as no conflict is discerned, no decision to be made, no moral dilemma presents itself and no moral decision has to be made. My moral dilemmas arise when I want to do two things but can do only one—which one should I choose to do? Or when I experience a conflict between a desire and a feeling of obligation, I want to do this but think I should do that instead.

Moral philosophers have argued about the relative value of different judgmental criteria—whether pleasure or happiness, stoic resignation, hedonistic indulgence, aesthetic satisfaction, or moral self-development is to be taken as a guide to decision. They have argued about the values by which decisions should be made and also about the method to be followed in resolving value conflicts. Some, for example, have urged that we acknowledge a supreme good to be achieved and then appropriate means to achieve it. Others, citing the aphorism that the road to hell is paved with good intentions, have urged instead a rigorous standard of right and wrong that does not take account of anticipated future effects which may ensue from present action.

However such disputes may be and however our sympathies may be directed, one thing seems clear. Moral decisions are not about the past, which cannot be changed, or about the present moment which is fleetingly actual, but only about the future.

All moral decisions presuppose the irreversibility and the onward march of time. We may condemn an evil deed, but we cannot undo it: we can either ignore it or seek to atone for it henceforth. To accept a moral responsibility, in any serious sense, means to resolve a solution henceforth, to read the situation as offering a possibility for development that I undertake, to try to build a value judgment into its future course. A moral decision activates a hope or belief that my decision can indeed alter the development of the future, can make a difference in how things will yet be. All my moral decisions are temporally structured decisions that relate to a future regarded as in some degree open to my intervention. My moral decisions are decisions about what ought to be that I might help bring to pass—with regard to others and my own self.

All moral decisions, then, are temporal decisions in two distinct senses. They relate to the future by means of possibilities which presently seem to offer themselves for realization—and so they exemplify the structure of experiential time. But they also embody action-commitments to the use of oncoming time in specific ways, for the realization of specific values, for the creation of a future deemed to be different in the absence of my active involvement. Not only are moral decisions temporally structured; they are also decisions about the use of time, about how a forthcoming temporal situation in which I find myself engaged shall be altered from what it otherwise would be. A moral decision—regardless of its specific reference, the values built into it, or the number of persons involved—is a decision about time use; it presupposes the reality of temporality, the presence of responsibility in determinate situations that are yet open-ended. A moral decision decides how the future of the world, in this particular regard and using the materials at hand, is to be created. Not only is a moral decision temporally structured and directed to the use of time. It also is forced by time. I cannot do all the things I want to do; I cannot do all the things I feel myself obliged to do. Most of my decisions are not between blatant evil and incarnate good but between alternate goods. In the dynamic press of the continuity of change I must decide between approvable alternatives. And I cannot refrain from decision—because not to decide is a deciding.

Time thus forces decision because time "finitizes." It forecloses all conceivable possibilities into just these few; it forecloses my pursuing all my values or goods into just these few among which I must still choose. It makes any specific finite choice a largely blind one just because I cannot see all the repercussions which will flow from it. And it makes my decision an irrevocable one as it closes off this particular situation and rechannels the direction of what comes after. Friedrich Nietzsche to the contrary, there can be no recurrence of the same because the continuity of temporal development introduces novelty into what may seem, at first glance, to be identical situations.

Not only are my choices finite. My life of choosing and deciding is itself finite. Behind every decision I make lurks the knowledge that all deciding as such will pass away, that there will come an end to my facing choices and resolving dilemmas. The time for all deciding is intensely finite, for death is the eclipse of life. The knowledge of impending death is indeed a part of life, but the experience of death is beyond life; we can experience the process of dying but death itself is beyond all possible experience. Death, the ultimate possibility we each will actualize, as Martin Heidegger pointed out, is absolutely incommensurable. We cannot fathom it, for our only experience is with the activity of being and not with the complete negation of being.

Yet death is not an unfortunate misfortune without present meaning. Its hovering promise is what forces choice, decision, moral reasoning, commitment upon us; it compels us to define our interests, our values, our pursuits, and thereby our own selves. I cannot investigate everything and so must decide what knowledge to pursue and what ignorance to accept. I cannot try out all values but must decide which I shall build into my self. Because my time is inherently finite, I am continually compelled to decide just how my biographic becoming will be directed and defined.

Time then is exemplified in moral reason in at least three ways: (1) my moral reasoning is temporally constituted, (2) it is concerned with temporally fluid situations, and (3) it is pervasively limited by its irrevocability, by the range of presented possibilities, and by the extent of time available to function. My temporality pervades the opportunities and the limitations of the possibilities I may make my own. And it is this ultimate temporal limitation on all that I can think and do and be that most prominently brings us humans to face our most ultimate concern, the mystery and abiding and pervasive reality of temporal finitude.

"What May I Hope?"

Time is, within human experience, the mark of reality and of being. The hope for life after death, for immortality, is the hope for continuing reality, the hope for the ongoing of the temporal. The prospect of the end of individual time has induced men in all cultures and levels of civilization to nourish the hope for life after death; even when this has been couched in terms of a somehow nontemporal eternal present, this is still but the hope for more time.[9] The hope for immortality thus underlines the fundamental import of time for us.

Whether we may have life after death depends on the nature of the universe, the structure of ultimate reality, the operational moral logic of its continuing functioning, for time is not only the mark of change but also the mark of continuity. It seems somewhat irrational and indeed wasteful that the individuality cultivated through life does not in some way continue. The quest for immortality is not only a quest for more time; it is also a quest for deeper rationality in the moral economy of the reality of the world. If rationality is, in any sense, goal-oriented behavior, the hope for immortality is the hope for purpose or goal justification in the struggles of life, the hope for an abiding rationality in the constitution of the universe.

The hope for continuance after death has been a prime impetus behind the postulation and conceptualization of a transcendent order and, in the biblical religions, of one supreme being, of God as the creator and conserver of order and rationality and meaningfulness in the scheme of things. If God is indeed a living reality, then the functioning of the world has a director; it is then reasonable to believe that purposive rationality is built into the fabric of things, that the governance of the universe is such that moral economy may prevail, that life is not a meaningless waste but has some transcendent destiny.

Because a life after death is beyond all possible experience in experiential time, one cannot prove or disprove the truth of any assertion concerning immortality, one cannot truly judge the validity of any such hope. Because the reality of God is likewise beyond any verification or conclusive denial, neither theism nor atheism can be demonstrated by finite human reason.

With regard to traditional theology, one must make a strong distinction between alleged proofs of God's existence and good reasons reaching beyond what reason can establish which yet justify a belief accordant with reason. Indeed, this is the outcome of Kant's deliberate destruction of the traditional attempts to *prove* the actuality of God's being. Human reason, Kant argued, cannot make cognitive statements that extend beyond the bounds of possible human experience. But knowledge is not enough for the living of life (or even for science). In a way that leads to the pragmatism of both Peirce and James as well as to the existential phenomenology of Heidegger, Kant insisted that knowledge is not enough: that to live, indeed to develop and use knowledge in living, we must employ rational beliefs, beliefs which go beyond what knowledge has established because their claims cannot yet be verified, but which are accordant with knowledge and seem implicit in human reasoning, even if this reasoning cannot establish their truth.

Knowledge can only tell us of what is determinate; we may have well-grounded hypotheses or expectations, judgments of probability and tentative claims to factual description, but until such cognitive claims have been verified, they qualify as perhaps justifiable opinion but not as known fact. Knowledge also can only be of what has been established; to the extent that the future is open, to that extent any possible cognitive claim goes beyond its evidential justification. But in any action, decision, or commitment, in any act of living we are stepping into a future which is not yet completely determinate, not yet reduced to fact; we are thus stepping beyond what knowledge, in any strict sense, can establish. Without a living commitment to beliefs which cannot yet be proved but which must yet be acted upon, we could not make a single rational decision. To live into the future, into what is not yet but still may be, is to live into the existentially unknown; to the extent that the future is still open and unresolved, it is to live into what is presently unknowable. Reason's only reasonable demand for rational beings is that their belief and value commitments to unverified and unverifiable beliefs be in accord with what reason has demonstrated and within the limits of what reason leaves open. What James called the necessity of the "will to believe" is the necessity to will to live, to commit myself into the unknown, the will to act and thus make a difference in the ongoing history of the world.

A belief in God's reality, then, has nothing irrational about it. Indeed, it would seem that the irrationality is rather on the side of disbelief. The possibility of belief as such is necessitated by the fact of futurity.

And indeed, three of the prime motives justifying such a belief come out of the forward-looking human stance: the hope that the end of individual life will not prove meaningless, the belief that the principles of morality will be validated, and the faith upon which all science must rest—that the order of physical nature and of human thought will be conserved and maintained.

Indeed, the fact that belief in God cannot be proved has been seen to be a point in its favor, for theistic religions usually regard the commitment to a belief in God as itself carrying with it moral virtue. We generally do not applaud the moral character (as distinct from scholastic diligence) of the schoolboy who learns his multiplication tables. But precisely because the reality of God cannot be proven, the commitment to belief is judged as any moral commitment is judged—as a sign of the commitment of the self to something beyond the self and thereby a moral virtue.

But this is to say that a belief in God, in any religiously meaningful sense, is not a merely intellectual or conceptual matter. In contrast to a merely intellectual judgment, a commitment to a belief in God should make a profound difference in the way one approaches the business of life. If one truly sees oneself as living in a God-governed universe, the context of one's every act and decision is radically different from the existential context of the committed atheist who believes himself to be living in a godless universe. As an existential matter, then, one must conduct one's life as in one kind of universe or the other; agnostic disavowal is an intellectualist evasion and is not existentially viable. For the committed theist the statement "God is" becomes a first premise, beyond all possible proof, of every vital consideration. The moral import of a belief in God is that the belief should make a moral difference to the believer. The existential belief in God is then itself redemptive.

But if we believe in God's reality, in what kind of a being can we believe? We have generally taken God to be, in Saint Anselm's words, that "being than which nothing greater can be conceived."[10] But the theological tradition by a logical jump has generally transmuted this to mean that God is absolute in power and in knowledge; when so conceived as not merely supreme but as absolute, the concept of God, by a further logical jump, is held to have no touch of our temporality but to be somehow timelessly eternal. So conceived, the idea of God is so exalted beyond all human attributes and predicates that one concludes that God is beyond all description by us, that God can be described by us only in negative terms.[11] This view, known as negative theology, poses very serious problems for a living religion (as distinct from a merely speculative exercise of thought), for if the God of religious commitment is beyond all possible attributes by us, an uncrossable gulf has been posited between God and man. We are then asked to believe only in a denial of all we know ourselves to be; such a belief, though perhaps intellectually intriguing, is religiously irrelevant. If our conception of God may have no positive attributes that are commensurate with ours, then any ethic of an "imitation of God" is meaningless.

We can only speak of, believe in, emulate, or even be aware of beings having something in common with us. Whatever its place in speculative thought, negative theology has not been taken seriously by lived religion even if some of its phrases have been thoughtlessly iterated. The God of religion, as Blaise Pascal insisted, is not the conceptual abstraction of philosophers or theologians. The concept of God that functions in religion is of the God to whom one prays, in whose will one hopes, a being who has purposes and reasons and judgments. But this implies that the only concept of God that is relevant for religion is that of a finite transcendent being commensurate with our own temporality.

Exploring the ramifications of the idea of divine finitude would take us into issues of metaphysics, epistemology, and value and would thus lead us far afield. Let me focus, rather, on two considerations directly emerging from the present discussion of human temporality.

First, if the pervasive temporality of our experience is not merely illusion, then it reflects something of the nature of the world, for our experiencing (even if somewhat illusionary) is itself still as much a part of the ongoing world as the objects of which we have experiences. But this says that, in at least some sense, time is real. If time is real, then God is necessarily neither omnipotent nor omniscient; if time is real, then God is necessarily a finite being. On several levels Aristotle already seems to have seen this; specifically in terms of time he noted that at least this "is lacking to God, to make undone things that have once been done."[12] If the time order is real, then God can neither know how to reverse it nor be able to do so; unable to cancel or annul it, God is thereby bound by it. God may see more clearly and wisely than we can, but he cannot see any way in which to negate the factuality of what has been.

It is remarkable how often these superlatives of power and of knowledge have been insisted upon while specific reservations were simultaneously entered in. It is not clear from just where this notion of an absolutely all-powerful being comes. The pages of the Bible are replete with stories about God's problems with men and the consequent necessity of divine intervention in order to rearrange forthcoming events in order to resolve them. Even the creation of the universe, according to Genesis, required six full days of divine laboring. In the philosophic tradition, Plato's deity was not even a creator but an architect who put preexistent matter into a temporal order.[13] And Aristotle's was seen to be necessarily passive and thereby ignorant of all change. Anselm did not speak of absolute power or knowledge but of the ultimate reach of the human understanding. Descartes, who regarded God as absolute and perfect, did not deem God capable of deceiving the proper use of the human intellect. Leibniz, who defended the notion of the absolute nature of the deity, still maintained God's inability to transgress the laws of mathematics and logic. Most wisely, Kant saw that the dogmatic ascription of positive, as well as negative, predicates to God as he may be in himself beyond the reach of the human outlook has no warrant precisely because it violates the discipline of finite human reason. As James urged, it is not God's power or knowledge but the belief in his goodness that is of religious concern. Only when taken by us to be finite in knowledge or power or both does God meet "the terms in which common men have actually carried on their active commerce with God."[14]

Indeed, we generally speak of a divine "plan" and a divine "will," but "plan" and "will" refer to a time order, to futurity, to the genuineness of alternative possibilities, to finite options, to tasks yet to be accomplished and goals yet to be won; they imply a distinction between ends and means and the temporal distance between them. A truly omnipotent being, as John Stuart Mill cogently argued, would have no need for means; his wish alone, much less his pronouncement, would suffice.[15] The use of terms such as "plan" and "will" thus serves to confirm the thesis that the God of religious relevance is a being conceived by us to be bound to the consequences of temporal order.

But let us go to the second consideration—from the hypothesis that time itself is real to the encompassing temporality of human existence. If all human thinking is time-structured, if all cognitive claims concern temporal existents, if human thinking functions by focusing on temporally available possibilities, then human thinking cannot possibly attain any meaningful conception of that which does not share its temporality. Even if human temporal dimensions, as we understand them, do not strictly apply to God, even if God is somehow beyond the human understandings of time, nevertheless, as Kant pointed out, we first must think of God not as strictly timeless but as a durational being; second, we must acknowledge that "time is the only possible means available to us to represent this [divine durational] existent [*Dasein*] . . . to us."[16] And Heidegger, whose examination of the structure of human temporality is the most exhaustive, has followed Kant in this by arguing "if God's eternity may be 'construed' philosophically, then it only can be understood as a primal and unending temporality" (with the explicitly stated consequent that the whole tradition of negative theology is thereby reopened).[17]

The implications of these considerations for a reconstruction of the traditional theological theodicy are far-reaching. At the very least they set aside, as indeed spurious, that problem which has occupied the theological imagination, the problem of evil—the task of reconciling the goodness of an all-powerful being with the reality of misery, disease, evil, and tragedy. It is not God's power but God's goodness that is of religious concern. If God is discerned not as all-powerful but as a finite being concerned with the good or the right, a being bound by the conditions of time, then religion becomes, as William Ellery Channing urged, a matter of transcendent friendship and allegiance with a deity who works in and with time.[18] Indeed, Kant had already suggested that what joins man and God together is that both are bound by the moral law. God, conceived as a transcendent moral being, bound by time, is a deity whose struggle is concerned not with the reconciliation of evil to power but with the problem of the good, the problem of helping us recognize it so that we may help in achieving it. If there be any plausibility to this way of thinking, then the morality a religion urges, as a central message to its adherents, takes on a transcendent meaning and gives rational meaning to the condition of time.

The point here is a simple one. The God in whom we claim to believe can only be conceived by us in temporal terms, operating in time and with time by means of a time order commensurate in some ways with ours and thereby bound to the finitizing consequences of involvement in temporal order. In contrast to any notion of an absolute timeless being, a view such as that suggested here is immediately accordant with the scientific portrait of nature as a historical process, with the thesis of biological evolution, and with a developmental view of human history. By the principle of conceptual economy (of Ockham's razor), it would seem that such a conception is rationally preferable.

If then God, as the focus of our religious concerns, is to have a religious meaning for us, if life itself is to have a religious meaning, we must be able to conceive of God in the only terms by which we can discern meaning, terms commensurate with our own temporality and accordant with whatever little knowledge we may already have attained. Whatever God may be beyond our temporal way of seeing and understanding and acting, God can only be meaningful to us insofar as his being, his activity, and his will can be seen by us to have relevance to our temporal ways of seeing, understanding, and being.

The Unity of the Three Concerns

What God may be beyond our horizon of temporality we cannot comprehend. What ultimate reality is beyond our temporal horizon we have no way of knowing. What time itself may be beyond our horizon of temporality we cannot say. The mystery of God and of reality are then equivalent for us to the mystery of time. We cannot define them as they may be in themselves; we can only come to work with them as they are able to enter into the temporality of the human outlook. Our approximating conceptions of them must be temporal conceptions. To the extent that we acknowledge the temporality of our working and approximating conceptions of them, we are enabled to work with them within our human framework, for doing so gives voice, and thereby meaning, to the kinds of beings we are, beings whose every way is to be pervasively temporal.

What God, reality, time may be in themselves is beyond our capability to comprehend just because we cannot transcend the inherent limitations of the human point of view. Like futurity, they remain unknown; but just as we delineate futurity in terms of necessities and still-open possibilities providing clues for action, and as we recognize the temporal nature of the futurity that enters into us, so we may attain some partial understandings as we recognize their entrance into our own temporality. And just as with futurity, so with God's reality and that of time itself, we have no choice but to proceed forthrightly with conviction beyond actual or possible knowledge and commitment beyond known fact. Life, it has been said, is an adventure of the spirit; it requires a conviction of freedom, conviction in courage, and a readiness to go forward into the unknown.

Our basic concerns on every level, trivial or profound, are concerns about the future. As we enter into futurity, as futurity enters into us, our knowledge and ignorance, fears and hopes, intelligence and faith join together to prescribe the tasks to be accomplished, the goals to be won, the hardships to be endured, the triumphs to anticipate. Futurity is the form of our concerns and of the meanings we see in the days of our lives. The character of futurity then provides us with the ways in which we define our ultimate concerns and fundamental convictions.

Our ultimate concerns and convictions are concerns and convictions about the meaning of the temporal. Whether we speak about science, freedom, morality, mortality, or deity, we are speaking of the temporal. When we ask about significance or meaning beyond the momentary present, we are asking about the meaning of life and so about the meaning of future time. The ultimate questions we ask, the convictions which guide us, are but expressions of our one fundamental concern. This one ultimate concern expressed in our three basic questions, the ultimate concern of all religious questioning and conviction is for the meaning, the significance, the nature of the temporal—the nature, within the human perspective, of time itself.

Part 3

Metaphysics—as If Time Matters

6

Are We *in* Time?

Are we in time? Are we really *in* time—as our ordinarily casual statements seem to suggest? Consideration of this most ordinary kind of locution quickly shows up the misleading nature of metaphors built into our casual language. More important, this consideration opens us up to the far-reaching philosophic ramifications of the pervasive temporality constituting our human condition. Before these ramifications can be fruitfully examined in detail, it is important to develop a comprehensive overview within which more detailed inquiries may find their context. Thus, this essay tries to spell out a generalized argument that touches many areas of concern and issues in a programmatic orientation suggesting the way in which a metaphysic that "takes time seriously" might well proceed.

"Time" in Language

The pervasiveness of our temporal concerns is readily acknowledged. We talk of the fleetingness of time that nullifies all permanence, that makes everything transient. Against its steady beat, we either race or dawdle. We talk of triumphing over it or being subdued by it. Often we curse the inability to stop the clock so as to gain more time for completion of a task. We bemoan the rapidity of its passing when enjoying an activity or trying to beat a deadline; we are buoyed up by its promise as we labor against discouraging odds; we wince at its inexorable pace when pressed by conflicting demands; we complain of its leisurely pace when we are bored by unavoidable delay. We casually refer to clocks and calendars as providing objective demarcation of specific events. We mark out birth dates and death dates as somehow defining the lives that tran-spired between them.

Yet we casually describe ourselves, things, and events as being in time. Somehow we picture our temporal progress along a line, marked out precisely along the way in seconds, hours, days, years. Time is the container within which life's journey is traveled; we are *in* time, we say, and mark out our journey across the time-box in which we travel as journeying up the diagonal across a rectangle. We plot just where we are, from what precise point we started and, in looking ahead, at least can point to a point beyond which we do not expect to be traveling anymore.

Our basic metaphor is that of a boxlike container; within it we plot the course of a line clearly marked out by a ruler. When this gross spatial reduction is questioned, we quickly substitute the picture of a perfectly balanced pendulum inexorably and without variation ticking away as we measure our progress against it. Our sequential moments are seemingly announced by a super-celestial clock ticking away in august transcen-dent splendor as we traverse the spatially marked moments of our jour-ney. Whether time-distance is measured by the analogy of a spatial metric, or is presumably governed by a precise gearwheel grinding out its moments, the temporality of our experience is not illuminated.[1]

A container-notion of time does not explain the pervasive tempo-rality we readily acknowledge in all experiences. Merely being in a time-box does not explain why a pervasive temporality inhabits our lives, our thoughts, governs all we do and say. Different people can respond to a common spatial condition—like being earthbound—in different ways: some crawl and others learn to fly. But crawling or flying, each must take account of the irreversible nature and essential continuity of sequential time. Even the pacing of a governing pendulum does not seem to ring true. Experiential time does not run this evenly paced course: some-times it seems deep with complex action, sometimes it dissipates into shallow transparent boredom. But the pictured pendulum ticks on with-out any apparent relation to what it is supposed to be measuring.

And so we substitute a different spatial portrait: time is not a pen-dulum, it is a stream. Time flows. That accounts for continuity as well as change, for the fact that we cannot really divide one moment from the next. Sometimes it flows deep and sometimes shallow. But it flows. And we see ourselves wafted downstream by the current—and mark our progress by noting regular points along the riverbank, all carefully marked out for us in advance by a thoughtful surveyor just so we can tell how far we have come and how rapidly we are traveling, even if we can-not see around the next bend.

How far may we push these metaphors? If time is a stream, what are its banks? From whence does it come? To where is it going? Our floating boat is moving with and in the stream, in time—but what is the stream? How seriously may we ask, as we may ask about the water, of what substance is this stream of flow composed? And how shall we explain the contemporaneity of those other boats which have either preceded us downstream or are following in our wake?

When pressed about parallel or simultaneous events, we often seek to objectify the chronological relationship by a cliché commonly used by each of us, by public figures, by philosophers who ought to know better: we seek to pinpoint the precise temporal "location" with the phrase "at this point in time." What is really meant is a particular network of interacting durational events. But what is pictured is a momentary notion of temporal reality in which past and future are relegated to the netherland of illusion while only the immediate present is portrayed as real. We presume some clearly marked-off surveyor points along the bank of the time-stream, or the pendulum marking off real moments along a timeline. When either is taken in any literal sense, we are led to Descartes's perplexity about how God manages to get us from one sovereign moment to the next.[2] When pressed, we clearly see that the metaphor of the stream, as of the pendulum, when taken seriously is seriously misleading.

Our experience of time, our time-bound experienc*ing* in its continuities and discontinuities, surges and lapses, and its yet essential coherence, cannot be reduced to geometry; experiential time cannot be squared with such spatial locutions, metaphors, and models. Time is not space; spatial pictures of time collapse just because they subsume time under spatial rubrics, portray it in terms it does not accommodate. "All statements ordinarily made about time," R. G. Collingwood noted, "seem to imply that time is something which we know it is not, and make assumptions about it which we know to be untrue."[3] We should be forewarned against looking to the peculiar expressions of our own parochial language for insight into the nature of time and temporal experience. Our everyday metaphors only succeed in distorting our understanding of the temporality we each continually manifest.

Experiential Clues

When faced with serious questioning, when I am cross-examined on the witness stand, when I am charged to explain a course of events or justify a particular decision, I do not present a neutral photographic report of a spatial panorama. I do seek to recall selected happenings which strike me as related to the particular question I face. I seek to correlate my observational or decisional complex of then-unfolding events which were still open-ended and which I had judged to be intertwined. I find myself explaining, not some "point in time," but a spread of durational activities as I now recall seeing and interpreting them to myself, activities that were still openly problematic when observed, specific activities extracted out of all else that was then going on because I now judge them relevant to what I try to explain. My explanation is essentially referential to, and expressive of, my individual perspectival judgments, my comprehension of unresolved and overlapping activities as I now recall having originally taken them in.

When I try to make sense of any experiential events, I am voicing, while unveiling my perspectival outlook onto the world in which I find myself, the perspective that forms the particular selective interpretive experience that is mine. When I try to explain my role in a problematic circumstance, I try to avoid being trapped by the thoughtless clichés, misleading metaphors, and ontological imputations built into my language; I do try to explicate the ways in which my experiencing activity, and its experiential judgments, were authentically constituted.

To do this is to begin to understand my own self, my own mode of experiencing my own course of experiential activity, the ways in which I function, the values which guide me, the capabilities I discern, the limitations I must accept. To do this is to begin to make some sense of my experiences of people, things, and events which I distinguish from myself while somehow finding them constitutive of the eventful happenings of the particular integrating experience I call mine. In order to clarify the import of the time references I use when I voice, describe, or justify my experiential judgments, I turn to some systematic introspection: I try to confront my own self in its experiential activity, to comprehend my own manner of experiencing my own experience. Temporal aspects of such self-examination quickly come to light.

However we probe the various facets of our experiencing activity, we find that temporality is radically pervasive. Our most innocent thinking, John Locke pointed out, is consciousness of a train of ideas, a sequential movement in which any one idea that attracts awareness presents itself as in a sequence of ideas, before some, after others. This first phenomenological discovery of introspective self-examination is that thinking itself is inherently a temporal process.[4]

Locke's discovery raises many issues, two of which are vital here: the continuity of change and the ability to be aware of sequence. Consider each of the following two primal aspects of rudimentary thought.

1. Unless we take that "train of ideas" to be going very rapidly, Locke's metaphor may be misleading. The content of dynamic consciousness does not present each separate idea-in-focus as discernibly distinct from its sequential neighbors (as one railroad car is independent of the others). Rather we find a continuity of movement: the precise boundary of each experiential idea blurs into the next—as when watching a rapidly moving train. Taken in this way, the train of ideas in consciousness presents a primal experience of the continuity of change—each item of focus seemingly arising out of what is yet to come as it melds into what has just been; each idea presenting no sharp demarcation from those abutting it. Even the most disciplined concentration manifests this continuity as presenting movement, some touch of lastingness, and sequentiality within itself.

2. If we are not to be captivated by each momentary presentation in turn but are to be aware of the sequence, we cannot be blind to all but the immediately present idea. In order to be aware of sequence and change, awareness must retain what was immediately previous as tied into what is immediately present but moving into the past. Presupposed in the experience of sequence is the ability to retain in mind what was but is no longer as tied into what is immediately present but fading into the immediate past, seemingly pushed on by what is just emerging. In order to be aware of sequence, I must be able to hold some lastingness or durational spread in mind as supervening the immediate focus of attention.

When we turn from a specific act of simple introspective thought to a specific act of perception, we again find that any perpetual object is a temporally framed sequentiality within a supervening durational presentation. The simplest perceptual glance is one of minute lasting and minute changing.

Neither sense-awareness nor thought is timeless. "Sense-awareness and thought are themselves processes," Whitehead pointed out, thus joining a conclusion reached by philosophers as various as Kant and James; they are processes that continually and inherently exhibit continuities of dynamism.[5]

Whether we seek to root experiential activity in sense-perception, in thinking, or in a synthesis of the two, temporal activity would seem to be intrinsic to our experiences, to our capacity to engage in experiential activity, intrinsic to any particular experiences we might have. We can find no example of timelessness in experiential consciousness. Time would then seem to be the essential form of any experiential consciousness, the form in which, or through which, all experiential content comes, the form of even the most passive experience we might imagine.

The truth of this thesis would seem apparent. Since Leibniz, Kant and James, Bergson and Husserl, I do not think it has been seriously challenged. As a foundational truth about human experiencing, one might expect serious thinking to take it seriously—as a point of departure and a pervasive fact of all human thinking and its cognitive claims. But it is generally and conveniently ignored, even in discussions to which it is crucial. Yet the thesis is not particularly new: Aristotle had already raised it by identifying consciousness of self with consciousness of time.[6]

The Cognitive and the Practical

If we take up this last clue and consider the broader range of personal activities, we find that all activity—cognitive and practical—is temporally structured. I have grave doubts as to the legitimacy of this traditional dichotomy, but these doubts notwithstanding, let us look at each in turn.[7]

With regard to the cognitive, we immediately note the central imaginative role played by memory. As perceptual recollection of the immediate present rolls out into the past, memory is invoked in order to maintain awareness of the continuity of process being witnessed. An act of memory is temporally intriguing: it is a temporal act that disengages from the perceptual field in order to place it into a wider context of continuity and meaning. In any act of memory-recall, what is no longer literally present is rendered present to the thinking mind. This capacity for memory-recall, this ability to commit a temporal act that at once disengages the narrow confines of the observational present in order to reengage a broader temporal perspective, betokens our ability to observe the separated "moments" of the passing parade while reintegrating past with present in order to comprehend continuity.

This ability to disengage and reengage temporal perspective is crucial to the capacity to read meaning into what we see, select objects of attention, direct activity, and hence to engage in freely determined courses of activity. In memory-recall, as in anticipation, we meld the immediately present field with what is not literally present; doing so enables us to broaden out the visual present into a net of continuities and meanings which permit evaluation, discrimination, focus, choice, decision.

"Every serial succession of which we are conscious," Royce pointed out, "has for us some sort of meaning"; it is this meaning that unites discrete elements into one continuity rather than leaving us with a disjointed staccato of myriad pictures.[8] To discern a particular event out of the passing flux is a selective perspectival judgment that "extracts" from a complex of activity in the perceptual field a particular chain of continuity as the object of focus, while relegating the rest of that complex to the status of a "background" of no particular interest or concern.

To describe a series of identifiable changes as one process presumes a selective judgment of sequential relations taken as presenting a discernible thread of meaning. Be it noted that the meaning is not merely in the result but in the process itself taken as an integrated series of conceivably discrete stages. A comprehending perception is then an interpretive activity in which one seeks meaning out of an observed presentation. Interpretive activity arises out of selective questioning—and questioning has a guided interest, purpose, or concern. Any report of a passing scene thus has built into it the biases and interests of the reporter who has focused on those aspects of that scene which respond to his own questions.

The meaning I read out of an observation is an interpretive report of a durational complex; it is animated by my line of questioning, which animates the selectivity guiding the way I look, focus, and interpret what I am witnessing or investigating. Two observers, facing the same panorama with divergent interests or perspectives, will seek out divergent meanings in what they look at, report disparate continuities, pursue different interrogations. *Questions precede answers.* In the temporal logic of the case, any question looks to future responsive interpretation. Questions, and the animating meanings sought, are thus essentially futural in outlook; their anticipations are what beckon us into those interrogations that direct our selective attention and our interpretive reports.

One can go to two rather different kinds of philosophers for the disclosure of what is involved in this futural bias of human cognitive activity. Its detailed examination in Martin Heidegger's existential analytic is well known. But it was already present in the pioneering essays of Charles Peirce. Let it suffice to point out that, like Heidegger's existential analytic, all of pragmatism rests on this thesis: human cognitive activity is founded on the capacity to anticipate futurity and bring that anticipation into the constitution of the present activity. Meaning, Peirce had argued, is to be found, not in a "speciously present" moment, not in present perception, but in expectations, desires, hopes, and fears—which conspire to motivate present investigations, present questionings, present interpretive constructs, present animating meanings.

These strictly noncognitive but temporally real aspects of present thinking provide the rationale for present selective observation, present criteria for evaluation, present judgments of meaning. In defiance of a long tradition, Peirce had urged that cognition is not the contemplation of currently apprehended information, but intellectually grounded expectation actively seeking out the future presentation of a fulfillment guiding us through an "extended" present. Cognitive activity is deliberate investigation into selected phenomenal sequences, in response to specific questionings. This activity is neither caused nor bound by the past but freely uses the past; by means of memory-recall and conceptual recollection, those aspects of what has been, which seem relevant to the problematic at hand, are unified with it as a key to development of meaning. Cognitive activity is essentially and pervasively temporal and time-binding in the ways it is constituted.

More dramatically perhaps, practical reasoning exhibits that same pervasive future-oriented temporality. All authentic deliberation regarding possible activity is focused not on what has been, not on what is literally present, but on the future that is not yet but is yet conceived as presently open to alternative development. But again, this is not really new. Aristotle had already made this clear:

> No one deliberates about the past, but about what is future and capable
> of being otherwise, while what is past is not capable of not having taken
> place; hence Agathon is right in saying, 'For this alone is lacking even to
> God, to make undone things that have once been done.'[9]

Practical reasoning involves deliberation concerning what is not yet but yet may be; it requires the presumption of the reality of time so that one may plan one's moves. It means organizing a course of action, that is, to commit a "stretch" of oncoming time in the light of a vision of what is to be accomplished. Practical reasoning is purposive reasoning; its essential temporality is exhibited in at least two ways: (1) it finds its rationale neither in the past nor the literal present, but in a judgment of possibilities for an actualizable future; and (2) it functions by bringing a commitment to a possible real future into defining and directing its activity out of the present decisional moment.

The presumption of the reality of time is requisite for planning; it is acknowledged in any response to a situation posing a dilemma calling for action. For it is time that forces decision and choice upon us. Our temporally structured action-commitments are themselves necessitated by our temporal situations. When we find ourselves called upon to act, we face a necessary decisional choice that cannot be refused: for to decide not to decide is itself deciding.

Most of our moral dilemmas do *not* (as first Rousseau, and then Kant, claimed) arise from a conflict of desire and obligations. Even Kant's man of good will could not, in any temporally defined situation, do all the things he might think he ought to do; his moral dilemma, in strictest rectitude, arises out of a conflict of moral obligations. The pressure of time forces decision between alternatively defensible right actions, alternate claims of moral conscience. Most real moral dilemmas do not present simplistic choices between incarnate good and incarnate evil, but rather between alternate goods. A moral dilemma arises, for the moral individual, just because, at a given temporal juncture, he cannot seek both goods, cannot perform both defensible acts, but must irrevocably choose one to the exclusion of the other. We cannot do all the things we want to do; we cannot, in most human situations, do all the things we think we ought to do; we cannot meet all the demands the most righteous conscience might demand.

Just because of pervasive temporality, every decision must be made as singular, irreversible, irrevocable, unalterable. I may seek to atone for a grievous error, but I cannot undo that error. Any decision or act initiates a new sequence of events that closes off all alternate chains of possibility-actualization; any particular act is radically restrictive of the future one can give oneself. Time not only forces decision; it forces the necessity to choose into the dimly seen future. Each temporally forced decision commits the use of time to construct the delineation, definition, and continuing development of the deciding self.

If practical or moral judgments are concerned with possible actions, commitments to the use of time, and the shaping of personal futures, then all decision, commitment, judgment, action is concerned with dilemmas concerning the use of time. The question, "What should I do?" concerns the use of oncoming time; the judgment or decision "I should do x instead of y" concerns the use of oncoming time. All moral reasoning would then appear to be concerned with the ontology of the temporal, for time is the concern of its quandaries, considerations, resolutions. Time, then, is the form of all cognition, deliberation, will, decision, commitment, action; it is the form of that self-development in the continuity of selective becoming that is the biography each person is in the process of constructing.

Whether we see ourselves as beings who cognize or decide, whether we focus on the quest for knowledge or the determinations of choices, we find that we are constituted in essentially temporal terms. Our cognitive processes, decisional processes, are pervasively structured as temporal. Time predicates are not incidental or accidental; they are constitutive of any individual being and of any particular situation in which he may find himself. As Leibniz had urged, time as such is not a thing and that is why it is not perceivable; but time-relations are built *into* each one of us as essential predicates of his being; time-relations are manifested *in* every expression of biographical becoming. The relations which are inherent in our thinking, observing, evaluating, deciding, and acting are temporal relations. Without them no reasoning or planning, no choosing or deciding, in short, no experience would be possible.

Sociality

With good reason, one might well protest that I have been considering the individual without regard to relations with other beings or with the being of nature itself. None of our experiences, it would be correctly said, is entirely personal. Our temporal biographies are inextricably enmeshed with, and incorporate, relations with other people, other living beings, and the processes of the inanimate things of the natural world.

Even casual observation readily reveals the pervasive extent of the temporal relations investing our sociality. We carry watches and calendars—created to public standards—in order to coordinate temporal activities, make appointments, structure our days. We freely talk of spending time with some, avoiding others. The acute temporality of our social relationships is rapidly evident.

It would, however, be wrong to leave it at that. Merely noting our common dependence on clocks and calendars suggests something too casual and external. These time-organizing instruments and the temporal relations that ensue from their use are not incidental or accidental to our being; they are intrinsic to it. My living activity is not left untouched by a change of appointment, casual as that might seem. My response might be trivial, in which case its triviality is itself an important aspect of my being. Or, it might importantly affect and redirect what I am currently about. In either case, these temporal incidents become new facts in my life and the ensuing repercussions carry on, whether strikingly marked or barely noticed.

We are not self-contained beings who somehow flit untouched and unscathed through a social whirl that does not really matter. Inherently we are social beings. We define ourselves to ourselves, as to others, in terms of our relations with family, friends, school, church, club, employment, nation. The complex of our particular social involvements and isolations defines the grammar of our daily lives, thereby the particular experiences we have—and thereby the preoccupations of our attentions, perceptions, thoughts, concerns, and plans.

We think in and with a particular language, which again is not incidental to who or what we are. It brings into us a particularly prejudiced historic distillation of the development of a particular cultural tradition; it helps to form the ways in which we see the world, the categorical concepts which organize our thinking, the grammatical forms and idiomatic expressions and metaphoric shorthands that serve to express and thereby shape our views and judgments and convictions. The grammatical categories, ontological imputations, and conceptual models built into a particular language during a given historic period conspire to reflect a historic cultural outlook; they guide and form and shape the questions we ask, the kinds of answers we seek, the ways in which our own individually peculiar viewpoints are shaped and shared with others.

Each person has grown up within a particular social matrix—of family and friends—who shared certain values as grounding all discussion, certain permissible disagreements as allowable options, certain dogmas beyond question, certain interests, commitments, loyalties. Each has thus been nurtured within a historically developing ideational complex, a way of looking, which he carries with him, even as he may use some of these presumed judgments to criticize, reform, and reformulate his own judgments on his individuated heritage and his still-developing relationships with it.

The host of descriptive predicates by which each individual sees himself and by means of which he gives expression to the person he finds himself to be are grounded in the multifarious ways in which the social temporality in which he is nurtured forms and molds the individuality he most prizes. Detailed explication of this grounding sociality would itself contribute to the present argument. But since I am unable to do so here and yet unable to ignore it, let me use a kind of philosophic shorthand by invoking the historical line of thought that a more adequate discussion of this special topic would carry forward. Such elucidation would utilize a Greek tradition of thought that, in modern development, comes out of Leibniz, Rousseau, Kant, and Hegel; it is the common tradition of philosophic idealism out of which both pragmatism and phenomenology arose. Its essential thesis here is that the social is more primordial than the individual, that individuality is not a thing but a process, a process that is essentially social in nature, that the process of individuation is a development building out of and feeding back into social temporality. Peirce and Royce (as well as Dewey) have forcefully argued that even the individual "assurance that outer nature exists apart from any [one] man's private experience [is] inseparably bound up with our social consciousness."[10] Quite similarly, Heidegger has argued that the individual self is only able to discover itself as already being enmeshed in a world of other people and of things. In quite different language, but to much the same point, they have joined to argue that self-consciousness and the consciousness of time arise together out of that net of relationships which we find built into ourselves and that enables us to become aware of and to develop individual perspectives as elements of the temporal perspective of the social whole. This social temporality is not an accidental accretion to individual being but ingredient to it and foundational to its emergence.

What then of physical nature? Most of us presume to take physical nature as somehow primordial to our own transient experiencing. I do not want to question this belief because I share it. But one must add that physical nature cannot be reasonably seen as the whole of reality, for my ideas and fears and hopes and motives, as the scientific laws I take to be governing the physical things of the world, are as real in my experience within the world of nature as any merely physical entity.

However this may be, precisely how should physical nature as such be understood? It is readily apparent, as Royce forcefully argued, that our current conception of nature is a social conception; it arises less out of untutored individual experience (dependent on what we euphemistically describe as "common sense") than out of this specific cultural tradition which has raised us to its standards and outlook which defy "common sense."[11] This tradition presents us with a developing body of scientific beliefs which we accept as authoritative, even when we cannot understand or explain them; this continued dogmatic acceptance is the more remarkable when we consider the continuity of revolutionary breakthroughs in the scientific understanding of nature, each of which sets aside what a previous generation was led to accept as unquestioned dogma of sophisticated knowledge.

It should really occasion no surprise or alarm that scientific conceptions of nature grow and thereby change. For the science that tells us of the nature of nature is itself a human product. Despite its transcendent pretensions, it arises out of human investigatory procedures, which are engendered by human questions, that express the temporal constitution of the human outlook from within the contemporary cultural matrix of its historic situation. It uses a man-made methodology, which is culturally conditioned, for its investigations; and a man-made logic, arising out of the grammar of this particular cultural tradition, for the validation of its reasonings.

The currently changing but currently developing beliefs of the scientific community, which scientific investigation uses as its point of departure, arise out of human questioning, and thereby exhibit the peculiarities and finite competencies of the human temporal perspective onto the world as we are able to see that world within which we try to develop sophisticated, reasoned understandings of it. Science is a human interpretive activity and thereby cannot properly present an extra-experiential portrait of the whole of nature; as human it is bound within the human outlook from within nature: it cannot tell us of the ultimate nature of nature itself, as many of its spokesmen too often claim to do. Rather, human science presents answers to sophisticated human questions from within nature which try to comprehend the surrounding developmental phenomena of nature, but always from within a limited human, temporal perspective on its own developing environment. Conceivably, another creature with a different time-span of attentive perception would focus on events we do not even suspect. As an imaginative experiment, contrast the outlook of a mosquito with a twenty-four-hour life span, our own outlook, and that of a transcendent and conceivably omniscient deity.

This is not the occasion to face the Kantian question as to whether this essentially biased human outlook can penetrate to the ultimate secrets of nature itself. However revealing or veiling our scientific insights may be, it seems clear that the behavior of nature appears to us as a network of irreversible processes: the acorn may become an oak tree that may produce acorns, but the oak tree cannot revert to its original state and itself become an acorn. At any stage of its life, the potentialities the oak tree carries with it depend for their realization on the environmental presentation of genuine possibilities for incorporation into its perduring being. At any stage of its life, the oak tree embodies a living synthesis of its own perduring nature, its individual history, and the proximate future which it incorporates into itself. Natural processes appear as developmental—as inherently durational, irreversibly sequential and time-binding. To use Peirce's term, the "habitual patterns of nature's behavior" appear to us as pervasive patterns of irreversible process, temporal continuity, and temporal integration. This is to say, in a word, that the behavior of natural phenomena appears to us as inherently time-ordered.

This time-ordered facet of natural processes may once have been seen as completely independent of human experience. And this apparent independence may have been a reason for the belief, most prominent in seventeenth-century Western thought, that man is an irrelevant spectator of independently operating courses of nature's systematic working. But the sciences that developed out of that period, incorporating historically developed conceptual tools out of a developing historic culture, are themselves creating a historic revolution in the history of nature itself. The refined techniques of human temporal investigatory procedures are increasingly involving larger areas of physical nature *in* human history. I do not mean by this merely the human appropriation

of increasingly wide areas of nature's being; I do mean that human investigatory activities are increasingly becoming part of nature's own historical development. Human development in Ionic Greece was already
able to demonstrate the inherent temporality of nature as manifested
in its intrinsic time-ordered processes. Contemporary technological
achievements—finally being accorded serious philosophic scrutiny—
are now demonstrating, in our own historic era, that nature itself is
amenable to temporal modifications of its processes, as man's increasing
interferences in the processes of the natural order are increasingly becoming part of nature's own historical development.[12]

This is to say that William James was not off course when he urged
that, after all the differences between the living and the nonliving, and
the mental and the physical, the one common predicate all existents
seem to share, the one common tie all have to each other, is the mutuality of temporal structuring.[13] However different man may be from other
living creatures, from the lifeless things of the physical world, this seems
to be the one pervasive tie that binds man to nature, enables man to in-
terrelate with nature, allows man to mold nature as nature molds man.

The pervasive reality of time, as intrinsic to the existence of man
and nature, Peirce argued, must be presumed if we are to be able to
make any sense of either.[14] Sharing in the common predicate of internal
time-order, Royce concluded, is what is "common to [both] matter and
to mind."[15] This commonality of being-temporal has even been seen to
have a theological reach: for Heidegger has followed Kant in urging that
even God may be conceived by us only in inherently temporal terms.[16]
However this may be, it does seem clear that the only reading we can
have of nature, as of ourselves, is that time is the one predicate that appears to be essential, pervasive, ingredient to all experiential being,
things, ideas, and entities, to all becoming. Time is, it would seem, the
essential predicate of any existent entity of which we may know, the
bounding context of any theory we may hold, the essential attribute of
any kind of reality of which we may intelligibly speak.[17]

Some Programmatic Consequents

I have suggested some of the ways in which the pervasiveness of time is
manifest in what and who we are, what we may do, how we think, how we
may know and act. Time seems to be the form of all consciousness, decision, action. It appears to be the form of nature as well. It appears to be
the essential tie binding each individual to the continuity of his own

being, to other existent individuals, to the other members of what Leibniz once termed "the common citizenship of this cosmic republic."

Are we then *in* time? I think I have shown that this common locution voices a misapprehension of our language. The reverse would seem to be closer to the truth: we cannot be in time because time is *in* us. It permeates every activity of the being of the self; it orders the continuity of change in all the complex relations that constitute a self; it permeates the relations each has with others; it appears to be equally pervasive in that dynamic relational system of nature we inhabit and to which we belong. Time, then, appears to be *ingredient* to ourselves and to every aspect of our world insofar as we can come to know ourselves and our world. Within the reach of the human outlook, time would appear to be ontologically foundational. Whatever else time itself may conceivably be, it does seem to be just this complex of relations internal to the continuity of the self in the continuity of its individual ties to its world of people, ideas, laws, and things; for it is these relations that constitute the social individuality each knows as one's own.

If we are to give these considerations systematic philosophic formulation, we find they conspire to urge us to retrieve and reconstruct, in temporalist terms, that central doctrine of the idealist tradition, the theory of internal relations.[18] For time appears to us as that network of developmentally constitutive relations which characterize any entity in its own qualities and characteristics, as in its relations with the other entities with which it finds itself. Time appears to function as governing rules of existent entities, for time-relations do make an essential difference to the variegated ways in which such overarching laws become ontically manifest.

A retrieve of the theory of internal relations—as the network of temporal constitution (not in the usual terms of logical entailment)—in its speculative reach finds more in common with the metaphysical visions of Leibniz and James than with that commonly associated with the name of Hegel. Avoiding the universalizing identity of a monistic system, it would build on the fact that temporal perspectives are individually unique, while time-relations are yet uniquely integrated in the ongoing becoming of individual entities. Its speculative hypothesis would then be a conception of reality as an interconnected time-order that is itself pluralistically constituted; it would recognize that individual perspectives and relations are yet related in a common time-system which appears to be individuating in its operative functioning.

A temporalist retrieve of the theory of internal relations could well commence from clues already to be found in Kant's "Postulates of Empirical Thought." If we rethink his three modal principles in terms more explicitly temporal than those in which he presented them, we find that "necessity" is effectively offered as our understanding of what is conceived to be trans-temporal condition; "actuality" as the content of the perceptual present; and "possibility" as the temporally governing ground of whatever may transpire within human experience.[19]

Such a temporalist retrieve would utilize Peirce's own retrieve of what he seems to have taken as a Scotist distinction between "existence" and "reality"—as temporally distinct categorical concepts: whereby "existence" refers to particular individuals incorporating specific temporal predicates; and "reality," as more inclusive, refers as well to what is conceived to be that system of overarching laws, trans-temporal predicates, and principles governing (and thereby manifested in or by) all temporally existent particulars. It would bring into development from Heidegger's analytic his own undeveloped distinction of those most traditionally confounded of metaphysical concepts, the "possible" and the "potential." It is the former, the "possible," in its continuing temporal offerings of viable contextual options that permits the latter, the defining capabilities we carry with us that we term the "potential," to achieve temporal development and embodiment by selective appropriations.

Working from such ground, we should be able to avoid the usual rationalistic reduction of sequential change to logical entailment and the consequent logicization of reality; likewise, we would avoid the empiric reduction of all sequential change to a mechanical chain of efficient causalities which by a projection of retrogressive sequentiality only succeeds in reducing the present to the past. If time is real in a dynamic world, the reduction of all sequential change, either to a first premise or to a necessary connection to a temporally first cause, effectively obliterates the efficacy of time-relations by portraying all causal links as reducible to either logical entailment or historical simultaneity. If this suggestion should prove to hold, then freedom, and perhaps also the notion of "chance" (which we find in both Aristotle and Peirce) would appear, not as deficient forms of necessitarian reason, but as authentic functions of temporal becoming.

A temporalist theory of internal relations would reformulate moral theory in ways accordant with the temporality intrinsic to all quandaries, situations, dilemmas, judgments, decisions. In method, as in doctrine, it would insist on taking seriously the historicity of human thinking in its forward-looking stance. Recognizing the sociality of individuality, it would comprehend the history of human polity as an ongoing development whose history is still before it; we could then face the contemporary need for a reconstruction of the theory of civil society that is consonant with the temporal continuity of human development, the import of freedom that any thesis of an open future demands, and the essentially prospective historicity of our living together in free individuating community.

This programmatic sketch is offered here only to indicate the far-reaching significance that ensues from a rethinking of the pervasiveness of time as an internally constitutive relational complex. Doing so would systematically work from the realization that we find time so compelling, so encompassing, so pervasive, just because it is the animating force and form of what we do and who we are. Philosophic thinking might then finally come to terms with the experiential integrity of that experiencing activity out of which it arises and which it seeks to understand, to explain, and even to guide.

7

Perspectivity and the Principle of Continuity

Everyday speech, like much learned discourse, often refers to particular things as first coming into existence and then later expiring. The reality of the particular entity or event is then discerned, identified, and even explained, in terms of the quantified temporal distance between these identifiable termini of its duration. This common manner of speaking and thinking presumes to understand particular entities and events as though the identity of each is somehow contained within its determinate temporal boundaries; we identify particular people, things, and events by means of their bi-terminal dates. And we speak of a person, a thing, an event in terms of its beginning and its end, as though these two chronological notations were preeminently intrinsic to the nature of its being.

Philosophic thought, like the sciences it has spawned, has generally declined any obligation to take a common mode of speech or thought at face value. Indeed, responsible philosophic thinking has served a critical function: the distillation and reformulation of those validities which lurk in the unreflective everyday use of language, with frequent misleading metaphors that too often mask perspectives and insights seeking expression. It does this in at least two ways: (1) by an essentially literary critique which seeks precision of meaning; and (2) by a metaphysical critique which exposes those presuppositions upon which such insights depend for their authenticity of meaning.

The intent of this essay is to point out some of the conceptual problems that arise when the rubric of "beginnings and endings" is used in any literal sense. Three groups of separable but closely related confusions are engendered. Collectively they demonstrate the very limited metaphoric utility which the rubric of "beginnings and endings" may serve in any discussion involving time or temporality.

To approach an object or event primarily in terms of its beginning or its end is to imitate the unimaginative surveyor diligently, but narrowly, pursuing his assignment; he cannot describe the land he measures but only the boundaries which mark its external limits. His employer, as a serious investigator, is concerned with terminal boundaries only because of his interest in what lies between them.

Interest in a particular event, examination of a particular phenomenon, attention to a particular person, are each excited by what it does, the functions it serves, the role it plays, the activity in which it engages— not supposed points of genesis and termination, but what lies between them is what engages attention or focuses investigation. This temporal "between" of an entity or event is its durational being, its lastingness, its span of activity; it is this "between" that gives meaning to its discerned terminal "points." To examine the entity or event primarily in terms of its beginning and end is not to discern it, but its limits. Its time is its duration; only within its durational extent is it itself to be found.

We generally mark the bi-terminals of a particular durational being by dating them. Yet we seemingly need a continuing reminder of the literal emptiness of this standard artifice; it is authentically descriptive of no existent entity. Rather, this descriptive vacuousness distracts our attention from what it allegedly "locates" and points us away from the centered "between" to its supposed temporal limits.

Dating indicators generally treat time as though it were some sort of container within which things happen—"at this point *in* time." The dating system then serves as a sort of spatial locution to "locate" the "place" of an event. Time is thus treated as a kind of spatiality and "locating" an event transforms temporal description into a kind of temporal geography. Such spatializing thinking, epitomized in a geography of dating, presumes a "container" model by which to think about time; as such it leads directly to the many incongruities and paradoxes which mark the literature at least since Zeno (ca. 450 B.C.). The many resulting absurdities and puzzlements which ensue from treating time as something it is not are signs of a refusal or inability to treat time and temporality in their own terms.

When we regard time as uniquely sui generis, as Lotze and Peirce among others have urged, we quickly see that a date is literally a term without any reference.[1] It is intentionally vacuous just because it literally points to no point at all. It claims to "locate" a temporal "point" which it names as a particular nonextensive "now"; but such a "point," as Aristotle had already observed, merely marks the junction of a specific "before" and a specific "after" and is literally nothing in itself, is not "in" time, and is certainly nothing temporal; it is but the mark of the boundary of a particular time—or, as we may now say a bit more precisely, the boundary-edge of a particular duration or lastingness of being.[2] The dating's only literal claim is to represent a fictional point on a fictional line. Useful as this may conceivably be, its literal descriptive force—as claiming to "locate" a specific "when?"—is fiction compounded and literally meaningless.

A date is nothing temporal. Descriptively false because it literally does not do what it claims, it nevertheless is extremely useful when not so misconceived. A date does *not* "locate" a mythic point "in" time. It *does* relate simultaneities and sequences of existents and events: it "locates" an event as related to other events. It tells us what else was happening when this was happening. It serves to relate this particular event with others at the same time, "overlapping in duration," "that was dying as this was being born," "this occurred before that began." The value of a dating system is intrinsically relational. Its prescription for testing the truth of a date ascription is to relate the event it "locates" to other proximate events—as when one "transmutes" the numbering of an anniversary from, say, the Julian to the Gregorian or the Chinese calendar.

As relational, a dating system illumines a particular entity or event as involved in a context of being. Its prime force is then to throw focus, not on the boundaries around but on the temporal context within which the entity or event manifests its activity of existing and reflects its existential colleagues within itself. As relational, a date demonstrates the contextual character of the existent to which it refers, the ways in which that entity or event reflects and builds its context into itself. As relational, a date forecloses the legitimacy of abstracting any entity or event out from the temporality of its existing and then treating that entity or event as self-contained. As relational, it points up the durational nature of what it "locates" and the ways in which that durational activity is in a continuity of relational mutuality with those other entities and events which share its temporal neighborhood.

When a dating system is taken as a metaphoric mode of describing, not terminal points, but a complex of dynamic relationships, it points to the matrix of relations inherent in any particular durational existent. When the function of a dating is seen as relational description, it precludes the legitimacy of severing an entity or event from its context; it urges that any entity or event can only be fathomed when seen as inextricably involved with, and expressive of, a continuity of temporal being.

When a dating is regarded, not as a mythic point on a mythic line, but as a sort of shorthand for a durational complex, we no longer regard a beginning or an end as more than a proximate limit: in a real sense, a beginning prepares itself, and an ending transpires over "moments" and carries on after it is over. As with any specific birth or death, we are immediately pointed to a process of alteration and change, to antecedents and consequents. We see ourselves looking back into a past that is no longer but is somehow still manifest in the entity or event before us. Our understanding of its activity reaches into the future that is already somehow manifest in the way we see what is before us as inviting possibilities yet to be actualized. When an entity or event is seen as a durational complex, we understand that its being is inseparable from its time, and its time is a continuity of being with all that came before and with what follows.

For any durational entity is itself an event without a precise moment of genesis or termination. As Santayana noted, "Events are changes, and change implies continuity and derivation of event from event: otherwise there might be variety in existence, but there could be no variation, since the phases of the alleged changes would not follow from one another."[3] We are not, then, bound to Hume's dictum that we can only "pronounce one thing not to be another."[4] Attentive observation of any particular entity or happening immediately points out its intrinsic temporal continuities with other things and events, and its own temporal spread no matter how precipitous it may be. Rather than speak of a "beginning" or an "end," we might better think in terms of progressive emergence and progressive decline. In this sense, the Greek terms of "generation" and "corruption" were more faithful to the facts of our experience.

Any presumption of efficient causality makes this clear. No particular thing is its own cause of being. Its present state manifests ties to an earlier condition, a process out of which it gradually developed, and perhaps some separate precipitating event which brought about that special transformation of its antecedents that makes it appear as new. Even the "big bang" cataclysmically initiating *this* material universe "took time" and was presumably the radical transformation of an earlier matter/energy complex, conceivably initiated by some separate precipitating event. Even the French Revolution, often described as the "beginning" of modern Europe, did not begin at a precise moment, carried with it

the heritage of prior problems and crises which precipitated its cata-
clysmic appearance, and shaped the ways in which it developed and the
ways in which it fed into what came after it died down. Unless one posits
a pervasive doctrine of spontaneous and uncaused generation, one is
bound to a view of nature or society that invokes any motion of efficacious causality as a process of temporal continuities and as carrying past
conditions in a transformed way into what comes after.

Any discerned and discriminated event, then, is a sign of both antecedents and consequents. Newness and variety—the new contours of
Mt. Saint Helens, the birth of a baby, the inauguration of a new governmental administration—whether in physical nature, biological emergence, or social history, arise only as transformations of what has already
been, as developmental continuities from previous states and ante-
cedent conditions, as the actualization of possibilities already available.
What we regard as specific, efficacious, or precipitating causes of particular transformations are themselves dependent for their being on antecedents. Any particular entity or event, then, is initially complex in its
developmental history and its pervasively historical continuities in the
world.

If the other entities and events with which it interacts are likewise
enmeshed in their own temporal continuities, then the temporal continuities of any particular entity or event do indeed stretch far beyond it,
involving it in a dynamic matrix that is essentially organic in character.
Any particular entity or event, as durational and developing, is then inherently involved with, and truly inseparable from, the continuing temporal continuities that characterize the existent world as such.

If time is the mode whereby one entity or event is related to the
others, to the world in which it is acting out its own state of developmental being, then such time-relations cannot be accidental or
nonessential to it; they cannot be merely external or arbitrary ap-
pendages attached to, but removable from it. The time-relations of an
entity or event are *intrinsic* to it, to what it is and how it is—not only as existent, but as exist*ing*, develop*ing*, chang*ing*, matur*ing*, declin*ing*. Any
entity that *is,* any event that occurs, is then constituted by its time-
relations—which have made it what it is be*ing*, activate what it is do*ing*
and the functions it is serv*ing*. Its time-relations are then constitutive
and, in the traditional jargon, are relations *internal* to the essence of its
individual identity. Because internal time-relations are inherent in definition and in structure, no entity or event can be understood or explained while its essential temporal constitution is ignored.

If time is inherently relational—whether externally or internally
considered—then time cannot be exclusively linear in character. Time-

relations cannot be simply characterized in terms of before-and-after sequentiality, although that sequentiality is certainly ingredient to them. As a network of functioning relations, time involves any particular entity or event with others. As a metaphoric shorthand—but at risk of gross oversimplification—we may discriminate time-relations as either sequential or simultaneous, but to take these terms as clear and distinct differentiations with full exclusive force is to treat them as accidental attributes and not as constitutive ingredients; to do so would also be a reversion to the naive simplicities inherent in a temporal geography that "locates" the "place" of a thing in terms of precise points within a spatially conceived box. To reduce time-relations, then, to mere sequentiality and simultaneity in an exclusive way is to preclude the possibility of comprehending the being of an existent entity, the meaning of a real event.

If time is inherently relational of real entities and events, and as such intrinsic to them, then time-relations must be conceived as real. However we may evaluate the descriptive competence of human reason's cognitive claims—whether we believe that human cognition may somehow penetrate to the heart of reality itself, or we find that human cognition is necessarily restricted within the a priori confines of its perspectival outlook—clearly any cognitive claim is predicated on the presumption of some kind of temporal realism. Any knowledge claim, restricted as it may be in its cognitive reach or certitude, must engage the presupposition that time-relations are somehow real, as real as the things and events we seek to comprehend, real at least as they truly appear to human awareness. One may or may not believe that objective reality fully appears within the outlook of human cognitive competence; but even the skeptic here must presume in his cognitive investigations that the temporal continuities which appear to human cognitive reason seem to have an objective ground independent of the modes of human thinking, as objectively independent as the things and events that appear to be constituted by them. And both must recognize as well that the activity of human thinking, reasoning, cognizing is itself temporally constituted—for any awareness of external change is itself a temporal event in the activity of the apprehending consciousness.

If particular entities and events are constituted and bound together by temporal ties—manifesting themselves as continuities of dependence, causality, purpose, function, interaction—then there can be no gaps in time or nature. Whatever discontinuous changes seem to appear, we necessarily presume that such discontinuities reflect a limitation of our understanding, and set a task for investigation; we presume that such discontinuities are not of the real order of events to which understanding is directed but in the understanding itself. The notion of a timeless gap between two distinct sequences is a contradiction in terms and devoid of intelligibility or ontological meaning.

As Leibniz urged, when formulating the law of continuity, we necessarily involve the premise that time is the form of the "continuous temporal modifications in the universe."[5] In carrying this forward, Kant had argued for a primordiality of temporal continuity and unity: the concepts of succession, simultaneity, and duration, he pointed out, all presuppose one time-order insofar as "no time is apprehended except as part of one and the same boundless time. . . . [For time] is the principle of the laws of continuity in the changes of the universe."[6] More primordial even than the laws of reasoning, continuity is at least a "first postulate" of the notion and experience of time.[7]

Whether we speak of the ways in which we can understand nature, or of the nature that is to be understood by us, if in any sense, we are in nature, then the requisite continuity is not only the primordiality of temporal continuity of nature but also of us. As Kant was quick to note, our possible knowledge of "all changes and successions" depends, first, on temporal continuity in the observed world; it equally "presupposes the perdurability of the subject."[8] Indeed, William James effectively carried this forward by urging that time is *the one* form of being common to both knower and known, to man and nature, and thereby the ground of the possibility of man's knowledge of nature.[9]

The principle of temporal continuity, then, has at least three subordinate principles: (1) the continuity of the phenomena constituting the natural order; (2) the continuity of the human subject who seeks to understand it; and (3) the continuity of their relationship in a mutuality of temporal being permitting knower and known to meet together in a common temporal field. The principle of temporal continuity is, then, a first principle for the understanding of external objects *and* of our own selves.

What we term a "beginning" or an "ending" cannot then be, within this one world at least, *ex nihilo* or *in nihilo*—out of nothing or into nothing. Beginnings and endings of particular entities or events can only be taken as noticeable transformations which activate potentialities already present, actualize possibilities truly genuine, and are continuous with and inseparable from them.[10]

The judgment that a particular transformation is sufficiently dramatic to occasion designation as a beginning or an end is itself a change, an event, in the consciousness of the beholder regardless of its descriptive truth. No judgment is a merely passive report of what is transpiring "out there." The most passive spectator kind of judgment, which does not disturb the continuing flux to which it refers (as the unobtrusive spectator does not affect the drama he witnesses), is already a selective report on what is claimed to be transpiring before one's eyes. One cannot claim to describe the infinite detail of what is before him in its totality; he thus necessarily focuses attention and selects aspects of it that excite his interest and respond to his ensuing questions.

To speak, then, of a beginning or end of a particular entity or event is to interpret specifically selected sets of continuities—the changing color but not the fragrance or the sound—regarded as important or significant to the reporting interest; but "important" means "important for something," and "significant" likewise refers to and invokes a standard of evaluation; to regard a set of continuities as important, then, immediately implicates the valuational categories of the speaker. One's judgment of a particular beginning or ending is the voicing of a particular perspective and its operating judgmental standards: the judgment has its cognitive meaning, then, only within the terms of that perspective. When considering the truth of any assertion, then, one needs to implicate the value structure—the criteria for significance, importance, focus, selectivity—of the perspective from within which the assertion is made. This perspective is, itself, a dynamically particular continuity of interpretive activity: as such it is durational, cannot be reduced to momentary states, and is inextricably involved with the context of its being.

If any judgment or knowledge-claim is inherently selective, if it depends in any way on its own (perhaps unspoken) criteria or values, it is no merely passive report; for it probes the presentational flux with its own interests, standards, and its questions: its report, which is the response to these probings of interest or concern, is an inherently interpretational activity. The selectivity of perceptional focus arises out of the needs or interest of the observer's attentive thinking; his judgment is structured by the modes of thought invoked to respond to the questioning interest that initiated it and brought it forth. Thinkers as disparate and yet similar as Leibniz, Kant, Peirce, Royce, and Heidegger—and Plato, too—have presented cogent reasons for this thesis that perceptual attention and consequential judgments constitute interpretive activity arising out of the particular thinker's peculiar finite perspective.[11]

Interpretive thinking is itself a process of temporal continuity that is, perhaps logically but not really, separable from the continuities to which it claims to refer. An act of thinking is a response by the thinker to what he sees and not merely a reaction to a perceptual stimulus. An act of thinking is animated as much out of the needs, concerns, interests, and desires of the particular thinker as out of the object about which he speaks: an act of thinking cannot, then, be reductively explained as the mere causal effect of the observational field.

A specific act of thinking, the interpretive understanding of what is transpiring before one's eyes, is oriented forward in terms of problems to be solved, confirmations of expectations to be secured, answers to questions being asked, purposes to be pursued, discerned lacks to be filled—in terms of conceived anticipations which beckon one onward. Within the activity of what is being observed, functions are discerned, purposes are seen as being frustrated or fulfilled, experiments are conducted, activities are planned, expectations are tested. These are discrete modes of human thinking—all of which look ahead to what is conceived as possibly yet to come; they feed on a vision of possible futurity and feed it into the present activity, taking up only those specific causal chains from the past which seem pertinent to the conceived task at hand. These are human activities which presuppose a new kind of continuity—a reciprocity between present and future.

Within the standpoint of the present, I can look onto the past from which the present arose and discriminate from that complex the specific sequential chains of developmental events which I understand to be *the* causal strands leading into the current focused matrix—as the weaver can discriminate those strands being taken into the particular pattern he is now developing from those that have already been used or will only come into other areas of his rug.

Thus I can explain the present in efficacious causal terms as being dependent for its being on specifically selected sequential chains from the past. But I cannot comprehend my own activities of planning, experimenting, or anticipating in this simple reductionist manner; for these current directive activities presuppose a vision of yet-unrealized possibilities that are taken as genuine and that as such feed my present decisions and acts—in a kind of running back-and-forth of continuities between future and present that are nourishing each other.

Present directive activity presumes a view of the future as somewhat open and thereby somewhat dependent for its specific development upon my present judgment, decision, activity. Mere chronology is thus confused in any description of such mental activity just because it inherently involves the mixing of the not-yet futurity of anticipation with the now of the immediate present. But, clearly, any deciding and planning presupposes firm conviction in the possibility of counting on continuing continuities into the future that is not-yet. And, clearly, actional judgment necessarily steps beyond cognitive certitude as it advances (by an invocation of rational faith) into its future which is, in any strict sense, unknown (and unknowable) just because it is not, by definition, presently determinate. What is involved in this reaching-into of futurity that is necessarily present in thinking activity certainly requires extensive development.[12] But what is crucial here is this: the principle of continuity is not to be seen solely in the causally sequential chains from the past that are presently manifest; this principle of continuity works forward in both the human act of interpretive understanding *and* in the developmental activity of the things we seek to understand, use, transform. Projection of continuity between present and the not-yet-but-still-can-be is thus intrinsic to any act of thinking as it seeks to deal with selected aspects of the world.

If perceptual and interpretive activity are selective, problemoriented, and judgmental, they depend upon the evaluative standards which constitute the continuity of the outlook and modes of thought of the particular human subject; for it is by means of these evaluative criteria or standards that individual attention is focused and directed, judgments made, decisions resolved, activities committed. These evaluative standards, which constitute any individual perspective, are then primordial to the selectivity of perceptions, the idiosyncracies of individual tastes and biases and commitments.

Any assertion, then, of a beginning or an ending is a selective interpretation of the continuing flux from the particular viewpoint of the particular speaker. Any such assertion can only claim to be a report of a discerned transformation of a particular aspect of the continuing flux *as* selected for focus in terms of the predilections and questions which the individual brings to his observation or investigation of it.

The primitive witch doctor and the typical Western physician will describe the same patient in terms of different kinds of transformations, report different "discontinuities" as a result of diverse examinations, anticipate different pathological development, and prescribe dissimilar remedial courses of action. Any attribution of efficient causality, as any directive activity, presupposes the principle of continuity; but the specific continuities selected out for discernment, evaluation, investigation, the specific continuities projected as the "henceforth" presupposition of deliberate activity, are dependent on the evaluative standards constituting the individual outlook of the person concerned.

Thinking, then, is itself a creative, interpretive structuring of presumably open situations with a problematic orientation and a point of view; it ties past into present by means of its structured focus and future into present by means of decisions and ensuing activities. Both taken together, in a synthetic whole, constitute the particular perspective from within which it reports, evaluates, and decides. The particular strands of continuity one abstracts from the presentational flux, in which one is

already involved, are judgmental interpretations from the outset; they finally depend at least as much on the values, interests, categorial structures, and physical dispositions of one's outlook, as they do on what is
actually transpiring in the reported field. The claim of a new beginning
is then inherently fallacious if it either suggests denial of literal continuity with progressively changing antecedents, or pretends that the particular idiosyncratic perspective of the speaker is irrelevant to his claim.

Different qualified observers often interpret the same presentation in dissimilar ways. Interpretive thinking cannot be explained as
merely the caused effect of the observed presentation. If thinking is selective and interpretive it is not reducible to prior causes, mechanistically conceived, because its activity consists in questing for reasons to
justify belief. It is thereby itself selective and thereby insofar free. Interpretive thinking presupposes the continuity of process and connection
in what it thinks about, but also its own selectivity of focus, the weighing
of reasons, the invocation of evaluative criteria and their examination
and refinement. Interpretive thinking thereby presupposes the ability
freely to engage in such discriminating and self-directive acts.

If I am to escape error in judgment—as Descartes had already
clearly argued—if I am to test my hunches, explore alternatives, evaluate
evidence, I must be able to direct my attention, control my thinking,
govern its investigations, and refrain from premature suspension of
questioning—until my own evaluative criteria for the fulfillment of my
quest have been satisfied.[13] Responsible thinking is, then, a free project
which is itself constituted in terms of its own temporal continuities.

Most considerations of human freedom have been in terms of
moral endeavor and practical reason. What is suggested, however, is that
any conception of perception as selective, any appraisal of thinking and
judgmental decision as evaluative and interpretive, bespeaks not only
the primordiality of perspective; insofar as an individual's perspective is
selectively interpretive, it is forward-looking in terms of evaluatively discerned possibilities not yet actualized. That resultant evaluation cannot
be explained as neatly reducible to what already has been or to what is
literally present, because it represents a step into the problematics of a
future not yet resolved. Evaluative selective thinking thus presupposes
the continuity of freedom in the durational existence of conscious evaluating beings. Acknowledgment of the functioning of freedom in the activity of thought only underlines the primordiality of the individual
perspective in the assertions the individual makes concerning aspects of
the changing world in which he finds himself.

We cannot, then, legitimately speak of any beginning or ending in any literal or absolute sense. Any discerned beginning is but a new transforma-

tion that itself is a process—whose precise genesis can hardly be dated with exactitude, and whose nascent temporal context can only be proximately pointed out. Any discerned ending is a transformation that carries into what follows or arises out of it; its further implications, like the ripples in a stream, can hardly be definitively delineated. The assertion of a particular beginning or ending is a selective, interpretive judgment from within the perspectival framework of the speaker, and brings to bear both his focus of interest as structured by the evaluative categories he uses and the freedom that is manifest in the reasoning he does in applying them. And that dynamic reasoning is itself a temporal process that cannot be severed from the temporal continuity of his biographical becoming.

Such judgments and outlooks, then, presuppose the essential historicity of durational activity: the temporal continuity of the speaker and his concerns with what he speaks about, the separable but not separate continuities of each, and the historical continuity of the cultural matrix from within which he has developed that individual distillation of his cultural ethos into the outlook he has made his own. On each of these variegated levels is presupposed the continuity of what is no longer with what is not yet but may yet be.

To assert a beginning is to point out a process which itself reaches out to what was and what may yet develop; it is a process which reflects an environment of currently transpiring interaction. It is to bring to bear on that complex happening an evaluative framework which justifies the speaker, from his own judgmental outlook, to speak of a birth rather than an emergence, a new turn rather than the maturation of an earlier activity.

What, then, of the utility of such a term as "beginning" or "ending"? By them, we ought to name the prominent part of a process and not a mythic point: a procession that ties the separable continuities of transformational complexes, represented in what is seen and in the evaluating observer, together into the event that includes them both. Our assertions concerning what we claim to describe merely give voice to the values incarnate in the outlook which chooses to speak. We thus describe, not the process being discussed, as the grammar might indicate, but the response to questions of selective evaluative import, the testing of expectations whose own continuities are only somewhat dependent on, and logically prior to, what is being allegedly described. To pronounce a judgment of beginning or ending is a proclamation of a new transformation that is, in a sense, taken as an interpretive "discontinuity" from within a continuous field.

This essentially metaphoric locution cannot legitimately serve as a framing concept that directs attention to the borders of the entity, or

event. When locutions such as "beginning" or "ending" are taken as relational and referential, they point to the durational reality within those
borders and equally to what lies beyond; they regard such temporal
boundaries as artificial selective impositions called for by the speaker's
purpose to direct focus, and not as truly descriptive of the entity he is focusing on. Such locutions, authentically comprehended, point in at least
two directions at once: to that to which they claim reference *and* to the
perspective (and its reasons) which voices them. Their authentic function is to point to a general area of interactional existence and not to a
particular determinate and allegedly self-contained event. Their function is not to frame, not to locate precisely, but to point out, to direct attention toward, the generally temporally constituted contextual area
within which an interpretive set of evaluative canons is claimed to have
some specified degree of pertinence.

8

Res Cogitans: The Time of Mind

odern philosophy, it is generally agreed, takes its point of departure from the work of René Descartes. Whatever else this genesis provided, at least we can say that it made the conception of the thinking mind central to all subsequent philosophical thought.

The first known certainty, Descartes insisted, is not the nature of the physical things perceived as external to consciousness; rather, it is the thinking mind itself in which consciousness of such perceptions arises. Systematic introspection becomes the new path to scientific or systematically grounded knowledge. Its function is to ground cognitive thinking in the thinking mind—which lodges all true knowledge and must certify all knowledge-claims. The nature of the individual thinking mind thus sets out, in advance of any specific use, the grounds of legitimacy for the admission of knowledge-claims and thereby the legitimatization of certainty for those knowledge-claims it deems to be properly admitted. Descartes's "Cogito ergo sum" ("I think therefore I am") becomes the first principle of modern thought, the necessary presupposition of any individual cognitive thinking, and the irreducible evidence of individual existence.[1]

Descartes's fundamental concern, however, was not to elucidate the nature of mind as such but rather to validate Galileo's new mathematical physics; to do this he needed to justify the applications of the mathematical concepts he found as innate qualities of the thinking mind to the objects comprising the experienced physical world.[2] In order to ground this, he posited the thesis that the world is composed of two radically different kinds of substances: physical things that occupy space and are thereby subject to the mathematical descriptions of size, weight, resistance, and place—later enumerated as the "primary qualities" characteristic of space-occupying entities with which science deals—and "mental substance," which is essentially describable by the *negations* of these spatializing predicates.

But what kind of an entity is this "mental substance"? Mind, as an existent functioning entity, is only described by negations of the predicates rightfully attributable to physical objects.[3] Although mind is portrayed as a kind of "substance," the only *positive* description we have of mind is that it is *res cogitans*, "the thinking entity," a nonspatial substance characterizable only by the *activity* of think*ing*.[4] This formulation bequeathed to what followed: the notion of mind as grounding all experience, but aside from specifying it as our source of mathematics, its nonspatiality, and its nature *qua* activity, Descartes left its inherent nature in the dark.

Some Ensuing Questions

Subsequent philosophic thought carried these general theses in diverse directions. Some philosophers have taken as seriously fundamental the stated Cartesian thesis that mind and body are actually two radically different kinds of substances: body as inherently spatial and mind as inherently nonspatial. In pursuing this they are enveloped by the question of *what kind of thing* mind, as a nonspatial entity, might really be. And they have been concerned to pursue some of the questions this twofold ontology suggests. If mind and body are so different, how can one communicate with the other? Can mind justifiably be reduced to body? Is the mind then merely an epiphenomenon of the brain? And if Descartes is correctly read as having suggested that we are each enclosed within our own individual thinking, how can we each truly face the question, not so much of "other bodies," but of "other minds"?

I propose an alternate route from this Cartesian genesis because I think it one more fruitful to explore. It seems to offer greater developmental possibilities and to suggest more sophisticated responses to that kind of inquiry.

I am rather entranced by at least this somewhat paradoxical consideration: Descartes (1) refused to reduce mind to the mathematically describable spatial; and (2) he only described mind by what it does: as *res cogitans*, as "the thinking entity." But (3) this is an activity description, and any activity requires a real temporal spread of continuity so that it may function; (4) yet Descartes attributed neither temporal predicates nor continuity to mind. (5) Indeed, he seems to have had problems with the very idea of temporal continuity, epitomized in his conviction that each moment is a somehow irreducible, real, self-enclosed atomic point in the structure of this universe, and is devoid of any sustaining continuity with any other moment.[5] Mind is described only as an activity; yet no temporal predicates are ascribed to it! If mind is knowable by us only as the "think*ing* entity," whatever else mind might conceivably be, it can only be understood by us as pervasively temporal.

Consequent Philosophic Development

It was not long before this kind of thought seems to have been taken up in somewhat different ways by both Locke and Leibniz. Despite their historic controversy—which sets out the contemporary divide in all subsequent Western philosophy—they each effectively set aside the notion of "substance" as the prime characteristic of mind; for both insisted that mind is known by us as a temporal activity.

John Locke, in his *Essay Concerning the Human Understanding* (1690), pointed out that even the most systematic introspection presents not the thinking mind itself, but rather a "train of ideas" which succeed each other in consciousness.[6] Each idea as momentary object of thought is transitional, progressively disappearing into the past as it is pushed on by a new idea (or altered object of mental focus) seemingly coming into present attention out of the future.

Leibniz, in his *New Essays on the Human Understanding,* epitomized and carried forward this view of mind as a dynamic processing of ideas when he explicitly argued that "to think and to be thinking are the same."[7] This conscious thinking, he had said, is "not only of my thinking self, but also of my thoughts, and it is no more certain that I think than that I think this or that."[8] (This consideration clearly suggests itself as pointing to a phenomenological notion of intentionality.) Because these ideas, which are the content of my thinking activity, are immediately reflective of the world within which I find myself, Leibniz transcended the Cartesian problem of an isolated mind; for mind now is not only in cognitive contact with the world; it discovers its own inherent structure only as it functions by thinking about the things in the world reflected within its thinking activity.

This intellectual development reached its full expression in Immanuel Kant's *Critique of Pure Reason* which, to this point, argued that time, as the form of consciousness—which Kant, following Augustine in *On the Free Choice of the Will,* called "inner sense"—is the form of all of our thinking. This, he went on to point out, means that our cognitive thinking must be organized by time-structured categories, that it can only generate knowledge, as distinct from conjecture and speculation, when it is concerned with time-bound sensory presentations.[9]

This Kantian thesis brings us into the main currents of modern philosophic thought. Taken up by prime movements of nineteenth-century thinking, it has molded prime schools of contemporary thought. American contextualistic pragmatism, announced by Charles Peirce and William James, made the pervasive temporality of all thinking its central point of departure. Josiah Royce, in terms of philosophic idealism, and John Dewey, in terms of philosophic naturalism, gave it further development by carrying it forward into every area of intellectual consideration. In our own local epoch, the centrality of time in human thinking, and thereby the essential temporality of mind, was underscored by Henri Bergson's *Time and Free Will* (1889) and Edmund Husserl's *The Phenomenology of Internal Time-Consciousness* (1905–10). Their thrust has been most forcefully developed in the work of existential phenomenologists, particularly Martin Heidegger's *Being and Time* (1927) and Maurice Merleau-Ponty's *The Phenomenology of Perception* (1962).

The Historicity of Our Thinking

This historical overview might be regarded by some as perhaps interesting but essentially extraneous. I do not think so. For I am aware of no thinking that starts "from scratch" and transpires in an ideational vacuum. Any act of thought starts by taking up a given ideational heritage. Any act of thought arises in response to questions we have been asked, experiences we have undergone, and the ensuing hopes and fears we have set out to realize or avoid. Any act of thought incorporates into its central structure a set of originally unexamined valuational judgments regarding what is important or unimportant, and proceeds by a logic which it accepts as legitimate.

Your thinking and mine both arise in this present historic context of ideational social development. Our thinking picks up some inherited theses concerning both doctrine and method we accept as "obviously true," calls some of the ideas handed to us questionable, and openly challenges others. The cultural context in which each finds personhood is essentially historical. Often taken as something of an allegedly temporally transcendent "God's-eye view," any act of thinking is nevertheless culturally bound: its present formulations are initially framed in accord with the particular parochial culture within which it finds itself and which is but one contemporary distilled version of an entire civilization's current legacy. The landmarks of a culture's development can be pinpointed, in an oversimplified way, as I have just done in terms of one theme, by pointing to key thinkers along the way. However, we need to recognize, if not always take the time to acknowledge, that each of these landmark thinkers was himself responding to an ideational complex of ideas which was itself developing while he was encountering them and which would not have been recognized at any stage of development in precisely the same form by his grandparents.

The content of any individual's thinking is thus a present individual response to his own historic inheritance. This inheritance provides the parameters we each use to guide our own thinking: the valuational standards and distinctions we invoke, often without question or conscious awareness; the questions which we raise in the face of proffered answers; the problematics we see in what members of an earlier generation may have taken as assured doctrine. Royce once suggested that each of us is born with an overwhelming debt, a debt to the entire historically still-developing civilization which has received us into its currently expressed localized form. All thinking, I think we will all agree, is contextually bound. But the context is first of all a dynamically historic one, which is to say that it is the temporal context of our inherently historical sociality.

Any individual thinking is thus historically situated. The immediate context within which it finds itself is a complex of individual interactions which have arisen out of a developing history that presents itself as a contemporary environment—our understandings of sociological and political and economic structures, family mores, and religious or ideological allegiances, many of which are never articulated but nevertheless heedlessly taken for granted. Its historicity is thus not only grandly political. For the family setting within which each individual develops is itself a particular historical ongoing process within the larger continuously developing social world.

Our conscious thinking utilizes a language, let us not forget, as an instrument of thought. And this too, historically developed, imposes a set of canons and procedures and presuppositions which only come into view when deliberately compared with other languages, particularly those of radically different cultures. Any individual's thinking activity thus reflects the historical milieu which is continually nourishing him even while he is developing his own distinctive judgmental outlook from it. No individual's thinking can then be "objective" beyond those culturally induced categories which are transcendentally operative in his thinking.[10] No matter how dispassionate one may seek to be, one can but express a particular kind of outlook on the historically developing world within which one finds oneself functioning.

As social beings, any individual thinking thus necessarily incorporates particularized time predicates, as particular differentiating descriptions of the historically developed social milieu out of which whatever individuality we each manifest has arisen. Because each individuality is idiosyncratically reflective of the nourishing culture, it is historical, thereby temporal, from the outset.

Time and Thought

As we progressively narrow the societal area of consideration, we finally come to the individual who reflects, even in his most strident individuality, the entire historical ethos which, in his own biographical development, he had absorbed into himself—and of which he must always remain an, even if critical, expression. However important this sociohistorical ethos may be in structuring the process and context of individual thinking, however pervasively our thoughts may be socially stimulated and socially directed, thinking ultimately is an individual matter. For each individual finds his own bond with, and differentiation from, his social context in his own self, in his perception of his own identity and individuality, in his own evaluative outlook and his relations with the other people and things that comprise the world in which he lives his own activity of being within which he develops his own perspectival understanding of his world—the content that he attaches to *his* verb "I think."

For let us not forget, as Leibniz pointed out, that one cannot merely think. Any act of thinking is not only in a context of thought; it is *about* something—an idea, representation, desire, or thing—that is the object of the verb that itself but names an activity of being. Any act of thinking is other-directed. My thinking is the activity of relating myself conceptually to whatever it is that I am thinking about. "I think" always means "I am thinking some-thing"; "I am thinking x—chair, enemy, friend." This is clearly recognized by each one of us: when you confront me sitting like Rodin's statue, buried in thought, you ask, "what are you doing?"; when I reply, "I am thinking," your immediate response is: "but what are you thinking about?" One cannot think without reaching out from the act of thinking to the object of one's thought. Conceivably, one can think about the nature of thinking itself, as Aristotle's God was eternally supposed to be doing, but even here, one is thinking about something other than one's immediate thinking self. The phrase "I think," like "I eat" or "I want," is a transitive verb and requires an object, even if it may on occasion be reflexive. One cannot think without thinking about something, even if that something, as in the case of some mystics, is about the presumed nothingness of all being.

Whatever it is that one thinks about is itself time-bound, an event or happening that itself consumes duration—whether it be an idea demanding attention in consciousness or an event or durational entity in the world presumably beyond individual consciousness.

It is not only the object of thought that is inherently temporal. Regardless of what one is thinking about, the activity of thinking itself "takes time." It may be momentary or leisurely, but no matter how fleeting, it incorporates duration. Thinking does not only occur in a historic setting; it takes up into itself historically developed parameters of thought, and refers to conceptual objects that themselves incorporate temporal predicates. Thinking itself necessarily consumes time. It incorporates time into itself. It is spread over those so-called moments—seconds, minutes, or hours—we use as a convenient externalizing metric for comparing experiential durations with each other.

Any specific act of thinking transpires in culturally developed, thereby historical, situations, thus incorporating and thereby expressing a temporally framed orientation. It refers to ideas, notions, or representations that are themselves durationally constituted as the objects of its referential intentions. And it does all this, as a process or activity, by itself utilizing spreads of time in order to do so.

The Temporal Structure of Our Thinking

Some of these observations do require development, but I would think it strange to find them regarded as particularly controversial. However, let us now proceed one step more—to a brief consideration of just *how* our thinking uses time for its own process of activity. What I want to suggest is that no kind of conscious thinking is devoid of temporal constituents, that all types of conscious thinking embody the integration of the thinker's past, present, and futurity into the thinker's outlook, and that this integration usually functions under guidance by what, in the standpoint of the present, is conceived as future.

Conscious thought may, I think, be roughly discriminated into at least three kinds, each with temporal characteristics peculiar to itself—while yet embracing crucial similarities with the others.

1. When I just stop, perhaps in awe or wonder, to gaze at a beautiful sunset or a beautiful painting, I am not usually conscious of the

continuing pulse of time. I am, as it were, caught up in a seemingly temporally seamless duration of aesthetic response or religious awe. My attention is fully consumed by the object that commands my gaze.

But is this truly a nontemporal experience—as many aestheticians and mystics have often claimed? Doesn't my present experiential moment connect what I see with what I have seen before? Doesn't it *press* to maintain its continuing present against distraction from future interruption? And if, while enthralled, I am conscious that this experience must itself terminate, isn't my continuing entrancement itself something of a protest against its impending presently future ending? Most crucially, doesn't the meaning I read into this presently consuming presentation represent my projected integration of past experiences which I immediately find either similar or dissimilar, the present activation of my aesthetic education, the aesthetic norms I have been taught to value, and my hope for its continuity into at least the immediate future? And, when the aesthetic experience—which must be durational in order to be experiential—has itself ended, don't I note its termination and yet carry the memory of the experience with me? Don't I regard the experience itself as a discontinuity within the continuum of that experiential flow in which I find my own being? Aesthetic, like mystic, experience, it would seem, is an experience of a durational present which is imbued with meaning by the past I bring with me and the future I either anticipate or fear.[11]

2. When I am faced with a problematic situation, a task to be undertaken, a conflict of desire or obligation to be resolved, I face what we generally term a practical problem. I face myself facing the question "what should I do?" That "should" directly refers to the future, to what is not yet but is shortly to be judged within the area of feasibility. The past we say is over and done with and the immediate present is what is now actual—and neither is subject to any decision I might feel called upon to make. But a problematic situation defines itself in the guise of the future presenting itself to me as somewhat open, as presenting a finite range of alternate possibilities. Between these possibilities which I judge as viable, I must select a course of action bridging the temporal interim between the immediately present moment and the state of resolution which I seek to achieve. Any action that is not a mere reflexive reaction is a deliberative practical action that is responsive to, and thereby guided by, a present vision of the possibilities for the future, for the not-yet but the yet-may-be. In forming my decision, I bring into thought those aspects of the past which seem pertinent to the problematic I see before me. But their selection, out of all my uncountably myriad past experiences, is of those few that strike me as presently germane to my task at hand.

Practical action situations most clearly present a future-orientation. They project one out of the actuality of one's present and past into what is, in the most literal sense, presently unknown and unknowable. They are guided by a judgment of possibility which may be secure or merely hopeful in its outlook. But it is this reading of possibly alternative future actualities that brings me to commit myself to one specific course of action. If this were all, it would be enough to support the argument that all thinking is inherently temporal.

But something more is crucial. The meaning which I read into my present problematic situation does not come out of the past and is certainly not dictated by the immediate present. For I read my present as itself closing off some possibilities I might like to pursue and as opening up those other possible courses of action which I regard as viable. My interpretation of any problematic situation, the very way in which I define it to myself, is by means of those possibilities for the "henceforth" which, for whatever reasons, I see it as offering. My present vision of possibility is not only an invitation which calls me to action. The problematic meaning I see in my present situation is itself essentially structured by these conceived possibilities—encapsulated in the question "what should I do about this?"

Any situation which I comprehend as demanding a response on my part is imbued by me with the meaning I interpret it to embody—not by an ambiguously indefinite past and not by the immediate present, but by those specific alternative possibilities of futurity I see it as commanding me to decide between.

3. At first blush, the cognitive situation might seem somewhat different. Like the aesthetic, it is focused on the content of the present presentation; for, in contrast to the practical, it is focused *not* on "What should *I* do?" but on the content of my awareness. It calls for a suspension of the personal, a call to depersonalized acknowledgment of the cold truth of factuality before me. But, let me suggest, it cannot avoid the strictures of practical reason, because it presents any momentary choice before me by means of the question "if anything, what should I do about it?" My answer to this question structures the meaning I read into the presented situation. Does the panorama I look at call for a response by me? If so what kind of response should it be? My answers to these questions delineate the meaning I read into the situation and structure the way I interpret and thereby understand what I am seeing. This is to say that no conscious perception of mine is devoid of judgmental factors I bring into it. No perception of mine is devoid of my projection of my subjective outlook. No perception of mine is then devoid of questioning in terms of possibilities of the future.

As epitomized in the popular picture of scientific objectivity, science eschews all subjectivity and asks us merely to recognize "the facts." Which facts? Not the myriad details in the panorama before us, but those which are selectively judged to be relevant or important. Judged by what criteria? Only by invoking evaluative norms can I regard some aspects of the panorama as trivial, recognize others as central to my focus, and respond accordingly. But this is an interpretive procedure; I am not merely reporting the myriad details before me; I am selecting some for interpretive attention and read them in terms of the meaning I see them as bearing according to canons I accept; without this deliberate intrusion by me as the committed investigator into the situation of the factualities of what I am trying to discover, I could discover nothing. We are asked to recognize the actual facts of the case, not by a passive unresponsive gaze, but by an active procedure of deliberative investigation. One need only consider that a physicist, chemist, biologist, and poet looking at the same oak tree in the yard will provide radically different descriptions of their common object of attention—just because each description is a response to the differently framed specific questions each chooses to ask. Or I may set out to learn "the facts" of the case by an attentive concentration on learning—which is to say, by an active course of temporal commitment into what, in the standpoint of the momentary present, is a choice of possibilities not yet actualized.

And again, one should ask about the motivation for undertaking such a course of action. Is it not to attain a knowledge that one does not yet have, to attain or avoid a possibility of a future state of accomplishments, reward, or chastisement? Is the activity of the most dispassionate student or investigator comprehensible without cognizance of the goal he foresees? This is to ask for the evaluative criteria to which he has committed himself as the justification of the procedure he chooses to follow. One of the more thoughtless clichés of our time is that the scientific endeavor is value-free. Without a high evaluation of depersonalized truth, without the approbative evaluation of specified judgmental criteria, indeed, without an existential commitment to very specific investigatory procedures, modern scientific objectivity could not be.

And let us note, as something of a footnote, that the procedure of any investigation or of any learning procedure invariably involves the investigator's handling and manipulation of aspects of the physical environment—be it a microscope, a pencil and paper, a piece of chalk on a blackboard—and thereby of practical skills in deliberately manipulating selected components of the physical environment, for a purpose. The entire procedure of following out a commitment to pursuing a goal constitutes itself by a series of smaller steps: to use that test tube I must first walk over to get it; to insure that the experiment is not besmirched by unwanted input, I must first clean the test tube. As Dewey once pointed out, every course of action, which we first grandly sketch out as a set of intelligently chosen means to a desired end, is itself but a continuum of interim means and ends—each one, let us note, futurally oriented. And the end itself—learning the multiplication table, discovering the atomic structure of this pencil, cooking something to eat—each step in the necessary process is itself an interim goal that is yet a means to something later, while the possibility of the realization of the goal of the action— being able to use the multiplication table, comprehending the atomic structure of this pencil, actually cooking an edible meal—is not intrinsically treasured for itself but for some still further end, goal, or value even more temporally remote.

These three kinds of thinking are not only durational; each involves some kind of unification of memory-selection from the past, selective sensory awareness of the immediately actual present, and the anticipation of possible futurity. Each necessarily seeks to recollect only what is deemed relevant to the present task—by selective acts of memory-recall which bring selective aspects of my past into my present awareness. Each takes its stance in the immediacy of the focused present presentation. Each interprets the meaning of what is presently seen as possibilities of continuance into the future or imperatives for action-commitments to possibility-realization in the future.[12]

This interpretive function of the human understanding—taking time, structured by time, oriented to temporally presented actualities and temporal possibilities—enables us to be ourselves as beings who operate into the future. For our primary mode of evaluative judgment is directed to what-may-yet-be but is-not-yet; our primary mode of evaluative judgment is directed to what appears to us as possibilities for development which are dependent on what we decide. This futural orientation of all human thinking allows us, indeed requires us, to project our own evaluative judgments into the "what-is-not-yet"; it requires us to project ourselves into the future, and to bring futurity into the constitution of the lived present. No action that is not commensurate with this description would appear to be experientially comprehensible. As Leibniz once said, we are like "little gods": by virtue of our interpretive judgments which determine all our responses and actions, we are creators, each in his own domain, of what is not yet but yet shall be. In the activity of thinking, we each project ourselves into the future that is now literally unknown and thereby make and form the oncoming future present that will yet be known.

The Essential Temporality of Mind

These phenomenological considerations do, I think, demonstrate the essentially temporal structure of human thinking. They show that any kind of thought integrates the three temporal modes of pastness, presence, and futurity into the interpretations of meaning seen as embodied in the living present. They also suggest that of the three, most kinds of conscious human thinking are primarily oriented to what-is-not-yet, to what-yet-can-be, to the possibilities of futurity which the present situation is judged to present as its crucial meaning.

All thinking, then, is not only a time-durational process. Thinking is not merely concerned with temporally defined objects—whether they be things in the world as such or thoughts in our thinking. The thinking process itself is the continual interpretive integration of the three temporal modes of the thinking activity that is the self; it provides the meanings that are developed in the commitments brought forth as imperatives for action. It is this continuing process of continually integrating the continuity of temporally framed and temporally structured experiencing that enables each to find his own selfhood in the continuity of the "I" who does the thinking.

Mind, then, appears to us as essentially temporal in every way that it manifests its activity of being. Its activity is thinking which, like any process or activity, "takes time"; it is oriented to objects, whether events in the "external world" or to ideas or notions that are the fleeting objects of thinking itself; in its thinking it incorporates its continual synthesizing or integration of the temporal modes of pastness, presentness, and futurity, which essentially characterize every experiential awareness. Mind, as *res cogitans,* appears to us as a temporally structured ideationalizing activity—revealing selfhood to the self while it is continually incorporating temporal predicates in every aspect that it is presenting for our discernment.

Some Philosophic Implications

I began with Descartes, who is generally credited as having provided the innovative force—almost five hundred years ago—that impelled the development of a new way of philosophic thinking, the thinking out of which our contemporary views have evolved.

What has been repudiated in the preceding discussions is not only the Cartesian notion of mind as a self-enclosed entity, but also the claim of the Platonistic thesis that mind finds truth only by escaping temporality.[13] The notion of timelessness is not experiential; it can be reconciled with neither the temporal objects of experience nor the temporal structure of thinking itself. We may, indeed, legitimately claim to know truths that stretch across the expanse of human temporality and are thus for us "trans-temporal"—but we know of no way to experience truths which relate neither to the temporally constituted objects that provide the content of our experience nor to the temporal constitution of the experiencing process itself; we have no way of relating to truths which are incapable of temporal instantiation and thereby of temporal predicates. The laws of arithmetic, for example, are deemed by us to be applicable to every "moment" of experiential time; thereby, they are to us trans-temporal, since they are continuously validated by temporal predicates and find their meaning for us revealed in every temporal moment in which they are tested. Like any other "necessary truth" that may find instantiation throughout our particular experiences, they are (transcendentally) presupposed by us as universally necessary conditions of our experiences; nothing, however, is thereby said about their ontological status beyond the constitution of our possible experiences.[14] Whatever an allegedly timeless truth may be in itself, it is, as such, only available to us as a possible object of temporally constituted experience, and is thereby, within the range of possible human experience, inherently time-bound.

Insofar as any allegedly transcendent truth-claim needs to be tested by us within a temporal context, we have no experiential basis for claiming an insight into any truths to which time predicates are irrelevant. What has then been affirmed is the thesis that any truth within the possible human ken, like the thinking that develops it, is inherently temporal in every aspect of its knowable being.

I have sidestepped Descartes's thesis that mind is some kind of nonmaterial substance, but I have explored the meaning of his only positive description of mind: that whatever it may conceivably be in itself, it only manifests itself to us as a thinking-activity (*res cogitans*). In propounding this thesis, Descartes had seen, I think, further than his own historically time-bound thought could carry him; indeed, he has provided us with a way of thinking about the nature of mind that stretches beyond his own historically bound finite vision. In a nutshell, he has provided us with the most succinct description of mind we have; when we explore its meaning we come to focus not on what mind "is" but on what it "does," on the ways it manifests its presence to us in everything we do and think. Only in its continuing particularized functioning do we find awareness of the biographical particularities that constitute our own individual being.

Were it now possible to continue this discussion, I would like to develop some of the wider philosophical implications of what I think has been established. For philosophy, as I see it, does not look to any final answers. Rather it seeks out the further questions which any resolution of earlier inquiries opens up for further exploration.

In this vein, let me conclude by suggesting that if the foregoing general argument is deemed to be experientially valid, a number of questions immediately present themselves for further discussion.

1. The activity of mind appears to be essentially a continuity of interpretational activity that is temporally structured; if so, is it really legitimate to understand mind in any mechanistic sense of efficacious causal determinism? For such causality reduces the present to the past—while this phenomenological description sees a mind as an activity that is rooted, not in its past which it only *uses* for its own discriminative evaluations, but in its future as conceived possibilities which it necessarily faces as somewhat open.

The modern claim of universal legitimacy for explanation by means of efficacious causality is generally traced back to Descartes. But Descartes himself never universalized such explanation; he demanded it merely for explanation of the things of nature, physical things that are spatially describable.

It was not long before Leibniz denominated such efficacious causal explanation as but one species of the Principle of Sufficient Reason, reason sufficient for explanation of an event. Entirely appropriate for the study of physical nature, it hardly begins to explain the reasoning activity of mind—which is more generally explicable in terms of purposes and motives which, in contrast, do not seek to reduce the present to the past, but look to visions of the future as a means of explaining present deliberation and action.

2. If so, this temporalist conception of mind provides a defense of the notion of evaluative or interpretive freedom as crucial to the explanation of all mental activity.

Indeed, in his "Fourth Meditation," Descartes himself suggested this by arguing that our differentiation of truth from error depends upon the ability or capacity of the mind to freely suspend final judgment until it has rightfully judged that all the relevant evidence was in. Descartes was apparently careful to maintain the distinction between: (1) the mechanism he saw as tied to the spatiality of the physical, and (2) the freedom of judgment he reserved to *res cogitans*. Unfortunately, much of modern philosophy has focused on the mechanism and made it more pervasive than even Descartes ever appears to have suggested; it has thus, without any explicit justification, resolutely come to read the functioning of mind in terms that Descartes himself had reserved to what he called "body."

The Leibnizian protest against this was taken up and developed by Kant, who is the first modern philosopher to have faced this distinction with utmost seriousness. His own adaptation of the Leibnizian distinction between the phenomenal (as the physical order of sequential mechanism) and the noumenal (as the governing reality of rational freedom) argues that they are but distinctive aspects of the one real world—in which both the necessitarian determinism of physical matter and the freedom intrinsic to the rationality of mind inhere. For the world as one whole *includes* in its unitary wholeness our own thoughts and acts initiated by our own minds' rationally grounded interpretive decisions about what is yet to be done.

However one may find this Kantian development, the portrayal of mental activity as a continuity of interpretive integration—of futural possibilities (which are necessarily understood as presently open) with consequently selected aspects of present perception and selected retrieval of the past—reopens the contemporary discussion of freedom-and-determination on a new level; that discussion has been largely conducted by presuming the *universal* legitimacy of the model of efficacious causality, a conceptual model which this present discussion urges is severely limited in justifiable application.

3. If this interpretive perspective has any merit, then another area of speculative thought is opened up: for if mind is not only continuously temporal, but is largely oriented to futural possibilities—rather than being chained to determination by the past or pinned onto the fleeting actuality of the present moment—then our growing knowledge and directive control of the things constituting the world presumes the possibility of a free temporally structured mind to attain true degrees of understanding of the world itself.

One of the most ancient of Western philosophic theses is that "like knows like." If so, then mind can only attain any understandings of the world to the extent that the world as it appears to human consciousness is somehow accordant with the structures and categories of the knowing mind itself. The world as such, at least insofar as we may come to understand it, cannot then be a completely determined system, every detail of which was inherently set out on the "first day of creation." If the human mind, as *an activity within the world,* is a continuity of interpretive thinking that continually operates on principles of temporally open possibilities which are subject to somewhat free interpretive decisions of rational intelligence, then we can begin to understand how the human mind can indeed attain degrees of insight into the world of nature. For, if this human mind's intrusions into physical processes can indeed redirect aspects of their development, then at least some particulars of the world's developmental being are still open, and the limits of free human decisions define temporally operable limits of temporally bound real alternative possibilities.

4. Although I have gone beyond Descartes—bypassing his notion of mind as a kind of "thing" and postulating the essential temporality and thereby the essential continuity of the thinking mind—this consideration takes us right back to the original Cartesian postulate, if with a difference. Mind is somehow different from the physicality of the things of the world we seek to understand, but we can only understand the things of the world insofar as they correlate with conceptual categories found intrinsic to the thinking mind itself.

If mind is somehow a trans-temporal continuity; if it uses time in its activity of thinking to seek comprehension of the temporally constituted objects which appear to its outlook by using temporal predicates for its understanding of their relationships to each other and to itself; then mind is a "thinking entity" that continually uses time, continually functions by means of temporal terms, and cannot find its own being except by means of the continuity of time. In short, mind must find temporality not only intrinsic to its own self but also intrinsic to any external intelligibility with which it can deal.

We may then face Descartes's opening query: "what" is mind? We find that we can only know it, as he originally declared, as the "thinking entity" (*res cogitans*), as the thinking activity in which each of us finds awareness of his own being. Whether we can attain any insight into *what it* is beyond *what and how it does* is a question which must still remain open.

5. However this last speculation may go, whatever *kind* of thing an individual mind may inherently be—a question Kant had set aside as inherently unanswerable by us except as possibly revealed in the continuing experience of rational freedom—we do know that each of us only experiences his own mind, his own self, as a self-conscious being who is a socially rooted individual, and who is pervasively temporal while facing all the vicissitudes of being free. This inherent time-bound freedom of individual minds then becomes primordial.

This primordiality does suggest some important rethinking for the systematic study of the individual psyche. This primordiality also proposes some crucial theses for valuational priorities when theorizing about the moral obligations of citizens of organized societies—about the criteria for intelligent judgments concerning those policy decisions that are appropriate rational procedures for the political organizations in which every contemporary individual, as an activity of finite freedom, finds its own individual being.

Each of these questions would take us far afield. Each requires a separate and detailed treatment on its own. I mention them only to indicate that examining the essentially free temporality of the "thinking entity" that each finds himself to be, is no pedantic exercise; rather it is an inquiry which has importantly pervasive implications for myriad questions beyond itself.

9

Toward Experiential Metaphysics: Radical Temporalism

ismissing all "metaphysicians from Descartes to Hume" and defending the thrust of the Kantian rejoinder, Peirce explicitly gave voice to the essential Kantian orientation by explaining "we can never attain a knowledge of things as they are. We can only know their human aspect. But that is all the universe is for us."[1] As Kant consistently urged, we can only speak cognitively from within the scope of human thinking, from within the structure of the human mode of looking out onto the world within which we find ourselves.

Our mode of "looking out" constitutes our attempts to understand both the functioning of the natural order in which we participate as we find ourselves apprehending it *and* also our ways of participating in it.[2] But we can only do this by means of the free decisions we make concerning our ways of studying it and using it for the ends we find ourselves setting for ourselves. Our ways of looking, directing, and using the structure of our human outlook combine to constitute the particular perspective we bring to bear on whatever attracts our operating concern.

The Primacy of Perspective

In order to comprehend our way of looking out, we first have to "look in" so as to discover the structure of that outlook we bring with us in every attempt to understand and understandably deal with the aspects of the world in which we find ourselves functioning. If every species is, as Leibniz repeatedly urged, to be defined by its mode of representation, then this peculiar outlook on the way in which humans look out upon the world defines in advance of any empirical particularity the essential common nature of the human species, the parameters within which, and by means of which, we humans may justifiably claim cognitive insights into the nature of the world in which we exercise the activity of living. Before any speculation concerning the nature of that supervening reality that transcends and undergirds our particular experiences can be justifiable, it must explicate and accept the enabling-and-limiting structuring parameters of the human outlook from which it emerges. Accepting both its own finite capability and reach at the outset, it can then seek to go beyond what has been established with some degree of cognitive certainty to those rational beliefs that human reason's self-understanding cannot demonstrate but nevertheless sees as implicitly coherent with what it already claims to know.

A systematic metaphysic has then a twofold task. It needs to delineate, first, the categories of thought by which it functions and, second, the situational parameters which it necessarily takes up into that thinking. Taken together, these set out in advance the specific ontological characteristics it is able to discern in any object or entity that comes within its ken. Its first task, then, is to become self-conscious about the peculiarities of the particular selective perspective it brings along. For it can only justify its particular questions, and thereby evaluate the answers it discerns, by first making explicit the point-of-view or concern by means of which its inquiries are generated. Only after this can it properly turn to that more exciting realm of rational speculation concerning the cosmology within which it sees itself as functioning—by an imaginative extension of its grounded cognitive claims to the ultimate nature and structure of the things of the world and the world itself as one whole.

Systematic metaphysics is, then, from the outset bound by its own interpretative categories. It cannot be reduced to intellectual reporting; it cannot claim to provide particular factual truths describing specifics of the world. In its speculative reach it is an interpretive, not a cognitive, discipline. It offers canons of interpretation for the comprehension of particular kinds of experiences within a unificatory outlook that is ultimately more concerned to discern meaning than fact. As such, it is a necessary human activity. Although it often yields answers that cannot be demonstrated, these answers respond to questions that we have to ask—questions concerning the essential meanings that undergird the cognitions we have succeeded in establishing. The answers we develop serve as guidelines for using the degrees of knowledge attained to resolve the problems that define the actions marking our lives. The legitimacy of both the questions we ask and the answers we develop are grounded in the nature of the human inquirer; our understanding of our questions and our answers must take into account the structure of the human perspective and the role that that perspective seems to play in the world, the ultimate nature or meaning of which is being interrogated by our activity of thinking.

Aristotle had argued that insofar as thinking is deliberative it is not about the past or immediate present but about the future, which is yet open to some degree of determination by what we decide to do (consider, for example, *Nicomachean Ethics,* bk. 6, chap. 2, 1139); the function of our speculative beliefs, then, is to guide us beyond the limits of presumably established certainties into that future that we necessarily take to be somewhat open and thereby in its specificity presently unknown. Part of the limiting bias of our speculative thought then is not so much to understand the world as it, in a Parmenidean sense, "really *is,*" but rather how it can be rationally seen as coherent with the situations out of which our quests arise. Although all speculations do not appear to be equally justifiable, alternate frameworks for speculative insights appear to be defensible. The validation of conflicting speculative beliefs would then seem to require at least a correlation with, and reasonable extension of, what already seems evident about ourselves as we find ourselves functioning in our world.

Each of us is then thrust back into himself as he finds himself in the world as he sees it functioning about him. How do I find my world not only in what the current authority of the sciences tells us, but in the ways in which I develop and experience those sciences themselves; my own encounters with our fellows; with my own self? What characteristics, norms, categories, structures, do I find animating me in interpreting my world as it presents itself to me? How do I define the ways in which I experience the experiences that are mine? In being thus thrust back on myself, I am not thereby thrust back alone—for each of us is essentially enmeshed in a network of relationships that helps us to define ourselves to ourselves.

As we meet ourselves only in meeting our fellows (from whom we progressively differentiate our separate individual selves), we seem to discover common facets of our outlooks and concerns, seemingly universal ingredients of human experience we share together that suggest something of the nature of the world in which human experience itself is taken as the prime experiential reality. If human experiences are themselves real, their structural ingredients suggest something of the nature of the world of which they are a part and which, in their ultimate wholeness, must somehow coordinate with that experiential reality which we, as humans, each experience as our own. If rational speculation is to be not individually or culturally bound, but justifiably giving expression to the universality of its human ground, its final test must be its ability to account for the origin of the viewpoint being expressed. For that viewpoint, however faithful or erroneous, is itself a part of the world-order that is to be understood and explained. Any comprehensive speculative portrait of the order of the world needs to account for the perspective within the world from which it arises.

This world-order can only be seen and understood by us from a human vantage point—employing the particular enabling and limiting factors built into human sensibility, understanding, and judgment. Any interpretative attempt to comprehend the world in which we find ourselves is thus biased in advance by the particular characteristics of the form of the outlook with which we see it. Each of us, then, starts from the peculiarities of his own thinking—those characteristics he shares with others, those idiosyncracies that distinguish him from them—and these peculiarities of outlook are themselves constituent components of the world-order, the understanding of which is being sought.

The Particularity of Experiencing

This may seem to suggest a resuscitation of the Cartesian cogito. Even Sartre found himself defending this as basic.[3] But, as even he recognized, no man can ever experience his own thinking in isolation as a somehow disembodied spirit looking out onto a world intrinsically separate from him. I am, from the first, in a world of other persons and things that are developmentally interrelated; I only find my own self in a contextually developing differentiation from them.

If I am to follow modern precedent and seek a first principle for my own thinking that is modeled on the Cartesian cogito while yet remaining true to my own experiential reality, it would seem immediately apparent that such a principle must differ from the Cartesian original in at least two ways. It must recognize that all thinking is temporally structured in specific historic situations that entail a continuing dynamic of all components comprising an experiential situation in continuously changing relations with each other. In addition, it must equally acknowledge the thinking act to be a social activity that continually engages with others—by virtue of the language, concerns, dependencies, involvements, and privacies that mark out the living of my life.

Yet, just because all experiential reality is what is experienced in some level of consciousness, Descartes's general notion of the cogito is a defensible starting point: for however explained, recognized, or defined, my experiences, separately or together, appear to me as the object of the verb "I think," even if he did not pause to examine the dynamic nature of the "I think" itself. If the I think, the cogito or *je pense*, must be the starting point of my own metaphysical reflection, however, it differs radically from the one Descartes proposed in at least two ways.

1. The cogito, the *je pense,* is itself a temporal activity; as Leibniz said, "to think and to be thinking are the same.[4] It is what Locke had already termed "the constant train—or succession—of *ideas,* in our minds," inherently a temporally structured process.[5] Thinking, on either account, is thereby already engaged in temporally developing situations; as an intrinsically temporally structured activity, it is always "in time," in temporally defined situations.

2. What is presupposed in every act of consciousness is its intrinsic involvement in and reference to what has variously been termed "intersubjectivity" or "community." No matter how individually idiosyncratic I might be, I presuppose in all my thinking (*a*) the historically developing language in and with which I think; (*b*) the historically developing society out of which I have emerged but still within which I am continuing to do so—as the mores, morals, and evaluatory norms that I accept or reject but which, in either case, I carry with me; (*c*) the things of the physical world that I take for granted and frequently use in accord with common understandings; and (*d*) the particular persons, whether seen as anonymous aggregates or individually discernible personalities, with whom I am (whether agreeably or otherwise) engaged.

A more appropriate formulation (of this second point) might then well read: "We think, therefore, I am." For it is only in the community of our thinking with, or with regard to, each other that each individual becomes aware of himself as an existent center of experience. The converse of this formulation appears to be equally true: "We are, therefore, I think." For the "we" is already presupposed in the "*je pense*" and thereby in the "*je suis*": "*Nous sommes, donc je pense, donc je suis.*" The free convertibility of this form of the cogito suggests that it points to something more primordial. In addition to Kant's set of categories setting out the universal nature of theoretical human reason we each exemplify, or Heidegger's set of existential categories we each manifest in our round of activities, we then find out that our individual perspectives are also enstructured by the ontological imputations of the particular language we each use to think and communicate; the evaluative judgments we bring into ourselves from our historically developing cultural, religious, and national heritages; and the whole set of social outlooks that are built into each one of us from the outset, defining the social parameters within which each one of us finds his own individual self.

It is then the particularity of the "we" that is primordial; the "I"— what German idealism denominated as the "ego"—is only found as a self-differentiating process within it.[6] From the outset, the "we" is experienced and understood as made up of individuals, although encountered in collections, groups, aggregates—often perspectively undifferentiated as duplicatable units rather than as discernibly different individual beings. Every existent is seen as a particular, an individual, an entity which, no matter how similar to those others with which it is originally associated, is nevertheless somehow also seen as being somehow distinguishable if not actually distinguished.

But however the objects of our attention may be individualized or grouped, we each seem to exhibit an individual particularity of perspective within whatever encompassing perspectival community is acknowledged. No matter how closely we may share the outlook, evaluations, and judgments of our fellows, we are each aware of individual differentiations within the common judgment. Indeed, it is that which we see in common that points up what Royce had often referred to as a "contrast effect," the idiosyncratic individual particularities that each of us denominates as "mine."

We each experience our common lived world as one particular organization of extant entities. Our experiential world appears to each of us as composed of individual beings sharing attributes of similarity and distinguishing dissimilarities, beings that are—in even a minimal sense—active in their being: each exhibits some quality of temporal lastingness or duration, which may be (partially or wholly) sequentially or simultaneously congruent with other entities, and also occupies at a particular time some spatial area only describable in relation to other existing entities—two ontological attributes any entity must itself manifest and share with the human observer in order to be directly observable.

What has so far been said would seem to be rudimentary because exception would be difficult to understand. To these must be added two noticeable experiential facts: (1) all of these particular existents appear to us to be somehow coordinate with each other by virtue of appearing to act according to some common laws or rules regulating even their differentiating behaviors, and (2) they seem generally to be divisible into two broad behavioral groupings: (*a*) those that appear to be passive or inanimate, i.e., only moveable (in regard to place or state) by the activity of some entity other than itself, and (*b*) those that seem to be, in some degree at least—and always within the bounds of the physical regulations seemingly covering *all* observable entities, including ourselves—self-directing in their activities.

Any human speculation about the nature of the world we inhabit would seem tied to such elemental observations. To the extent that a speculative outlook is to be rationally coherent, it will bring them together with related aspects of human experiencing into a unified "picture" of the structure of reality that offers instructive explanation of how particular aspects of individual experiences are related to each other and to the structure the experiencer finds himself using in trying to make sense of the experiencing that is his conscious life.

However far one's speculative reach may extend from within his own experience, it must be his. It must start from the presumption that the individual experiencing is real; that it is somehow truly a coherently explicable constituent of the world that is being experienced. It must also be able to account for the elemental characteristics of the human perspective. An acceptable speculative metaphysic must be able to account for both the sociality and individuality of particulars, as experienced and as experiential centers; of their developmental flow and spatial involvement; of the common patterns of dynamic stability in both perceiver and perceived, and yet the continual changing patterns of each and their continuing dynamic interplay with each other. Whatever may be said about individual experiences—singular, plural, or universal—human experience is our only intelligible point of departure. If such experience is to be regarded as genuine, its own attributes must be attributes of and thereby in functional harmony with the reality it seeks to comprehend. For the reality of this particular world, whatever it may ultimately be discerned as being, includes within its scope the multitude of particular human experiences and perspectives that seek to discern at least aspects of its nature and thereby its meanings, so that the individual experiencer may function as he does within it.

But however comprehensively conceived, we cannot hope to transcend a human point of view, a particular selective perspective that inherently carries its own capabilities, limitations, and interests with it. That human viewpoint is with*in* the world and its time. It is *internal* to the world, is thereby bound to some theory of internal relations, and cannot hope to see the world as one whole from some external perspective, as it may conceivably be perceived in itself.

The Temporality of Decision

The central strand of any individual experience appears to be its temporal structuring. Temporal factors denominate our self-awareness, our perceptions of the physical environment, the activity of seeking out and interpreting the meaning of what we see, and the ideas we have and use in all experiences (and that cannot be reduced to spatial "thingness"). The objects we see in the surrounding environment, like the content of self-consciousness, display a continuity of both lastingness and change. However different we may conceive ourselves to be from the inanimate things of nature, predicates of temporal structuring seem to be common to both. As James and Royce argued: after all the differences between the living and the nonliving, the mental and the physical, the mutuality of temporal structuring is the one common tie we each have to the things we think about and the ideas that constitute our thoughts.[7]

We each seem to have at least three somewhat distinguishable kinds of temporal experiences. (1) Our appreciative acts appear as a spread of *present* enjoyment or satisfaction, in which lastingness is the prime temporal mode; that appreciative present itself takes up an acknowledged continuity out of past moments (or more) as it looks to its continuity into the at least proximate future. (2) Our acts of reminiscence focus on events recalled from the past and contemplate either mere acceptance, satisfaction, or sorrow that they did or did not have a greater future continuity. (3) Most of our present acts are concerned neither with the past (except as a source of lessons to retrieve for present use) nor with the immediate present—except as presenting problems to be faced, tasks yet to be done, decisions or commitments yet to be made: any temporally present situation does indeed present us with the need for deliberate decision about what is yet to be done. If all deliberative thinking is concerned with what is not yet, with a future understood to be somewhat open and dependent in some degree on what is in the power of the deliberator, then all deliberative thinking is, as Aristotle pointed out, future-oriented.

The need for deliberative thinking is itself forced by the temporal flow of things and events. In any situation, not to decide between available options is itself a decision. Forced by time, any decision is a decision into the unknown concerning the use of future time. Futurity, as Heidegger suggested, carries with it the full force of the German *Zukunft*, that which is coming at us. We have no choice except to meet it by deliberately "wading" into it or else trying to stand still and then being overwhelmed by it.

Such decisions can concern trivial acts, which are often made without conscious deliberation; most of our daily routines, encrusted by developed habits, are made in this way and are dependent for explanation on earlier adoptions of behavioral habits. Indeed, it has been argued that one specific human attribute is the ability to economize on deliberative thinking by *not* having to rethink a specific kind of problematic situation each time it occurs; that is, the ability to depend, when nothing unexpected is offered, on earlier decisions embodied into an habitual mode of conduct.[8] We thus find ourselves "going about our business," implicitly making innumerable actional decisions, without any conscious deliberative effort. This may be as true of the scientist in his laboratory pursuing a methodological procedure as of the man in the street buying his newspaper before getting onto the train or bus.

But conscious deliberation is a different kind of experience. It depends on an assessment of the options with which we see ourselves presented and also the capabilities we see ourselves as carrying into the situation. Intelligent decision confines itself within the open area their integration appears to permit. Intelligent decision distinguishes those possibilities for future development that are genuine from those that are merely desired; it confines its discriminatory consideration to those alternative possibilities that are judged to be not illusory but from among which a future actualization can be regarded as feasible. Any such assessment also considers the capabilities, the power to effect decision, the potencies or potentialities one carries along. To write a symphony is a genuine possibility only for one who has the musical competency to do so; to discover a new facet of a law of nature is a genuine possibility only for the trained scientist in the field; to rectify a moral dilemma is a genuine possibility only for one who has some control or power of "input" into the moral situation. Any act exemplifies not only the Kantian principle that "ought implies can," but a broader one that "does implies can."

This is to suggest that, on one level at least, the old ambiguity between potentiality and possibility may well rest on a lack of discernment of temporal modes.[9] In any lived situation, "possibility" seems to mean the alternative viable offerings for the future that the present appears to hold open, while "potentiality" would seem to mean the defining capabilities or powers—which we bring with us out of our historical development and which have thus become descriptive predicates out of the developed past of our present being. Any temporal juncture of decisional action is then something of a synthesizing of inherent or defining potentiality brought out of the totality of past experience with the situational possibilities discerned as offerings of futurity that are seen as presented to us in the temporal present.

In a basic sense, this seems to be true on nonhuman levels of existence as well. A particular oak tree, at any stage of its life, carries with it developmental potentialities that depend for their realization on the environmental presentation of genuine possibilities for incorporation into its perduring being; at any stage of its life that oak tree embodies a living integration of its own perduring nature, its individual history, and the proximate future that it is, as a living entity, continually incorporating into itself. As with the oak tree, so with man; to live means the continual appropriation of as-yet unrealized possibilities—but with one crucial difference: although a particular individual person may find himself accepting into himself much that seems "destined," he also experiences himself as making *some* decisions about alternatives—passively accepting some presented possibilities while deliberately selecting some and denying others.

Potentialities, then, *at any given temporal juncture,* must be regarded as given: although one may act into the future, by deliberation or habitual conduct, to develop some potentialities or leave others moribund, one must start with what has been developed so far *and* with what is presently discerned. The mere assessment of one's potentialities, the becoming aware of one's present capabilities and limitations, thus involves discernment but in itself no selectivity. How specific potentialities may be sorted out and developed is continually dependent on possibilities that are situationally presented, not as immediate actualities, but as options for future development that are selectively separated into those that are accepted as action-commitments and those that are left by the wayside. As such, they orient one not to the past or the immediate present but to what is not yet but yet may be, to the future that is within grasp and can be developed. By accepting into one's present activity some particular possibilities instead of others, one is bringing into one's activity of being a particular commitment to a chosen future state that one is attempting to actualize. Insofar as viable alternatives appear, within the range of what is presented, their discrimination, appropriation, and incorporation into one's ongoing being depends on a process of conscious or subconscious selectivity.

Temporal experience, then, is a process of bringing potentialities along and determining which to develop in the light of proffered possibilities, while accepting those conditioning limitations that appear to be beyond present control. Lived temporal experience is the experience of a continuity of selectivity of possible alternative future states. In order for me to appraise apparent alternatives, interpret their meanings, set priorities, select some while dismissing others, and commit myself to a course of action into the future as I anticipate a particular transformation of possibility into actuality, I must be able to do so. But this is what is meant by freedom. Lived temporal experience is the continual experiencing of limited options: bound by potentialities generated from the past and possibilities appearing as offerings of the future, living is the continual experience, within these limits, of the exercise of freedom.

The Necessity of Freedom

However the standard arguments about determinism, chance, and freedom as the capacity for rational or deliberate choice may go, there seems little doubt that we experience ourselves as free beings who are continually faced by the necessity of selecting a particular focus, deliberation concerning alternative actions in both thought and deed, and commitment to decisions concerning actional commitments. Even so trivial a decision as whether to take a bus or a train provides an existential demonstration. Even if intellectually convinced that we have been fully programmed and are now merely acting out a preordained role, such a conviction does not set aside the *necessity* of appearing to ourselves as being involved in a continuity of possibility-selection and decision-making.

In this light, many contemporary defenses of determinism take on a somewhat ludicrous note: how does one explain in a conceivably fully determinist world the continuing *appearance* of freedom?[10] Indeed, if full determinism were true, what would be the point of advocating its recognition? By his own premises, the author of an argument for determinism, on his own principles, can rightfully claim to be doing no more than playing out a predetermined role. So why should we attend to his argument instead of his role? Further, why should he attempt to convince his doubtful reader? For the reader too, on his premise, whether accepting or rejecting his argument, is making no real decision, but merely playing out, as on a phonograph record, what was previously destined to be played.

However explained or explained away by speculative thought, the experience of freedom is at least part of the essence of what it means to have a human experience and thereby to be human. The philosophic roots of this contention, with all the ambiguities attendant on it, can be traced at least as far back as Augustine. Any intellectualist attempt to call a fundamental experiential fact of human experience into question should itself first be called into question. "Instead of saying that we are free only in appearance in a way sufficient for practical life," we might well heed Leibniz's admonition that "we should rather say that we are determined only in appearance but that in strict metaphysical language we are perfectly independent relatively to the influence of all other creatures."[11]

The issue of freedom is usually depicted in contemporary discussions as concerned with external choices and actional dilemmas. But Descartes has already given it a more fundamental ground: in the "Fourth Meditation," in tracing out the sources of error, he effectively argued that freedom to control one's own thinking is requisite to the attainment of any cognition. Freedom is intrinsic to thinking, to seeking out the questions to be answered, the conceptual connections to be used, the evidence to be admitted, the obligation to pursue lines of inquiry, the laws of nature and of thought that one accepts as binding, the test of conclusiveness that one finally chooses to accept. Arguably, all living is not reducible to thinking, as the Cartesian argument has been construed to suggest, but all thinking, as an exemplification of living, would seem to explicate that freedom which is intrinsic to conscious living activity.

If what this Cartesian argument suggests has any validity, then freedom is an enabling condition, not only of all morality as Kant had originally urged, but of any kind of rational activity as well. Indeed Kant, in his later works, came to this. For even cognitive thinking, the attainment of those kinds of cognitive assurances his First *Critique* was designed to delineate, Kant finally rooted along with morality in freedom as their common enabling condition.[12] The rationale of such a move is clearly evident in any problematic situation. Whether the problem is moral, methodological, cognitive, or even aesthetic, one faces, in any situation demanding deliberation or decision, one fundamental question: "What should I do?" The "should" is inherently future-oriented to what is not-yet but yet may-be or can-be within the range of possibilities presented and potentialities carried toward meeting it. The entire question of any "should" presupposes the capability of freedom—for if this were not so, the question of "what should I do?" on whatever level, would be meaningless.

Freedom, as Heidegger has argued, is thus the basis of all rational activity; for both "obligation and being governed by laws, in themselves, presuppose freedom as the basis for their possibility. Only what exists as a free being could be at all bound by an obligatory lawfulness." The ground-problem of thinking, of logic, as of any sense of obligation or responsibility, "*reveals itself to be a problem of existence in its ground, the problem of freedom.*"[13] To live is to exercise finite freedom, the selective appropriation of presented possibilities for the actualization of potentialities carried along as essential elements of one's individual being. To live is to be within a situational context that is historical in development, bound by incontrovertible necessities, a finite range of options or opportunities dependent for their ongoing development on the choice that the controlling individual makes. To live is then to re-form one's world and irrevocably alter, in at least that respect, its ongoing development—by closing off some paths and opening up others in the multitude of either/or choices one makes (whether by habit, predisposition, or conscious deliberation) along one's way.

One's present, then, is not a point but a field of focus, delibera-tion, action that is constituted "at any point" by the conjunction of po-tentialities brought with one as essentials of one's being out of one's own historic development, and those possibilities that are situationally pre-sented. But again, possibilities, if they are truly genuine, are not merely future actualities—the next few grooves on a phonograph record to be played out—but *alternative* courses of development, which are finite in number but in their finiteness constitute the specific options one faces. Living a life is experienced as a continuity of deciding between available options; lived life presents no alternative but the continuity of doing so. Whether to drift, which is inherently a decision, or to resolve to follow one path instead of another, is not a decision one can abjure. For the on-comingness of time is the oncomingness of options: at any temporal juncture, one faces the necessity of selectively focusing attention, dis-criminating between what is deemed important and what is not, discern-ing one's options, and committing one's course of action to one of them.

Freedom, then, is not itself free; it is itself not a free option the ex-ercise of which can be abjured. To-be is to-be-necessarily-free within de-finable limits. Every choice of alternative decision cannot be avoided and also has its price—always at least that of the excluded options; to-be-free is to be compelled to face specific limited options. No one of us is truly granted the option of whether to-be-free or not. We have no possi-ble "escape from freedom." To-be is to-have-to-make-decisions—of selec-tivity interpretation, emphasis, alternatives—in thinking as in active involvement with the environmental world and the continuing forma-tion of one's own self. To-be-free is to be bound by the necessity of the continuity of judgment; and whatever else judgment may entail, it does entail the continual necessity of evaluating, of deciding.

The context for such deciding, the necessity for doing so, does not come out of some abstraction. It comes out of the specific societal situa-tions within which we find ourselves—our comport with family, friends, colleagues, associates, acquaintances, and encounters with other per-sons who are anonymous to us (if not to themselves); the organized so-ciety that provides for us the prime environment in which we find ourselves functioning; and the physical accoutrements that demark the geography in which we exercise the time of our being. On multifarious levels, these contextual aspects of our lives continually present us with objects of selective attention, provocations for habitual responses, the basis of justifiable claims we have upon others, trivial choices hardly no-ticed as such in passing, and deliberative decisions we often struggle to make.[14] On whatever level, each is made in response to the question, often not even consciously asked (but explicable if pressed): "In this situation, what should I do?" Each is made in response to a living concern about facing the oncoming future that is delineated in any present perspective by means of possibilities—whether they are merely accepted as "obvious," discerned as posing a question, or discriminated as presenting "hard" decisions that one feels oneself called upon to make.

Freedom is no real option. It is *essentially* ingredient to the fabric of living. It is the continuing necessity to interpret the meaning of the lived present by means of discerned possibilities of futurity on levels both trivial and profound. *Freedom is not merely an open option to make choices; freedom is the continuing necessity to make interpretive decisions*—decisions based on an assessment of possibilities for continuing development along selected lines, decisions concerned with what is to be done, whether denominated on an intellectual or actional plane.

Lived freedom takes us beyond the bounds of any empirical knowledge. It takes us beyond the reports of the five senses, which can only really tell us about what has *already transpired*.[15] The necessity of freedom is not concerned about the past; its concern is with what can yet be done, with what is not yet actual, with that from which we cannot conceivably have any present sensory knowledge, with what can yet-be but is literally not-yet, with the future options the consideration of which constitutes our living present. The necessity of freedom is to live into what is, in the most literal sense, presently unknown. The necessity of freedom is the necessity of commitment beyond what can now be confirmed. The necessity of freedom is the necessity of *now* moving on into "mere possibility," into that which is not now actual but rather some kind of "no-thing" reality; it is the necessity to re-form the ongoing structure of the world in that area of its progression in which we exercise some degree of influence or control. The necessity of freedom is the necessity to make a difference, however picayune or grandiose that difference might be. For if freedom enters into the reality of a dynamic world, every decision—trivial or profound—changes the world's future *total* description, changes what Leibniz would have termed the *complete* list of its future descriptive predicates. The necessity of freedom would then seem to be the necessity to make a difference, by diffidence or decision on a thousand different levels, in the ongoing history of this one actual world in which we dwell and of which we are a part—and whose ongoing being is constituted by a genuine continuity of becoming, of changing possibilities, some of which will be discarded and some of which will be, by decisions of choice or chance, incorporated into the actuality of its ongoing history.

Real Being as Becoming

That the experience of freedom can, in principle, not be explained in terms of the categorial constructs needed for the scientific understanding of natural phenomena is a prime thesis of the Critical philosophy. Indeed, the formal presentation of the Critical enterprise ends with the assertion that freedom as "a matter of fact" not only grounds the "actual actions [constituting] . . . experience" but opens the way for the extension of human reason "beyond the bounds to which every natural or theoretical conception must remain hopelessly restricted."[16] (As requisite to our exercise of obligatory judgments, as of all cognitive activity and speculative thought, freedom then appears to be the root "category" of all human activity and thought, what Kant has called man's "supersensible faculty.")[17] What Kant seems to have been urging is that theoretical understanding of the necessary processes of nature as an efficaciously determining causal system is not adequate to insight into the nature of our world; at the very least, such efficaciously causal determinism cannot explain the fact of our experience of it and involvement in its development.

Freedom is not a speculative assessment of something external to us. It is our active involvement in our world and thereby gives us a kind of insight into the nature of our functioning world, which must be somehow primordially constituted so as to require its continuing appropriation of our true interpretations and decisions, which we see in its continuing accommodations to our decisions concerning its ongoing development.

Any real comprehension of natural processes comes by way of dealing with them directly—by the interpretations, decisions, and choices that one makes in doing so. Freedom is not a speculative attempt to look at the world as though we were somehow outside of it and unaffected by it. Freedom is the direct encountering involvement with a developing world *in which* we participate and which we are continually altering as we are continually affected by its ongoing dynamic development. Freedom is our continuing necessity to respond to the continuity of change in our own selves and in the environment in which we find ourselves by broadening interpretational and actional decisions.

Our experiential involvements usually lead us to seek an ex post facto theoretical interpretive understanding in terms of fixed laws of nature that explain its regularities and that we then often seek to use as a guide to future dealings on the ground that such understandings have more than a strictly empiric force. In the end, however, it may be questionable whether human attempts to discover unalterable laws of nature can possibly be successful. For, if man is a historical being—biologically as well as socially—in a historically developing world, human questions are being asked from a perhaps gradually but nevertheless continuously changing interpretive perspective, just as the world itself would appear to be a dynamic system in which changing is inherent even if with a perhaps continuing developmental direction.

However this in itself may be, the basic thesis of the priority of human freedom is to argue the priority of practice.[18] For practice looks to a future that cannot be seen but can only be passively expected or actively anticipated. Our pragmatic encounters tell us, on a firsthand basis, just how we may understand nature—that nature which includes our activity of being, which is a continuity of ordered becoming—and its encompassing reality, beyond the recollection of the relevant past and the immediacy of any present moment. Our plans and anticipations for dealing with those aspects of the world that provoke our responses tell us something of the nature of the reality within which we find ourselves—which theoretical understanding can only retrospectively seek to explain. It is necessary for us to accept this, for the human investigations of the nature of this, our world, are themselves transforming the nature of the world we are investigating—and also ourselves.[19]

The systematic human attempts to comprehend the underlying laws of nature's developmental being, which we understand as science, cohere with the futural orientation of the human temporal perspective. For science's method of testing its own hypotheses is by means of practical involvements with that particular selected aspect of the environment it is concerned to explain; and its prime test of truth is no mere logical consistency but a future-oriented predictability of particular occurrences. The laws of nature turn out to be not pure Platonistic forms but norms for the correlation of particular behavioral patterns. What is sought is not some law of pure chance, as both Aristotle and Peirce allowed, but "some principle of reason sufficient" to explain not only the general conformity of particular occurrences to general rules but also the particular deviations from them.

Whether we approach the world of nature in strictly scientific terms or in terms more explicitly commensurate with the subjective biases and outlooks of particular human experiences, we find essentially similar and compatible principles of the human outlook operating. The test of the scientist as of the craftsman is workability, and that workability is taken as showing us aspects of the reality within which we find ourselves functioning as somewhat free interpretive agents who are intrinsically involved with that with which we are working.[20]

The reality of the world in which we find ourselves functioning as finitely free causative agents appears in human experience as an interrelated dynamic process that cannot be reduced to its material components locked together by a completely determining efficacious causal sequence. If that were indeed so, the present state would be completely reducible to a temporally first cause that governs all details and allows neither any contingency nor the efficacy of temporal process in nature, much less in man; possibility would then mean not open options but merely future as yet unrolled actuality. But we do not experience our world in this way. We do experience our world as continually setting forth new tasks to be undertaken, new choices to be made, as continually demanding new interpretive understandings that are requisite for any deliberate time-situated action, and therefore the use of reason or intelligence in deciding upon action. We experience the world by means of ideas and principles, hopes and fears, which move us to seek out areas of control and redirection; the free use of intelligence penetrates into and thereby changes the developing character of physical nature itself and our own selves, as well as our growing experience of successes and failures, of mistaken judgments, fortuitous guesses, and insightful discernments.

The form of time that encompasses and structures our experience of our own selves and of our world suggests that it is in some sense an inherent aspect of the reality with which we continuously deal. The form of enveloping time seems to be somehow manifest as that Logos, that developmental rational order of our world, to which Heraclitus had originally pointed. The inherent temporality of our experience does not appear to be a closely knit set of Cartesian moments. Rather, it presents to us the dual aspects of continuity and change. This continuity of change would itself be impossible if continuity was not itself developmental. If human experience has any reality to it, then that continuity is not merely the motive power of originary efficacious causes and unalterable potentialities; human experience depends for its being on the genuineness of possibilities, of options not yet resolved, of alternatives not yet decided, of a futurity that presents itself as open to the contingencies of innumerable decisions—and of a perdurance that is not itself "permanent" but is a continuity of dynamic becoming, the driving principle of which might, as Heraclitus once obliquely suggested, itself be conceivably changing as it continues its continually operative force.[21]

Human experience may indeed be an experience of illusions or illusionary appearances, as some philosophers seem to have argued. But if human experience is not itself an illusion, then the reality of perduring time, like the reality of genuine possibility, also constitutes a real aspect of our experiencing—and thereby of the real world in which the reality of our real experiencing transpires. Genuine possibility depends for its being on the omnipresence of time so that discerned possibilities may be sorted out—some passing into the realm of first present actuality and then remaining as the actual retrievable inheritance of what has been.

If we are to seek for some ground principles by which we can come to a fuller comprehension of the human experience of the world, it would then seem that the reality of time, freedom, and possibility must be understood as joined together as the enabling, and thereby defining, ground of experience. In something of a Kantian sense, they must be understood as somehow noumenal, as characters of that ultimate reality with which we are always working and which, in our more speculative moments, we seek to comprehend.[22]

But to pass from a careful delineation of the kinds of ontological characterizations we project from our own way of seeing onto the world in which we are and we seek to comprehend, we must be careful. Our own ways of looking out, as social beings who function by means of synthesizing potentiality and possibility in time-bound situations that are themselves defined out of specific historically developing concerns, exclude in advance any possibility of achieving in speculative thought any assured insight into the ultimate nature of the things of the world, or of the world itself as one integrated whole, as they may be "in and of themselves." The ontology of our own structured outlook thus forecloses at the outset the possibility of any final "cosmology" of the things and systems of order that constitute our world. On this level, then, our speculative thought may attain degrees of coherence and insight but cannot attain to any final truth.

If this is so, then we cannot hope for any "final" metaphysic. For if time, freedom, and possibility are somehow or somewhat real, then the world is in some degree open-ended. New interpretive understandings emerge as the range of human experience widens and grows. There cannot then be, as Heidegger (among others) suggests, any "end of philosophy"; for the "love of" or "quest for that wisdom"—which is based on knowledge but seeks to go beyond knowledge—is a continuing attempt to comprehend the growing wholeness of the world within which the growing human perspective functions.

Each of us brings to bear an at least unspoken metaphysical assessment of what constitutes reality and illusion when we face the vicissitudes of our daily living. If any defensible metaphysical outlook, or way of seeing and comprehending our world, is indeed the intellectual understanding of what the content of the human perspective indicates, we explicitly need to accept as fact that it operates from within the world as a part of the world, that it can only recognize partial aspects of that world in terms of the ontological characteristics its own cognitive and existential "categories" permit as the delineation of its outlook, and it does so to use whatever insights it gains in order to continue its free use of intelligence to enhance its level of being in the harmony of the developing whole.

In seeking out clues to what Heraclitus had once termed "the hidden harmony" within or behind the whole, we might face the question that he implicitly raised but neglected to answer. The notion of harmony is itself borrowed from musical experience, in which the particular harmonic relation of the notes in a song or symphony is itself changing as their relations change while the piece is being performed.[23] Harmony, then, is a dynamic concept that transcends the particularity of any specific notes by binding them together into an integrative system that is itself never quite the same but is a continuing dynamic mode of creative developmental unification. If "the hidden harmony" is itself the Logos of the world-order, then perhaps it too is changing. For time, as the continuity of change, appears to be the encompassing form within which we necessarily understand our own selves as participating in the ongoing becoming of the world. However there may seem to be a continuity of principles behind nature and man, their exemplifications and thereby their meanings are continually, if imperceptibly and gradually, changing for us.

What we call "abiding principles" may indeed be truly transtemporal, but we have no philosophic right to term them "eternal."[24] And we should be especially careful in making even this limited claim. For changing continuity and the continuity of change mark the structure of our experiential world—as we are able to see and comprehend those aspects of the world with which we deal by the use of freedom in the employment of intelligence, which operates by taking possibility as well as potentiality seriously, and necessarily presumes that time, as their enabling and defining form or condition, is real.

If there is any truth to the ancient maxim of Empedocles that "like knows like," or that of Anaxagoras that "like produces like"—"like" does not imply identity; it merely asserts essential similarity—we would seem to have a presumptive right, if not a necessary mandate, to presuppose that the prime characteristics of our experiential activity, out of which decision and knowledge and understanding arise, tell us something of the nature of the world in which we find ourselves and within which we function as effecting members.[25]

Different as we may be from other constituents of our world, we find that (1) possibility seems to be genuine just because we cannot function without that presumption, (2) freedom seems to be real because without it none of our experiences seem to be intelligible, (3) futurity appears to us as finitely open just because, within given limits, deliberate choices by beavers as by men seem to determine what a future actuality can be, and (4) time seems to be a fundament of both ourselves and the other entities with which we deal just because it appears to envelop us all as the encompassing form of freedom, of possibility, of our being that is a becoming insofar as it appears within our ken. To the extent that a metaphysical framework for understanding our world is not only comprehensive but is also projective of our ways of understanding, its success in explanation will be marked by its correlation of the world—whether taken as physical, biological, historical, sociological, or moral—within which we find ourselves functioning with the ways of functioning we find ourselves able to utilize. Such a comprehensive understanding is no mere intellectual exercise. It too has a function. An understanding of the world to which we belong has much to say, in a normative way, to the ways in which we should conduct ourselves, the ways in which we should organize our moral conduct and social practices, the ways in which we may integrate our religious commitments, the ways in which we may justifiably interpret the cognitive claims of our sciences.[26] A speculative use of reason to comprehend the world, as human reason is able to take it all in, is itself a guide to how reason may finally come to guide that chief business of men that Dewey always pointed to, the organization of solving the multifarious "problems of men." To what extent any particular metaphysic may be finally "true" (aside from the coherence of workability), we really have no way of knowing; but to the extent that a metaphysic is essentially useful and rationally necessary in guiding the rational development of human concerns, it is itself functioning as if it is true. Perhaps, beyond all dreams of a Cartesian-like certainty, that is the best for which we may hope.

Emerson once said that the fins of a fish tell us about water as the wings of an eagle tell us about air. An experiential metaphysic will take the essential structures of human experience—the only experience, let us never forget, that we may directly know—as somehow indicative of aspects of the nature of the world in which it functions. The attempt of reason to achieve a speculative comprehension of the world in which we find ourselves can be both intelligible and useful only to the degree that it encourages us to explore it by means of structures commensurate with the structures of human experience—within which possibility functions as genuine invitation, freedom functions as enabling the use of intelligence, and time is recognized as grounding both the experiential reality of the world in which we function and of our own selves as inherently creative beings in a world open to creative development.

Part 4

Time, Freedom, and the Common Good

10

The Temporality
of the Common Good:
Futurity and Freedom

C onsiderations of public policy often focus on individual problematic situations in an ad hoc manner without discernment of their
relations to each other, to the context within which they arose, or
to the consequences that might ensue from alternative responses.
Needed is a coherent set of clearly articulated principles which bring to
political controversies of our time a unified perspective within which
questions may be asked, discriminations made, relations perceived, and
priorities established. If a prime concern in seeking out such principles
is for the reformation of the republic so that it may be assured a healthy
longevity, we should heed the counsel of Machiavelli's political realism
urging us first to seek the revitalization of its originary principles.[1] Insofar as a republic derives its ideational grounding from the developing
Western tradition, we can do no better than begin by repairing to the
fount of that tradition. Two key passages from Aristotle provide us with
an appropriate point of departure.

On opening the *Nicomachean Ethics*, we read its well-known initial
sentence: "Every art and every inquiry, and similarly every action and
pursuit, is thought to aim at some good; and for this reason, the good
has rightly been declared to be that at which all things aim" (1094a).[2]
The closing paragraphs of the *Ethics* effectively introduce the *Politics*,
which begins in similar fashion: "Every state is a community of some
kind, and every community is established with a view to some good; for
mankind always act in order to obtain what they think good" (1252a).

Taken together, these topic sentences suggest two separate theses
concerning the human condition. First, individual and communal activity

share a commonly defined objective, the quest for what is deemed to be good. Second, human reasoning is prudential: it is teleologically organized; human rational activity, whether individual or communal, is to be understood as goal-oriented behavior. This is to say that all rational activity is temporally structured: it is animated by the present perception of possibilities of the future which are not yet actualized but are nevertheless presently seen as attainable by appropriate human effort.

If, as Aristotle goes on to say, all human activity arises within a community context, individual and communal goods reciprocate. A community grounds the individuals comprising it while being carried forward by their combined efforts. The activities of the organized community have immediate repercussions in the lives of its members: by altering the actualities with which they must deal and the possibilities for going onward which they may rightfully consider.

These foundational observations raise four prime questions: (1) How are these two poles of our living together, our individuality and our sociality, intertwined? (2) How is our common good to be defined while it yet allows our pursuits of our individual goods? (3) How is the range of available possibilities preeminent in the functioning of our prudential reasoning? (4) How is our capacity for freedom already necessarily presupposed? I want to suggest that these four questions are not truly separable, that each involves the others. The prime thesis which is sketched out in what follows is that these questions, separately and together, presuppose the essential structure of forward-looking human temporality as the grounding condition for the exercise of all prudential activity, and thereby of our social assessments. After developing the distinctive principles these questions suggest, I intend to draw them together to adumbrate the moral of the tale.

How are individuality and sociality intertwined? Society, Aristotle told us, looks beyond the rudimentary "supply of daily needs" (1252b) while presumably yet presupposing the continuity of that concern. The organized society, the state, is so completely "prior to the individual" (1253a) that any individual absolutely independent of society is "either a beast or a god" (1253a). This priority of the social could be argued on diverse grounds. Aristotle's own stated reason is the fact of reason expressed in speech. Only as we are able to speak and reason with each other can we develop insight into evaluations, the difference between the "expedient and the inexpedient," or "any sense of good and evil, of just and unjust" (1253a). If it is because of our community of communication that we are enabled to develop moral insights and insight into our notion of the common good, it would be important to examine, in more detail than afforded here, just how it helps to structure the lives of men.

Speech is the expression of a common language and we each have been born into a linguistic community, into a family and social order using a particular language for communicating. That language, at the outset, builds into the communication of even the most rudimentary needs and desires a common vocabulary, system of grammatical structures, idiomatic expressions, linguistic shorthands, and ontological imputations. It thereby forms the thinking by which we organize our perceptions and the categorial concepts which structure our ways of expressing and shaping the outlook we bring to bear on the choices we see ourselves able to make.

That particular language, into whose outlook we are born, is itself a particular historic distillation of the evaluations and biases of a particularized cultural tradition. At the outset, it compels us to think and view and judge by means of particular rubrics and conceptual models.

But a language is not merely a set of particular rubrics needed for organizing communication. It is itself requisite for generational development, for history, just because it enables the accumulation of knowledge, customs, and valuations to be handed on. By binding us to a historically developing outlook, a language enables individual visions to be tied together into a common bond of cultural identity. A language is thus the bearer of the outlook of a culture; it is a prime vehicle whereby a community maintains its continuity within the dynamic of the outlooks, categories, valuations, and norms that comprise the heritage it is expressing while reshaping it and passing it on. Most crucial, that cultural heritage does not only take up a continuity from earlier generations; it manifests itself by setting out the parameters within which expectations and anticipations may develop. A living language is thus developed by the ongoing experience of the community it governs. It is a reflective process through which the historic development of a society is manifested. A language is one sign of the life of a community, a community that is, and understands itself to be, a continuity of ongoing development, growth, and change.

Any given society is itself a historic process. As Royce pointed out well, it "has a past and will have a future. Its more or less conscious history, real or ideal," is not separable from it but essentially ingredient to its self-definition.[3] It inculcates a reverence for its heroes, its habits, traditions, customs, and valuations by which it defines itself, the norms by which it judges its successes and failures. To the extent that its members identify themselves with its history, accept its folklore, regard its customs as theirs, identify with its problems and share its aspirations, they bind themselves to the identity of a common "we" and understand themselves as members of a greater whole with a history and a future, a commitment to a common good within which each is to find his own.

Even the development of self-consciousness is but a process of self-differentiation within a common bond. The growth of self-consciousness is a function of social consciousness. "A child is taught to be self-conscious just as he is taught everything else, by the social order that brings him up."[4] Individuality, however eccentric it may conceivably become, is socially rooted and socially nourished by the language, habits, and customs within which it is raised. Individuality, then, is rooted in historic community, a community that finds its own roots in a commonly acknowledged history while it is itself historically developing out of what it was into what it yet can become. Like any individual, a community is not merely an entity with dates in chronological time; a community, as Royce perhaps most profoundly saw, is itself a time-process; it is a "being that attempts to accomplish something in time and through the ongoing deeds of its members."[5] Its continuity depends upon the ways in which its individual members continue to interpret their common heritage and possibilities as the heritage and possibilities they share together.

Aristotle saw that we are essentially social beings, that citizenship—membership in a community—is requisite to being human. In our own day, Paul Ricoeur has restated this truth: "The threshold of humanity is the threshold of citizenship, and the citizen is a citizen only by means of organized society."[6] Social organization enables each to pursue those goods after which he strives, goods which he could not pursue, much less envisage, alone. The quest for individual good requires the ongoing continuity of society's quest for those goods deemed to be the common good for its members.

Society, then, is not a thing but a process, a process of our being-together in situations that are inherently developmental. Any society takes up its past in order to define its present; and it understands the meaning of its present as offering to it those open possibilities for its ongoing development which appear to it as accordant with its own nature, evaluative norms, aspirations, and anticipations for carrying itself forward. Living history is conceived as an ongoing process that is intrinsically temporal and oriented to a future of possibility-actualization.

History, then, is not the dead letter of a completed past. It *is* for us today that past whose lessons we can retrieve and make our own. It is presently functioning as presently interpreted by conveying meaning into our own lives; as we accept the lessons we read out of it, we provide

ourselves with the parameters we are able to utilize in carrying it forward by building what is not-yet but yet may-be. Our current understanding of our own past is primarily in terms of what it has foreclosed to
our present situation and the possibilities it has yet permitted us for
building our future.

Our social, like our individual, reality is perceived by us as a temporal process. Our present society, which defines the parameters of our
present existence, is understood by us as a continuing historicizing process within which we conduct our lives as individuals who continually reflect the historicality of our common social context in an essentially
time-formed outlook.

My immediate temporal outlook indeed varies with my current activity.[7] But whatever may be the rhythm of my lived time, whether it is
punctuated by a mechanical clock which ticks off its seconds, or follows
the more leisurely flow of a chess game or a picnic, my temporality—
as pragmatists had urged, as Heidegger's existential analyses clearly
demonstrate—is marked by a priority of futural considerations. The
lived present of any problematic situation is seen not only as arising out
of what has been; it is understood as offering alternative possibilities for
development. I may decide to try to continue or to negate a particular
development from the past or I may determine to initiate a new course.
But whether my task is winning a chess game, writing a paper, finishing a
book, embarking on a journey, or just loafing around, my lived present
is future-oriented in its structure. My comprehension of my present situation is interpreted by me in terms of what seems possible to do henceforth; by the light of the alternatives I interpret the situation as
presenting to me, I will retrieve from past experience whatever guidance
I deem germane to my present prospect.

However I evaluate the past futures that went into the construction
of my present present, I recognize that past and future are radically different; what has been is unalterable, unrepeatable, and completed, although its meanings can be read in differing ways; the future appears to
me as somewhat open and subject to those possible decisions I feel compelled to make. My only real concerns are my decisions, not about the
past, but about the future, about the henceforth, the what-next, the can-
be, about the genuine possibilities seen as available to me now. Kant explained this quite well:

> Men are more interested in having foresight than any other power,
> because it is the necessary condition of all practical activity. . . . Any
> desire includes a (doubtful or certain) foresight of what we can do by
> our powers. We look back on the past (remember) only so that we can

foresee the future by it; and as a rule we look around us in the standpoint of the present, in order to decide on something or prepare ourselves for it.[8]

As Aristotle had already urged, "no one *deliberates* about the past, but about what is future and capable of being otherwise" (1139b). Such discernments of philosophic common sense are quickly acknowledged and promptly ignored. But individual, like social, temporality is structured by each of us as we interpret the meaning of any presentation of futurity (as available but yet unrealized possibility) carrying us onward. All social questions arise for any generation, as individual questions arise for any individual, in specific historic situations—each understood as having grown out of earlier possibilities, actualized or discarded by earlier decisions, and as presently offering us alternative courses. However complex our social situations may be, all decisions are made by individual persons who understand and hopefully interpret their decisional situations within the context of their socially bestowed responsibilities. Some decisions are made by individuals for themselves, their families or friends; some by officials of social subgroupings—clubs, churches, corporations, unions, political parties—for those who accept their leadership; and some are made by public officials for those constituencies they are charged to represent. But whatever the scope of the particular individual's particular decision, it is made by means of his understanding of the possibilities available and is enlightened by his retrieval of past experiences deemed germane to the currently faced problematic.

If all deliberation and decision concerns what is not-yet but yet may-be, then all decision is engaged in building history. We are often accustomed to describing past and future as directions on a "timeline." But, as noted, past and future are ontologically different. What is done is done and cannot be done again; it is that tangle of actuality that has already been. Our understandings of that unchangeable and unrepeatable past can, however, be altered as we interpret selected aspects of its meanings in the light of our present prospects. For example, the American Civil War while being fought was interpreted as a struggle to save the Union; its meaning for us today is that it has foreclosed the possibility of slavery from the future of the American dream. We thus continually reinterpret the meaning of the factual past, socially and individually, in the light of those present options which illuminate our interpretations of the meaning of the present.

If I find myself retrieving lessons from the past, as from a textbook, which may be read in different ways; if I find myself selecting out of the myriad details of the present those which strike me as significant; if I am continually choosing among present possibilities I deem available those which shall be fulfilled and those which are to be discarded; if, in short, I continually interpret any factual situations in which I find myself by means of the sequential continuities they appear to offer for discriminative appropriation, then I must be able to do so. I continually find myself in responding to my current situations as a forward-looking being in an essentially dynamic historical setting. Restricted as my outlook may be, I find myself functioning as a free, deliberating being in a time-bound parameter. Like my fellows, I find myself acting by exercising a necessarily presupposed, enabling freedom—by means of which I find myself obliged to discriminate, interpret, understand, and decide, and to do so just because of the compulsion of what is termed "temporal passage." Freedom—the time-bound necessity to make interpretive decisions—is my existential condition. It is my grounding capacity to transcend my momentary "now" into a living present, to comprehend this living present as a field in which I must choose and act—and which compels me to decide just how I shall choose and act. I have no choice but to choose. I have no choice but to interpret my situation as presenting futural possibilities as nurtured in the past but which, while foreclosing others I might prefer, still beckon me onward. I have no choice except to determine which possibilities before me might be viable, to choose among them and to commit myself to the forthcoming action they demand. That meaning results from this necessity to interpret the present by evaluating divergent strands from the past; that we face the future by discriminating just which possibilities are genuine instead of spurious, means that any act in which we deliberate, interpret, evaluate, and decide exhibits and thereby presupposes not only the inherent capability of doing so, but that in doing so we are demonstrating ourselves as essentially temporal beings oriented to what can yet be, to futurity. We discover ourselves in the acts of living as free beings who are somehow endowed with a primordial capacity for self-interpretation, self-direction, self-commitment to what is not-yet but yet may-be; we discover ourselves as individuals in the exercise of freedom, a freedom to direct ourselves by our visions of our possible future.

That freedom is central to the being of man is a theme which echoes through the course of modern thought. Descartes saw it necessarily functioning in any cognitive act. Rousseau understood it as the essential potentiality of man that a free society opens up for development. Kant, insisting that it is requisite to morality, argued that it is the one transcendent aspect of experience meeting the Cartesian demand for certainty, the one tie we have, beyond all phenomenal appearances, to ultimate reality itself. Heidegger urged that it is the foundational principle of sufficient reason upon which all subsequent explanations of specific human actions must stand. Hegel seems to have brought their common thrust together (and perhaps gone beyond them) by announcing that the development of freedom is the meaning of our history.

The essentially enabling temporal nature of human living grounds the enabling capacity for freedom. And if individual living is social living, if individual temporality only functions within the scope of social temporality, of historicality, then individual freedom is social in character, for some degree of social freedom is requisite to the embodiment of any other social values or norms—justice, fairness, morality, equality, individuality, responsibility, peace. In seeking out norms of a just society, of a society designed for human living, the first question, then, is that of freedom. For freedom is the root of any evaluative activity and thereby of any notion of decision, commitment, or responsibility.

That this is really no novel thesis but has deep roots in our historic culture can be readily seen by looking back to Plato's *Crito.* Its concluding passages—the conversation between Socrates and the Laws of Athens—presume four theses: (1) the relation between a society and an individual is generational; (2) social participation carries moral obligation with it; (3) private property is socially recognized; and (4) most important for the present discussion, social participation and obligation rest on individual free consent, consent to be bound by a system of law, an obligation to obey those laws *and* to call to public attention those which are deemed to require change. As given, what might be called the "right to resign," the right to take one's property and leave without penalty, is spelled out as *the* essential socially recognized freedom undergirding any subsequent obligation; the acknowledged need for free criticism rests on that same primacy of individual judgmental freedom as the ground of any defensible notion of political legitimacy. Without this, how could we have any intelligible discussion of concepts of justice or any other social virtue? Aristotle's *Politics,* our foundational text for principles of constitutional government, makes a similar point; "a state exists for the sake of a good life, and not for the sake of life only; if life only were the object, slaves and brute animals might form a state, but they cannot, for they have no share in . . . a life of free choice" (1280a). If the function of the state is the promotion of "a good life," it must presume the freedom of its citizens, a free citizenry.

If freedom is requisite for all interpretive reflection, considered decision, and exercise of responsibility, then freedom is prerequisite to all those kinds of activities we understand as human. As the enabling possibility for the pursuit of whatever else is deemed to be good, freedom is primordial. Its defense demands a priority before any competing loyalty-claim which itself must rest on freedom for its ground, condition, justification. The political implication is clear: the only kind of society we can regard as legitimate, as meriting loyalty and respect, is one which acknowledges the social commitment to freedom as intrinsic to its definition of the common good—and takes that responsibility seriously by facing within situational possibilities the ensuing obligation to secure the social grounds of its developmental future.

But if freedom is primordial, how shall freedom be understood? Three points must be acknowledged (and each needs more development than present space permits). First, if individuality is always bound by interpretive recollection, limited foresight, and the perspective brought to any situation, then individual freedom, like individuality itself, is contextually bound and inherently finite. Second, if we are not separate atoms but essentially social beings, then all individual freedoms are within a social matrix. As Kant insisted, my freedom ends where that of others begins; my freedoms must be limited by those limitations requisite for maximizing the freedom of each within our common social condition; my freedom to seek what I deem good can only be a variant within the good of the sustaining whole. Third, and most important in the light of some recent discussion, freedom is not the mere absence of restraints; freedom is valued as the power to do, to engage in positive acts, to accomplish, to effectuate means to chosen ends. Freedom is positive opportunity, the positive opportunity society opens up, by enabling us to do together what we could not do separately, by expanding horizons we could not envisage alone, to pursue those individually desired options whose ultimate justification must be that they contribute to the good of the whole.[9]

Those specific freedoms or options whose exercise the society guarantees to protect are socially grounded opportunities for individual appropriation of possibilities, possibilities whose general availability is deemed to be in the common interest. Freedoms then need to be specified; however delineated in a specific social condition, they are inherently prescriptive of what possible futurity is to be closed off or opened up. Specific freedoms are opportunities sanctioned by the perception of the common good; they prescribe opportunities to pursue what is not yet actual but whose actualization will be deemed in accord with the interest of the common good; they may also permit, as specified liberties, those permitted (if not encouraged) activities which will be tolerated as not injurious to the harmony of the whole.

Freedom is a socially open condition encouraging individual initiative to pursue, for one's self or one's community, those goods deemed to be of social value. Freedoms are protected options to actualize in a

future present those possibilities whose availability is of social value. If
the common good is to be discerned in specific freedoms or opportunities for action, then the quest for the common good requires the temporalization of opportunities in specific kinds of situations so that they
may be appropriated and realized in concrete ways. The concrete freedoms a society sanctions—whether by communal pursuit of the common good or by inviting individual contributions to that common
good—are its prescription of what it seeks, its delineation of the kinds of
activities it commends. Individual freedoms, like the freedom of the social whole, are to be found in the pursuit of possibilities for the future,
pursuit of a future to be commonly shared. If all free deliberation, decision, action, is concerned with what is not-yet but yet may-be; if all deliberation, decision, commitment, rests on the freedom to-do, then human
freedoms, however specified, are freedoms-for-the-future. However finitized, specific freedoms represent to us those possibilities we are encouraged to pursue, those future actualizations to which we may aspire, those
unrealized goods which we are presently encouraged to make our own.
Freedom is then social temporalization: as specific liberties or absence
of restraints, of those activities which a society will permit if not encourage; as positive freedoms, of those specific kinds of temporal continuities of activity which a society encourages and promises to protect.

Four prime principles emerge from these considerations.

1. Individuality is inherently social—in its actual functioning as in
its grounding possibility. If so, then the philosophic ground of an atomistic liberalism is rootless. In our day, when technology increasingly
makes us increasingly interdependent, its rhetoric has an increasingly
hollow ring. Like the nominalism it presumes, any atomistic ideology
can only function by already presuming just what it denies—a grounding set of common social values and commitments. It cannot face that
criticism of Hobbes already voiced by Leibniz: if society were but the
mere aggregate of individuals emerging from a "state of nature," their
contract would be impossible if they had not already developed a common vision of a common good and a mutual commitment to adhere in
their future common state to what they had supposedly forged together
in their past pre-civil state. An atomistic individualism is a rootless abstraction—because it is blind to the presuppositions of its own common
commitment, because it ignores the temporal dynamics of social interaction, and because it can describe no known period of human history
utterly devoid of shared traditions or aspirations. Its philosophic destruction opens the way for the revitalization of the tradition of civic republicanism which traces its lineage back through Hegel, Hamilton and

Madison, Kant, Rousseau, Montesquieu, Leibniz, Machiavelli, and Cicero, back to Aristotle's polity.

2. Each individual finds himself in an historically ongoing set of social relations. Human action traces out the structures of what is now the past while building the future. History is the process of building a heritage to be handed on; doing so involves a continual reinterpretation of what has been in the light of new possibilities being opened up. Historicality necessarily points to human temporality—just because social decisions are made by individual men, whether they do so by imposing a ruling will, competing decisions which will meld into a common stream, or as interpreters of the general will or common consensus. Historicality points to human temporality on a second ground as well: society is the educator of the rising generation—not only by the common historic lore it passes on, but, as Dewey continually insisted, by the ways it actually behaves. Social historicality is the embodiment of social time and time itself represents not only change but also continuity.

3. Our working conception of time is formed by the temporal structure of our reasoning outlook. We each assess a problematic situation as posing the question, "what should be done about it?"; that "should" is considered practical, an intelligent and responsible exercise of prudential reason, when it is confined within the "can," within the scope of specific possibilities presently available. But human foresight, like hindsight, is finite. How often do we, as individuals or societies, embark on possibilities which do not work out, which spew forth results which were unforeseen and whose far-reaching effects ripple on into consequences yet to be discerned? But they ripple on—they carry into situations yet to be developed—thus manifesting the Leibnizian law that time *is* continuity. What has-been continues in dynamic force and persists through change, even as its shape is altered, sublimated, and redirected. Even at crisis-points, Royce noted, "points where one kind of process [seems to] end, and a process of a decidedly distinct kind appears quite suddenly to begin . . . there is no absolute discontinuity."[10] To rationally assess proffered possibilities is to evaluate just how they can take up and accommodate those, even undesirable, streams and voices from the past. Temporality, as Heidegger demonstrated, is organized by us under the aegis of futurity, the aegis of unrealized but available possibility; but the continuity of time urges the amendment that only those possibilities which incorporate the continuity, the taking up of the past, may be regarded as genuine options before us.

4. If we are to act rationally as social individuals and responsible citizens, we require a standard of judgment, a principle of selectivity by which to set priorities among those viable yet alternative possibilities we

face in any concrete situation. Is any norm primordial? The crucial key to the continuing possibility of rational decision is keeping open the grounding possibility of decision-making itself. To deliberate, evaluate, and resolve is to exhibit our capacity, our primordial potentiality to make free decisions. Freedom is our existential condition which provides the enabling ground for all our specific decisions. Freedom, then, is our condition of possibility, our "ground of all grounds," our fundamental principle of sufficient reason for all the particular reasons we can employ in the particular decisions we are able to make.[11] As such a primordial enabling ground, it demands our prime loyalty. For loyalty to freedom is our loyalty to the possibility of being loyal to any subsequent values or norms. Freedom is thus primordial.

If freedom is requisite for the pursuit of all particular goods, if individuality is inherently social, then individual freedom is manifested in those specific kinds of temporal sequences of goal-oriented activities a society invites or permits. If individual freedom is social, it is grounded in the healthy life of the society whose prime obligation is to maintain the stability of its commitment to the free future of its citizens. These considerations lead to some three consequents:

(a) Our specific freedoms vary with temporal conditions: in times of drought, the free use of water may be curtailed; in times of war, economic and political acts, normally encouraged, may be foreclosed; in times of technological advance, uses of pollution-producing facilities may be forbidden or controlled. If all specific options within a society derive from their instrumentality to what is conceived as the common good, then any individual options depend upon a prior obligation to give the common good a priority of concern before any claims conflicting with it. For it is the vibrancy of the common good that grounds the specific individual goods of its members. If the common good defines the state of freedom, then the society may justifiably interfere with such activities that conflict with it. Just as one may not rightfully claim unlimited water during a drought, one may not claim a right to utilize one's time, property, or social position for antisocial purposes. If all individual rights are social rights, then property rights, as one example, are but socially delegated grants of authority, and on two grounds: first, on the social presumption that private economic activity more efficiently contributes to the economic well-being of the society than does centralized bureaucratic dictation; and second, on the principle that the power inherent in property needs to be diffused for the political well-being of society's freedom.

Starkly stated, this priority of the social is not yet at variance from our accepted procedure. We generally recognize the right, if not always

the prudential wisdom, of a free society to share in the fruits of individual temporal endeavors by restricting ensuing property claims: by taxing
incomes and expenditures; by placing zoning, health, and use restrictions on homes, facilities, and neighborhoods; by limiting individual
ability to contract employment and working conditions; by limiting the
usage of productive property by employment, pollution, health, and fire
regulations. Beyond property questions, we today consider society obligated, in order to safeguard its future, to intrude into the privacy of family life by insisting on the education of the children. Such intrusions into
abstract claims of inherent liberties are direct societal intrusions into
how individual time may be used and enjoyed; such prescriptive intrusions are as requisite in a complex society for the greater freedom of the
individual citizen as they are for the future of the developing common
good.

(b) Freedom entails correlative responsibilities: by the individual,
responsibility for what will ensue from his exercise of those specific freedoms his society promises to protect and for the effects of those programs he commits himself to advocate; by those granted governing
authority (whether in directing subgroups or the overall political structure), to use granted power and commitments in accord with law and the
common understandings of the common good. Authentic responsibility,
as freedom, is not merely for what has been done; to take up specific freedoms is to accept responsibility for what can ensue. To freely commit
oneself to specific programs requires not only recognition of the effects
similar proposals may have already generated, but also imaginative concern for the concrete actualizations they are likely to produce—just because authentic responsibility is, before history, responsibility for the
future.

(c) Freedom entails power: A specific freedom is a social grant of
power—to do certain acts, to honor obligations, to utilize property, to
press claims on the social whole or, for the magistracy, to press claims on
the citizenry. Depending on position and function, it is thus the power
to make decisions that will bind others. Specific freedoms are grants of
power to control developments of future time. Such power must be finitized. Its excess invites corruption, as Lord Acton taught, and few among
us are able to resist its seductive rationalizations. As Aristotle might have
urged, its excesses become self-defeating.

Specific freedoms, as powers to control futurity, need restriction to
teleological adequacy. For ourselves, we need power adequate to exercise the specific freedoms we choose to utilize—but it needs to be moderated by distribution among fellow citizens. For our officials, we need
power adequate to discharge their specified responsibilities—but if not

checked it can become tyrannous, and if not prudentially moderated it can faithfully evolve into that overprotective paternalism which evaporates individual accountability. The free powers of any citizen are both invigorated and finitized by his participation in a society that, by seeking freedom for all, must thereby prescribe restrictions on the powers of each.

The problem of power is the problem of affording adequacy without excess. It is the problem of how to organize social freedom so as to ensure its future. This problem of power has been notoriously and irresponsibly neglected by the two extreme voices of contemporary discussion.

(i) Advocates of atomistic liberalism, in the name of a utopian vision of unbridled liberty for each, have forsaken any viable notion of a positive common good—which requires, in a technological age, unprecedented degrees of collective decision. Having denuded the concept of community responsibility, their proposals would mean that already powerful individuals would be enabled to make pervasive decisions binding us all. By defining liberty as property, as Locke did, the logic of their proposals would lead to an anarchy depriving most of us of our liberties and positive freedoms. If not fortuitously frustrated by the unvoiced mercantilistic heritage of free societies—that economic activity must ultimately function under social controls—they would have led us to something approaching Hobbes's "state of nature."

(ii) Advocates of Marxism, in the name of a utopian vision of unbridled freedom for the social whole coupled with the ideal of enforced equality of each, have forsaken any viable notion of individual freedom in their redefinition of the common good—which requires, in a technological age, renewed focus both on the potentialities of individual initiative and differentiation of the kinds of individual expertise needed for responsible social decisions. By arrogating total power and privilege to self-anointed elites, they have violated their own espousal of equality and have but succeeded in establishing the most murderous tyrannies ever known to man. By insisting that free societies, which afford them opportunities for advocacy, are little more than a Hobbesian "state of nature," they can only offer us Hobbes's solution, the imposition of a tyrannical peace by the force of an absolute state.

This common irresponsibility to the temporal problematic of power may well be grounded in intellectual rebellion against the open-ended structure of human temporality which continually functions by means of freely evaluated possibilities. Atomistic liberalism found its ground, not in history, but in a mythic prehistoric "state of nature" out of which we are somehow to have taken inherent property rights into a society whose prime function is to eternalize them by limiting itself to serving as their guardian—without any prescription for their proper (thereby limited) employment, any cognizance of the temporal dynamic of their temporal exercise, or any notion of an historically developing common good. Marxists grounded their doctrine, not in history, but in a claim to a timeless insight into a timeless law of history which precludes free development by foreclosing temporally conditioned presentations of previously unforeseen concrete options; in its name they deduce the demand that all differentiated groupings be deliberately obliterated in a peace to be imposed by force; rather than look to a prehistoric "state of nature" in a mythic past, their promise is to end history in a timeless mythic future.

We have no experiential notion of what a pre- or post-historic existence, of timelessness as a social condition, might conceivably mean. Neither an anarchy which can only lead to a war of each against all, nor a tyranny in which peace is imposed by the barrel of a gun can comprise any common good we can experientially envision. We must therefore reject not only the Hobbesian diagnosis but both sides of Hobbes's choice. We are temporal beings, whose temporality is freedom, freedom to develop our idiosyncratic individualities, our accepted obligations and privacies, our interpretations and proposals, within a common bond, a common bond within which the specified freedoms of each contribute to the continuing development of the social good we share together. We require a state, an organization of the whole, that presumes the reality of time and thereby is open to the unveiling of new possibilities that cannot be deductively forecast. Only a forward-looking temporality that is open to presently unforeseen possibility can offer us maximization of freedom accordant with changing problems, developing needs, and novel opportunities. We require organized social prescription and direction precisely because we are not able to do, each for himself, what we can do together. The privacies we each prize, the opportunities we each seek, the options we each use, the futures we each try to build—all depend on the continuing development of our common good in which the goods of all concrete individual freedoms continue to inhere.

If freedom is social freedom for the future, fundamental social decisions must be entrusted to those we choose, on multifarious levels, to make specified decisions for us; upon finite grants of finite authority and thereby power to our officials whom we entrust with finite control over specified aspects of our future. If freedom is to be organized with an end-in-view, our decision-making procedures need to be institutionalized in finite ways. Such institutionalization is inherently prescriptive: it announces how conflicts are *henceforth* to be reconciled; it grants limited authority to be used; it provides for occasions when power is abused; it prescribes those areas of common concern within which public authority will be exercised; it proscribes those areas from which it is foreclosed. The institutionalization of freedom is a constitutional order and as such it prescribes the future course of its society. However political scientists may argue the relative merits of one kind or another, any constitutional structure is a *writing-out in advance* of the procedures to be followed. It delineates what must be done, what may be done, what is foreclosed—from any discernible future. Most crucially, it anticipates the possibility of changes of the public mind by specifying how its grants of authority and its procedures themselves may be changed.

Just as jurists distinguish between constitutional and statutory law—the first prescribing the uses of authority, and the second but embodying the specific uses of that authority—let me suggest that a constitutional system is ontologically prescriptive to a given society just as its specific statutes are ontically descriptive of its functioning fidelity. Its ontological description is its formulation of its decision-making procedures, both in and out of its governmental structure, the form of its freedom as a free society; its ontic description, seen in its statutes, restrictions, permissions, and encouragements, comprises the content of the specific freedoms it enjoins. No free society can function without a time-oriented set of institutionalizations which allow and encourage an openness to the future by means of a content of concrete freedoms whose exercise it protects. If a society has ensured in advance its freedom to judge its own state of freedom, it does so by examining the specific ways in which its decision-making powers encourage the development of the future-facing freedoms by which it sees the developing interest of its common good. A free society then sees its common good manifested in the ontic expressions of its ontological commitments.

What has been sketched out are the social implications of what may be taken as an aphorism from Plotinus: "Engendered beings are in a continuous process of acquisition; eliminate futurity and at once they lose their being."[12] The being of each of us, individually and socially, is the openness of futurity, a futurity that is apprehended by us in the continuity of our ontic freedoms. Each of the four principles developed has spelled out an aspect of this temporal web within which each realizes its meaning: (1) individuality is socially and temporally structured under the aegis of futurity; (2) any individual, society, or group is itself a time-process engaged in building history by selectively taking up its past and redirecting its development into that heritage to be handed on; (3) historicality and temporality, as the two sides of the human condition, are manifested in the freedom presupposed in every act of evaluation and decision; and (4) freedoms manifested in our situational evaluations, decisions among alternatives, and commitments to courses of action comprise our power for the future.

If there be any plausibility in what has been suggested, we should briefly consider what its present meaning might be.

If our evaluations and commitments are responses to our continuing encounter with the reality of time, intelligent decision should accord with what appears to be the nature of time itself. Time is not only the sign of change, the continuity of change, but of continuity itself. As Leibniz would have urged, not only in nature but also in social development, there can be no gaps. We ourselves each represent continuities with the past. We are historical beings and carry pastness with us—by language, traditions, values, modes of thought, resentments, fears, anticipations. Any realistic proposal for change must square with that with which it must deal; any proposal, including our leaders as well as ourselves, must mesh with what we already are; failure to recognize what is being brought along only invites disaster.

It seems symptomatic that of the three great revolutions marking the modern age, the second two sought precipitous and revolutionary change and each ended in a reign of terror, ensuing war, and continuing question as to what happened to its utopian promises. In sharpest contrast, the American separation from Britain precipitated no radical change, no social explosion, but the creative taking up of an acknowledged past in the building of a redirected future whose structure, significantly, has endured without any comparable modern precedent. Even a crisis-point, as Royce noted, represents, perhaps, a sharp turning but yet a continuity of what has been into what can yet be. Specific possibilities available to a society are those possibilities it has historically developed; they must be possibilities which take up its past into transition. If there be any lesson from revolutionary histories it is that explosions, in society, as in nature, do not create; the reforms which endure are those honoring the historic heritage which may be transcended or redirected but cannot be aborted; history is evolutionary and, if not frustrated into recoil, carries itself forward.

If our temporality and historicality must honor the past, we cannot seek to duplicate it. What has been has been; its pastness demands being honored by its recognition as past. Time is not only sequential continuity but also the continuity of change. Growing out of our past, we still discern our problems by means of possibilities for the future and we modify our procedures and canons as we respond to those possibilities.

If all present decisions are decisions concerning our future, it would seem that the legitimacy of a political system or a specific proposal cannot rest on its genesis: governments come to power, economic arrangements emerge, proposals arise out of all sorts of conditions and contingencies, few of them ideal. Appropriate genesis is not present justification. Although we need to understand how a present situation came to be, the function of our evaluation is not to justify the past but to address the future. Our authentic proposals address, not historic antecedents which cannot be changed, but concrete possibilities presently available.

Instead of facing problems by regretting their supposed causes, leaping to utopian nostrums, or taking them as self-contained atomistic situations, imaginative foresight, acknowledging the continuity of temporality, seeks to anticipate new problems that might ensue from alternatively available resolutions, so that present streams of continuity might feed into a peaceful river rather than pour into a wild cascade. Noteworthy is Aristotle's chapter "On Revolutions"; it is concerned, not with how to foment them but how to obviate their occurrence, how to anticipate and correct potentially disruptive grievances before they explode.

As Leibniz, for one, had urged, "it is much better to prevent poverty and misery, which is the mother of crimes, than to relieve it after it is born." This conservative philosopher, who was also a statesman of his time, urged that the proper "definition of the state . . . [is] what the Latins call *respublica*"; its prime telos "as democracy, or polity, is to make people themselves agree as to what is good for them." Seeking to avoid the irrationality of "arbitrary power," he looked to "mixed government" and noted that a republic not only serves as a beacon of pluralism and freedom but makes "the common good the first object in [its] social catechism"; that the function of its "politics, after virtue, is the maintenance of abundance, so that men will be in a better position to work in common concert."[13] Looking beyond his contemporary economy, he recognized that abundance can only be created by productive enterprise; to this end, he urged social mechanisms to encourage manufacturing and the stimulation of the creative economic activity of the citizenry. In like manner, Alexander Hamilton, explicitly repudiating an atomistic economics of doctrinaire laissez-faire—in what can be construed as a neomercantilism—urged the new American republic to extend "the incitement and patronage of government" to the encouragement of manufacturing, to use the power of the whole—and indeed, "the public purse"—to encourage otherwise unused minds to make their own effective contributions to the common prosperity, "to foster industry and cultivate order and tranquillity at home and abroad"—because a high level of peaceful productive prosperity is the fertile ground which nourishes popular freedom.[14]

One prime effect of such proposals for an active stimulation of diverse economic activities by republican government has been to effect the historic diversification of economic power. Using the power of the whole, focused in government, to pluralize the freedom to create new social developments, pluralizes the sources of liberty and freedom in society, and multiplies that first principle of any constitutional government: power must be reined in by countervailing power if the freedom that is the common good may rule. Such historic development gives modern recognition to that principle of political realism Machiavelli enunciated: "all the laws that are favorable to liberty result from the opposition" of the diverse elements constituting a society.[15] The power of the whole, when effectively used, pluralizes the sources of power, checks tendencies to tyranny by any group, and gives every citizen a vested interest in maintaining the dynamic of a free society. It is pragmatically significant that such policy has produced increasingly middle-class societies enjoying the widest common prosperity ever known together with a sharing of educational opportunity and consequent social mobility undreamed of in the past.

What free societies have evolved, despite the prophets of social doom and necessary cataclysm, is a complex system in which the freedom to decide, the power to initiate new temporal sequences of activity with ongoing repercussions is so dispersed in government and the economy that it has passed the power of any individual or group to arrogate its control. By pluralizing the sources of new initiatives, by inviting diverse creation of new temporal sequences, by placing the protection of the whole upon the continuity of contesting for influence and authority over the creation of our future, we seem to have given effective recognition to the essential dynamic of the temporality of freedom, which consists in a continuity of contest within a common bond.

The authenticity of freedom is no mere abstraction. It is manifested in the diverse activities of individual citizens, and in the stability of social processes that permit each, as such or with others, to plan ahead for those improvements which are the living signs of the common good. The authenticity of freedom is found in explicit recognition that freedoms must be concrete and finite to be at all; concrete freedoms, as powers to build the future, are grounded in the pluralization of power to propose new programs, initiate new courses of development, appropriate new possibilities into the common heritage we are building together. Our specific freedoms, as institutionalized in organs of political stability and economic health permitting them to function, comprise the content of our common good.

But freedom is formed by temporality, and authentic temporality guards the openness of futurity. Freedom, then, is securely grounded only by a complex of political and economic institutions effectively pluralizing open options while effectively guarding against despotic foreclosure of genuine possibilities for continuing enhancement and development. The authenticity of our temporally structured social being is grounded when it is institutionalized in concrete ways by a society that identifies its common good with the possibilities of futurity. A free society defines its common good as the common freedom to build the future, the common good which each member of a free citizenry is encouraged to develop as his own.

11

The Process of Polity

Free peoples in the contemporary world live under what they generally describe as *democratic governments*. Strictly speaking, this general term is a misnomer. In point of fact these governments, whether nominally headed by a ceremonial monarch or an elected president, embody the principles of classical republicanism. Their citizens pride themselves on their freedoms as they go about their lives—even as they frequently or only occasionally utilize their time to discuss policies, debate programs, become politically active, or merely vote in elections. Yet this essentially temporal freedom from continual political involvement and control is rarely noted. And only rarely is it acknowledged that one prime argument for the representative republic is precisely grounded on this temporal freedom, a pervasive temporal concern that appears in several ways in any examination of our sociopolitical lives.

Five closely interrelated themes that explicate the essentially temporal nature of a free citizenry need to be sketched out. Each of these themes deserves a detailed examination on its own; but it is, I think, important to see them together. The practical outcome of these considerations would be to suggest often overlooked priorities which merit our attention when we attend to our public problems.

Time is as intrinsic to our political processes as are the evaluations and judgments we make about political issues—yet neither political theory nor contemporary political debate pays much attention to the import of the temporal nature of this political activity and this concern. Let us then turn to face these themes in order: (1) the nature of republican government and its historic foundation in a temporalist concern; (2) the future-oriented cast of political intelligence; (3) the temporalist distinction that places a premium on republican government; (4) the unbreakable interconnection between time and freedom; and (5) a clarification of the nature of pragmatic thinking which insists on facing the alternatives among which we must decide in authentically temporal terms.

As we all know, the concept of free government has developed from the ancient Greek invention of civil government, which claims to seek the welfare of its citizens. Aristotle, who wrote the classic text on the Greek political experience, delineated the types of government known in his time. Having lived in the free city or polis of Athens, he took its innovation of citizen-government as setting forth a standard for true civil government, a standard which he termed the "idea of polity itself." And his incisive examination, let me suggest, is still pertinent to the more complex situations of our own time.

Two central questions, he urged, need to be faced in evaluating any governmental system. First, how many persons select its officials; second, for whose benefit is political power used? A true *polity* is an organized constitutional government that seeks to function for the benefit of the entire citizenry. When its power is rather used for the sole benefit of the ruler(s)—whether a dictatorial individual, a dictatorial group, or a dictatorial majority—it is a perverse, or we would now say, an *illegitimate* government. Only when governmental power, however selected and distributed, is used for the generalized good of the whole, is it to be recognized as a *true* or *legitimate* government.

Pure democracy is not applauded; rather, it is grudgingly accepted as the least perverse of these deficient or illegitimate forms of government: least objectionable because, built on majority rule, its benefit includes most, not merely a few, into its concern. But it is still unacceptable because, incarnating unmitigated majority power, it deliberately rules for its own benefit while excluding all minorities from its concern.

In contrast, a true polity exemplifies a civically organized political structure that seeks to serve its entire constituency as an organized whole; it provides a constitution, which sets out procedures and limitations on authority that bind any majority within it. As such, a constitution is a prescriptive standard by which any polis may be judged: its effective dedication is to the common good of the society as a whole in which *all citizens* are to share. How may such a conceptual possibility be institutionalized as an actualized reality?

Aristotle's inherent pragmatism showed here brilliantly. In any general group of citizens, he argued, one finds two somewhat opposed camps, both of which are necessary for the social health: one prizes wealth, the other prizes freedom. For the good of the whole, *both* are needed to function together for the social health. Bring them to cooperate in one unified government and that government will necessarily serve the interests of all, the interests of the entire organized community, because all opposed interests are represented in its governing structure. Bring oligarchy, the rule of the few who have wealth, into union with the many who prize their individual freedom, and the compromises they must make among themselves for the sake of social harmony will encompass virtually all citizens into the common concern. The move from pure democracy to what he termed polity or *constitutional government* is what, since its Roman development, has been designated as a *republic;* it is the move from *most* to *all,* from the imposition of an unhindered majority will to the compromises inherent in a universal inclusion.

Such a governmental system spells out in advance a set of temporally prescriptive procedures for adjudicating disputes in the light of a common interest, for choosing officials to handle specific delegations of authority—and thereby also serves to relieve most citizens of the need to bind their own time to the minutiae of civic affairs.

The two key contemporary terms—*democracy and republic*—which are commonly used to denote the idea of polity, come from that heritage. We often use them today as virtually interchangeable, but when we attend to their origins, they clearly carry radically different meanings bound around some notion of equality. The term *democracy* has come to have diverse meanings: equality of the right to vote, equal subjection to the law, and especially a social meaning pertaining to the absence of rigid class divisions in the society and a high degree of social mobility. It is these meanings that permit us to distinguish democratic and undemocratic republics. But the other distinctive, and more historically sanctioned, meaning of "democracy" refers to political organization, and is completely at variance with the word *republic.* As *political concepts* these two terms point in two opposed directions, two different ways of handling a central temporal concern, and bear on the nature of freedom.

If government is to function *for* the people, the Athenians quickly understood, it must be under their control. Government *by* direct popular participation, by the *demos,* was the unprecedented Greek innovation. And this was clearly understood by them to mean government by participation of the people in the general assembly—what we today call direct or participatory democracy. As all citizens were regarded as fully equal and thereby qualified to serve in virtually all public offices, they saw no need for elections and so they filled most offices by lot, a practice still followed in the United States for the selection of juries.

Two facts quickly became apparent. The first was the general desire for general leisure. As all citizens were required to spend the bulk of their time in the public assembly or other public business, they were not free to control their own time; they certainly did not have the time to furnish their own sustenance. The Greek free citizenry, then, necessarily constituted a prosperous leisure class whose time expenditures were controlled by the public assembly, and who depended on a slave economy for economic support. It is paradoxical but nevertheless true that their invention of direct democracy or participatory popular rule not only foreclosed individual control over personal time by free citizens but also necessitated slavery.

Direct democracy, let us note, thus entailed a double restriction on individual freedom: the slave's time was constrained by his master, and the time of his master, a free citizen, was constrained by the majority of the popular assembly.

Second, it did not require much political experience to see that some citizens were better qualified than others to handle delicate or involved tasks, such as commanding the army in defense of the city, and so the idea of delegated authority was invented. Particular individuals were elected to represent the interest of the citizenry for a stated period of time in pursuing a specific kind of task. These individuals were given the responsibility to act for, and even to direct, the citizenry in accord with a specific instruction and the ensuing requirement to report back on how the office entrusted to their care had been exercised. And so the idea of representative government was also invented—although it was not until the Romans coined a new term for this: *res publica* or *public property* became the name for a state governed by representatives chosen by the people to handle specific delegations of public authority for the general benefit. It was the Romans who spread the institution of slavery through their conquests; yet, paradoxically, it was the Romans who developed the idea of republican government, which, in contrast to a pure democracy, does *not* require a servile population because it leaves the citizenry free to control their own individual time without yielding popular control.

It was the Romans who first developed Aristotle's perception that a government directed for the benefit of the entire citizenry had to bring all elements of that citizenry into the governmental structure. This idea of republican government, that it mixes into its structure the varied elements of its citizens, indeed, was the practical definition of polity or constitutional government. It was symbolically proclaimed by the Romans on the standards their legions carried as they carved out the core of the Western world—"SPQR": the Senate *and* the People of Rome.

Indeed, it was the inspiration of the Roman Republic that paved the way for the democratization that began with the onset of the modern age. Their experience, *the only experience of extended republican government* before the American and French Revolutions, was explicitly and judiciously examined by Machiavelli in his *Discourses*, by Montesquieu in *The Spirit of the Laws*, and by Rousseau in *Of the Social Contract*, as they started to work out the texture of modern republicanism. The Roman Republic provided the institutional concepts which enabled first Montesquieu and then Rousseau to condemn slavery as absolutely illegitimate.[1] Conceiving the modern republic as taking up Aristotle's description of free citizenship, they set out an unprecedented standard by universalizing the idea of citizenship as a rightful claim by all society members. Proclaimed as the one fundamental social right due to any person, citizenship as full membership in the polis became the foundation of all specific civic rights and obligations.

Specific rights of citizens, then, are social rights that are dependent upon the obligations ensuing upon full civic membership; these obligations while exacted from each citizen must be minimal because the popular will is to leave each citizen, as a free being, free to devote his own time not to civic affairs but to the securing of sustenance and enjoying of leisure.

These core concepts of modern societal life incorporate that temporal process of time-bound and time-formed development which *is* history. The historical experience, which produced the core concepts we use today, has often been a painful one. What this historical experience shows is that a polity, or a properly constituted civil government, is neither a *thing* that endures unchanged through time nor a somehow timeless idea; a polity is a *process* of be-ing together in a mutually conditioned temporal experience; the *process of being members of a polity is* a way of be-ing, a process that is certainly time-bound; as lived by each citizen it is also pervasively temporal. And one of its prime, if rarely voiced, concerns is how the control of the individual time of its citizens is to be allocated.

Indeed, the cyclical notion of time, which dominated all classical thought, led Aristotle to set out a theme which most subsequent political thinkers picked up—the notion that an organized community can be expected to develop through a natural cycle of generation, growth, corruption, and dissolution. It was only with the rise of the modern world that the cyclical presumption of eventual dissolution disappeared from the tracts of political theory—even as the kingdoms in which these tracts were written had already begun their process of dissolution. In a way, this is ironic, for, to the best of my knowledge, the last two serious discussions of this classical theme were presented by Montesquieu and Rousseau—who, for the first time, by foreclosing the legitimacy of slavery, bequeathed to us the essentials of the modern democratic republic.[2]

Modern free societies have taken up the heritage bequeathed by Aristotle's examination of the Athenian innovation of free government.

When we abjure their acceptance of slavery, and focus our attention on his descriptions of government that was constituted for the benefit of free citizens, we find that all the rudiments of a contemporary theory of republican government are already in play. We find the insistence that it derives from, and is intended to serve, the entire body of free citizens; the delineation of the three types of governmental activity—executive, legislative, and judicial; and the principle that they should be in different hands coupled to the principle that all elements of society should be represented in the institutions of government, yielding the full notion of mixed government. We find the warning against any tyranny—whether by one ruler, a ruling minority, or the ruling majority itself—tied into the crucial distinction between those policies that favor the ruler (individual, group, or majority) and those policies that are to benefit the entire society as one organic whole. We find the thesis that a society, for its own health, cannot be divided into two warring classes of the rich and the poor, and the remedy—a strong middle class that imperceptibly reaches into each of the other two and thus fosters social cohesion so that a mutuality of a common loyalty may unite disparate internal tendencies. These principles still guide us; they are commonplaces of theories of republican government. In terms of specific enactments, they sometimes occasion controversy, but generally they are taken in free republics as standards by which to gauge governmental policies.

Having generally accepted the standards for a government of free citizens which Aristotle had set out, it is strange that political theory has largely ignored the temporalist framework in which he had set them. Yet, at the outset of his work, Aristotle had clearly set out, on two distinct levels, a temporalist standard for political judgment. On the more general level, every state, as he suggested at the beginning of his *Politics,* is oriented to a future accomplishment: "Every state [or polis] is a community of some kind, and every community is established with a view to some good; for mankind always act in order to obtain that which they think good" (1252a).[3] This future orientation is not only a social phenomenon: it characterizes every individual intelligence: "Every art and every inquiry, and similarly every action and pursuit, is thought to aim at some good; and for this reason, the good has been rightly declared to be that at which all things aim" (1094).

If we think through the meaning of these two topic sentences, we can only conclude that when human reasoning is directed to practical concerns, it is essentially constituted in purposive terms and is thus temporally organized. A deliberate decision to act undertakes a course of activity in the present and commits a stretch of oncoming time to the achievement it seeks to instantiate. Whether on an individual level, or on the level of social decision, deliberate rational activity aims toward the future; it aims to bring into the actual dynamic state of existence certain values, norms, commitments, or even a pictured outcome.

Rational activity is purposive activity. Action is undertaken with deliberation to accomplish what has not yet been rendered actual; political intelligence seeks to invoke past experiences that are relevant to the course that is set out. But however wisely or blindly one sets out to pursue some plan or direction, one does set out to accomplish something that will be a new fact of the historical chronicle, something that will depend for its being on the efficacious use of planning intelligence, something that will not come to be unless appropriate steps have been instituted to bring it about.

Political reason, then, depends upon the appropriation of possibilities, upon the intelligent assessment of conditions, helps and impediments along the way, and on an intelligent use of an imaginative creativity that is as crucial to the practical as it is to the arts. The future, to which we aim, is not some "thing" into which we are to plow. The future is that which we are to create. What will result from our acts will either be a state of being into which we slide without any awareness of deliberate decision; or we will have created some new state of affairs which could not have come to pass without our own creative ingenuity in bringing all the contextual forces and conditions at our disposal into a purposeful harmony. If we are obsessed with our passivity through change, we will then discourse on the fateful necessities of historical development within which we will see ourselves as mere pawns. When we acknowledge the need for decisive action, we will recognize ourselves as fateful creators of history, as innovators upon whose efforts the outcome of historical development depends.

It is, I think, significant that in all democratic polities, in all truly representative republics, leaders are chosen who claim to be able to bend the perceived direction of ongoing development, who claim to be able to redirect the forces of history and create a future instead of merely acquiescing before it. Most of us perceive social time as open to challenge, debate, and decision. Most of us perceive the present situation—which is to say, take up the facts that have been established and acknowledge the possibilities they present—as the temporal site of options for the future, options among which we must decide, options which however limited they may be, yet present alternatives which are dependent upon our present decision for their eventual oblivion or actualization.

Political intelligence, then, is always future-oriented. It orients itself to what yet can be within the constraints of what must be. It functions on the premise that the future is at least somewhat open. It presumes that, within the realm of the possible, it still is able to resolve what will, in due course, become actual. This is to say, by whatever standards of judgment rational intelligence constructs the future, it does so in order to transform some presently favored possibility into historical rendered factuality.

This future-oriented stance is inherent in the description of polity as constitutional government. For, as already suggested, a constitution, by its intrinsic nature, has set out in advance a set of procedures by which a free citizenry shall determine the limits of allowable actions, the modes of social interaction, the ways in which alternate social policies may be advanced, debated, and how those debates will be resolved. A constitution is then a prescriptive set of rules enunciated or agreed upon to "henceforth" govern the complex lives of free citizens insofar as their activities may be anticipated as impinging on each other. It is designed to set out in advance of any conflicts the ways in which those conflicts are to be resolved, decisions taken, and authority delegated. To the extent that it is well crafted, it will lead to a social harmony in which differences may be encouraged while contained, and each citizen will be left with that degree of personal control over one's own time, which is the essence of one's freedom, consonant with its general enjoyment by all other citizens. As Kant summarized the intent of any constitutional arrangement, it is to "allow *the greatest possible human freedom* in accordance with laws by which *the freedom of each is made to be consistent with that of all others. . . .* "[4] Madison had defined *law* to mean a *rule of action.*[5] A constitution may then be described as that set of fundamental laws which a society accepts as the prescribed procedure to follow in formulating specific rules for specific types of actions that accord with its general animating principles and purposes.

Political intelligence is then prudential or pragmatic intelligence. It seeks to incorporate its values, principles, or goals into a course of activity. And it judges the efficacy of its acts by its success in incarnating those values, principles, or goals into what effectively comes to pass. Political intelligence, in Aristotle's language, is then inherently prudential—thereby entailing the need for close attention to practical sequences in its activities as the virtue of citizenship. To the extent that its guiding principles are moral principles, it is in Kant's language, inherently moral—thereby entailing a deep sense of responsibility for its animating norms. However framed, the test of an action or a program is its efficacy in accomplishing what it set out to do without disrupting other value-loyalties, virtues, or norms along the way.[6]

To acknowledge the priority of our orientation to the future in every deliberate decision is not to suggest that a society can start without acknowledging the legacy from its past. As Paul Ricoeur has noted, "We can perhaps 'transvaluate' [our] values, but we can never create them beginning from zero."[7] In the living present that looks ahead, the presence of the past is always prominent: in the language we speak, the cultural history it represents, the folklore we accept, the values we cherish, the customs we follow, the presumptions within which we have learned to work. Without awareness of the continuity from the past, we would hardly be prepared to face the task of creating our future.

And, indeed, we form the deliberate ongoing continuity of our society by teaching our children about its past, bringing them to share a veneration for its heroes, and finding the roots of a common community not in its supposedly unanchored aspirations but in its past record of successes and failures out of which these aspirations have grown. Without a strong sense of shared historic roots, there can be little sense of present community and a shared vision of what we are striving together to achieve.

Society is indeed a process, a process of historic development. Any particular nation, Edmund Burke pointed out, "is *not an idea only of local extent and individual momentary aggregation, but it is an idea of continuity which extends in time* as well as in numbers and in space." The ways in which a nation understands itself and the situations in which it finds itself come out of a development of "the peculiar circumstances, occasions, tempers, dispositions, and moral, civil, and social habitudes of the people, *which disclose themselves only in a long space of time.*"[8] A society is a history, a history not merely of accomplished fact, but more so of a common "we" within whose scope each "I" finds one's own motivating aspirations.

Significantly, as well as symbolically for the civilization that emerged out of the Athenian experience, Pericles had begun his call to the Athenian future with these words: "I shall begin by speaking about our ancestors . . . [who] by their courage and their virtues, have handed [this land] on to us as a free country."[9] Acknowledging the heritage of the past carries with it a responsibility for continually refining and developing what it has bequeathed; by doing so we enrich ourselves by using it as opening up opportunity for what may yet be wrought.

As citizens of free republics, we are fortunate in that most of the decisions we make, most of our daily concerns, are not political. Most of our decisions, most of the concerns which preoccupy our living time, are private concerns and decisions about personal matters. Most of our lived time is devoted to questions of livelihood or the leisure that it sustains, to family and friends, to hobbies and entertainments. One of the unspoken glories of a free republic which entrusts its affairs to freely chosen representatives is that its citizens are freed from preoccupation with public dangers and political excitements, as well as from the minutiae of governmental management. It is precisely because free societies are generally stable, because their procedures are dependably constant, that they serve so effectively as the enabling context for the personal.

As suggested, one of the rarely noted virtues of a free society is that it frees the time of its citizens from preoccupation with the business of administering the polis. Cheerfully, this is left to duly selected employees—who are expected to do what is required of them within the confines of their delegated authority with probity and responsibility and without requiring the time-consuming inefficiency of constant public supervision. Indeed, public anger usually arises only when officials have not been true to their charge, when public corruption or malfeasance is exposed, and personal attention has to be turned from the priority of the private to the intrusive responsibility of public concerns.

To minimize the possibility of such public disruptions while making sure that such potential exposures are pursued when called for, a self-policing system, often called a system of "checks and balances," was worked out since Montesquieu first devised it. That its proper functioning would not be compromised, free republican governments have insisted on the principle of being supplemented by a nongovernmental agency, a free press, whose legally protected carping is expected to sound the alarm when that self-policing system of checks and balances fails to function properly and in accord with the general will.

A free polity, indeed, usually prides itself on providing a stable public backdrop for the private concerns of its members. Because of a continuity of shared freedoms and liberties, we need not be preoccupied with their defense, but generally utilize them without much thought until we find them being attacked or subverted. Because of a continuity of duly constituted procedures for making public decisions, we are for the most part content to periodically take time out from more private concerns to debate and decide whether to reemploy or replace our representatives. The rules and procedures which govern a free people are deemed successful when they are not obtrusive, when they provide a stable public life which does not require constant attention, just so we each can be so much freer to devote more personal time and attention to our private lives.

Indeed, aside from the transformation of the city-state into the nation-state, the greatest departure from the governmental practice of ancient Athens that marks free societies has been the substitution of the republican for the democratic principle in its political life. Strictly speaking, a "democracy" as the Athenians invented it, and Madison explained it, depends on the full-time participation of the citizenry in the administration of the political structure.[10] Only a leisure class can conceivably afford the temporal luxury of active governmental participation.

When Montesquieu devised the principles of modern republicanism, he saw that no members of a truly democratic society, dependent upon the efficacious use of their time for their livelihood, could afford the time for direct democratic government, that no free people would *voluntarily elect* to spend their time in that way. If *the people* are to be the ground of their government, if government is to be, indeed, a *res publica*, a public affair and a public property dependent upon the will of its citizens, it needs to honor the public will that the members of the public be left free to pursue their own concerns instead of being tied to operations which were better left to hired hands or representatives.[11] And it must be so constituted that the whole people and not merely a leisure class are regarded as the ultimate authority from which that government derives its authority and to whom it must periodically report.

Rousseau, the most "populist" of all republican theorists, urged that a "pure democracy," or direct self-government, is appropriate only for the gods.[12] Condemning rule by both monarchs and landed aristocrats as unable to govern in the public interest, he joined Montesquieu in resurrecting the principle of classic republicanism by calling for rule that derives its authority from the people as a whole. If the people are to control their government, he argued, their only recourse is to what he termed an "elective aristocracy," the public selection of particular officials who are employed to "administer the constitution."[13] Such employees, like any employees, have designated areas of authority, specifically charged responsibilities, and employers (i.e., their constituencies) to whom they must periodically report.

This "republican" system of government, as Madison and Hamilton repeatedly argued, is the only feasible form of government for a free people.[14] This is so for several reasons, two of which depend upon the acknowledged import of the consideration of time. The first has already been outlined: the need of a free citizenry to devote their time to private rather than civic affairs. To this and to the famed principle of checks and balances, which they learned from Montesquieu, they added a new temporal consideration—a strict time limit on the delegated authority of all elected officials, a creative use of chronology to control the utilization of delegated political power. But more crucially, they recognized that individual freedoms depend upon limiting the power of governmental officials to intrude on the time of the citizenry. As Hamilton had pointed out, "[Government's legislative power] not only commands the purse, but prescribes the rules by which the duties and rights of every citizen are to be Regulated," which is to say that governmental power has the capacity to rule and control the time of its citizens.[15] Republican government, therefore, is necessary in order that a free people may control the social impositions placed on their individual control of their own personal time.

This central temporalist argument for a representative republic rather than a participatory democracy speaks directly to some radical proposals being offered today: if people are to be free to spend their own time as they see fit, *their* preference, especially when they are of moderate circumstances, is to devote their time to their livelihood and leisure, rather than to resolving the minutiae of civic affairs. To compel them into participatory schemes is to infringe their freedom to use their time as they see fit. The first freedom anyone desires is the control of individual time. To free a people to control their own time, while still maintaining their oversight over their common good, provides a test of any government that claims to be the government of a free people.

A free people is a people who prize their freedom to control their own time; such people have historically abjured rigid class structures and welcomed high degrees of social mobility, as inherently expressive of a free society. Just because of the great value which they place on personal time, they cannot afford and have therefore abjured the time-consuming luxury of participatory government. Their democratization is their generalization of individual time-control. Their republican principle of governance came into being precisely because the freedom of the people requires freedom from having to be preoccupied with details of civic management. Uniquely, republican or representative constitutional government facilitates popular control while leaving the populace free for other time-consuming pursuits.

Republican or representative government thus supports the democratization of a society by maximizing free time for the citizenry; it does this by leaving the nongovernmental activities of its citizens to the voluntary initiatives of its citizens—and on these voluntary citizen undertakings it not only depends but bases its aspirations for prosperity and progress. The expectation is that by limiting governmental agencies for the most part to procedural directives rather than direct intervention in the subsocieties—corporations, unions, churches, clubs—the authority of governmental agencies to interfere with the free time of the citizenry in their own community concerns is minimized.

And, indeed, the degree of personal control over one's own time is a prime mark of a free society, one that distinguishes free political and economic systems from those which are not. John Locke, who comes out of a philosophic genealogy somewhat different from the one outlined here, declared three individual rights as primary and intrinsic to any others—the rights to "life, liberty, and property" (although he showed no qualms in subordinating these individual rights to unmitigated majority rule). But he, and those who join him in doctrines of inherent rights, should have realized that the prime "property right" which anyone can conceivably claim to have is not that of any particular permission or possession but the right to use one's own time, as long as it does not harm the public health, as one sees fit. The degree of individual time-control is the first test of individual freedom: only a society that enhances individual control of individual time, in contrast to all systems of dictation and regimentation, is generally regarded as a free society.

In the organization of one's personal life as in the life of one's society, two themes come together: time and freedom. Indeed, if our use of time is in those pursuits that we consider good, we must be able to evaluate the prospects and possibilities before us, discriminate the desirable from the undesirable, the good from the bad. If we are able to pursue our values and normative standards by the use of intelligence, we must also be able to discriminate the important from the unimportant, the useful from the useless, the instrumental value of one pursuit to another and the relative value of alternate claims upon our time, our temporal efforts, attentions, and concerns.

If we find ourselves actually doing this in everyday life, we must be capable of doing so. This capacity to make evaluative judgments and to guide our actions by them is what we mean by freedom. No matter how one explains or explains away the experience of making free evaluative decisions, one cannot avoid continuing to do so. Even the sophist who proclaims that freedom is an illusion finds himself necessarily continuing to make the free evaluative decisions he claims to be a sham. However logical the argument against the reality of freedom may be, it fails just because it is incoherent with our lived experiences, just because it can explain neither the *experience* of freedom nor the fact that its exercise cannot be abjured.

The experience of freedom, of making evaluative decisions and acting upon them, constitutes the time of daily living. These evaluations may be habitual or deliberate; they may concern questions trivial or profound, but without them life would come to a halt. The continuity of these evaluative decisions we feel called upon to make cannot be aborted, because freedom is itself not free. Freedom is forced upon us because of the temporal constitution of lived experience: not to decide is to decide, and the dynamicity of temporal flow demands that it be ceaselessly filled out by evaluative decisions.

The ability to exercise this capacity of making evaluative decisions is the ability to control one's own time; it is what is meant by the power of self-determination. But this freedom of self-determination is socially bound. It is limited and enhanced by the constraints and opportunities which a society constitutes for its members. The traditional distinction between personal or metaphysical freedom and social freedom that characterizes much of philosophic history is existentially meaningless. For I can only exercise my capacity to make evaluative decisions to the extent that my society permits me to do so. The greater the degree of bureaucratic control, the fewer options for time expenditure are allocated to me. To the extent that controversial information and debate is inhibited, that education has failed to stimulate my intellectual capabilities, or that adequate sustenance cannot be earned, my ability to exercise and develop my capacity for making free decisions has been severely frustrated. What I can do, as a social being, presumes the opportunities that my society opens to me and the constraints that it imposes. The freedom to use my time is then first of all a social freedom.

This is why the claim to freedom epitomizes most social demands. For the control of time is control of the self; it is crucial to the entire experience of self-determination. It is for this reason that freedom is so highly valued; this is why the first mark of freedom is the freedom to control one's time. In this claim to-be-free is wrapped up that complex of rights and privileges and obligations and demands which even the freest society necessarily makes finite by organizing the freedoms of its citizens.

Freedom requires time for its exercise. And freedom is always freedom-for-the-future; as Peirce noted, "future conduct is the only conduct that is subject to self-control."[16] Our concrete freedoms are found in the ability to channel or delineate that time which has not yet been reduced to unalterable fact, to determine which potentialities shall be developed, which possibilities shall be actualized rather than being consigned to oblivion. Freedom is then essentially creative, for only in its exercise do we create what shall be. And freedom can only function if oncoming temporality hovers before it as a field that demands that it be marked out and designated.

If freedom requires time in order to function, then time is the condition which makes freedom possible. The reality of freedom, then, depends upon the reality of time. And if freedom is to be effective in a social order, that social order must steadfastly honor its own temporality. A free social order cannot forget that its own being is that of a process, one that brings a legacy out of the past for discriminative development into its future. It cannot forget that its future can only be the creative product of its citizens whose contributions will be limited by the opportunities they find and the restraints they share. To say that a society is not a "thing" but a "process" is to say that history is not merely the chronicle of the past, it is, in its broadest ramifications, the developmental career of the social body that is presently engaged in transforming the heritage it has received into the legacy it will bequeath to those who come after.

A free society calls its citizens into the ongoing building of its history by equipping them to develop their own contributions to the legacy it is constructing. To the extent that it has educated them well, to the extent that it invites their individualized contributions to the social dynamic, it will bequeath a legacy richer than it received. But to take living history as a living bequeathment is to insist that freedom entails responsibility. For the activity of freedom, on the part of the individual as of the social body, always changes the social milieu within which others will have to live. If freedom is inherently social, then all of our acts impinge upon others. And however one may regard his responsibility for what he does to himself, what one does to the time and freedom of others is from the outset a social responsibility.

As social beings we must live together. Whether we broaden or narrow the degree of personal autonomy we delineate for our society, our freedom-for-the-future always takes us into the lives of others just as the acts of others come into our own. We are social beings whose temporalities and freedoms tie us together.

Most of our individual decisions and actions have social consequences. Most of our decisions, even private ones, have an impact on others. We live in closely knit societies which provide degrees of autonomy but never isolation. Whatever we do will enter into the lives of others as their decisions and action will enter into ours. We cannot afford utopian gambits that ignore the social costs they might incur. The intelligent exercise of freedom, like the responsibility of a mutuality of citizenship, requires a discipline of evaluation, judgment, and decision that takes the principle of temporal continuity seriously and recognizes that it is inherently incremental.

Even our most rudimentary social concepts come out of a long history of practical application as well as intellectual development. The ideas we invoke and the concepts we use are not merely labels casually pulled out of a dictionary. And none of them was invented "from scratch." Concepts, like the people and the societies that use them, have a history that is crucial to their present meaning. They represent a development of experiments that failed as well as those that succeeded, and often transactions and events that were painful to those involved.

When honored for what it is, a serious concept presents a fund of experience that is often predictive of the ways in which it relates to other concepts and to the practices associated with them. This is to say, again, that a concept is not merely an idle set of words; as representing a historic strain in human experience, it points to practices that honor or defile it. When we think this through, four points, the criteria of a temporally responsible mode of social judgment, will emerge.

1. A concept refers to actual time-bound practices within a context stretching beyond it. To an educated understanding, it reports a history of what has been done in its name and commends and condemns future kinds of activities. It calls us to make evaluative decisions that can be tested in action.

The first mark of a system of socially responsible reasoning is to recognize that the concepts we use are inherently *pre*scriptive; they commend (or foreclose) certain kinds of practices to be undertaken in order to advance certain ideals, values, or norms.

2. Again, our orientation to the future needs some clarification. Too many ethical admonitions reduce this temporal concept to a spatial one, and too many recommendations and proposals and programs follow this spatial language by conceiving our temporally constituted lives as a journey into a "place" called the "future." Our temporally constituted situation is then misconstrued as the spatial problem of how to get from "here" to "there." The prescription for a journey is necessarily segmented into three independent considerations: first, the starting place; second, the destination; and third, all the various roads or routes between the two—to be clearly examined on a map. There is no intrinsic connection between them.

And we thus find ourselves ensnared in countless debates about whether the end justifies the means, whether it really matters which road we take as long as it promises to lead us, even if by a circuitous route, to the promised land. All roads may, indeed, lead to Rome, as we are told; but Rome will still be Rome once we get there. If we conceive our problem as a journey, then we are justified in separating "means" and "ends." But too much human misery has resulted from the postulation of a desirable end independent of the steps needed to attain it. The more utopian its pretensions, the less scruple seems needed to get us there.

But time is not space, as William James never tired of reminding us. And time cannot be segmented the way space can be. The future is not a *place* that is merely awaiting our entrance. The future *now is* but a nest of possibilities which suggest a condition of being *yet to be created*. And until it has been rendered actual it cannot be definitively delineated. What will emerge will conform to no preordained pattern but will be the result of *all* that has fed into its creation—including countless other streams of concurrent development that will only then emerge into view.

Rather than the image of a journey across the land, temporal development might better be conceived as the steps an artist takes in reducing an inchoate vision to a tangible work of art which can only be comprehended after its creation—or a *procedure* which a conscientious doctor *prescribes*.

Consider what this suggests. The doctor starts by discerning a problem as having emerged from the presence of a specific historic development which is intrinsic to his diagnosis; he then proceeds to effect a cure by trying out a sequence of actions. The resultant state of the patient's health will emerge from the congruence of these actions together with whatever other unknown factors may intrude. The future state of the patient's health is *not now* known because it is *now being created*. And the conscientious physician takes the prescribed procedure, not as a means to a predetermined end, but as a process to be tenderly nurtured and continuously reexamined along the way; he watches to see the responses to each step and quickly alters the prescribed course if an unexpected reaction ensues. There is here no divorce of ends-and-means. In a serious commitment to the reality of temporal continuity, a flexible prescriptive procedure is conceived to ameliorate the problem without creating a new one while doing so.

So, the second mark of a disciplined method of socially responsible temporal reasoning is to take the time of action in its intrinsic continuity of development with utter seriousness, abjure any distinction between means and ends, and rather recognize that what we do actually *produces* what will actually ensue. The future is not a place that will be arrived at; like a work of art, it is produced—and until the process of creation has been completed, the doctor, like the artist, cannot know precisely how it will turn out.

3. But we cannot each do everything. Take any remotely complex task, and most of us are unqualified to attend to it. Society is built on a division of labor. Each ideally has a function to serve and depends upon countless others to serve theirs. Our individual temporalities overlap each other by feeding into the social temporality we share together.

The third mark of a temporally structured responsible mode of social reasoning is an acknowledgment of limitation in a frank recognition of areas of competence. We *need* each other, and a prime mark of social responsibility is continued acknowledgment that responsibility is being inherently shared. We have a vested interest in the efforts of others and we are, if you like, each other's delegates and representatives in the

myriad aspects of our common endeavor: the mark of wisdom is to recognize our finite capabilities, our inherent interdependence, and
thereby just how circumscribed our particular responsibilities really are.

4. If the function of the present is to develop the future out of what
has been provided, then we must start by recognizing the *absolute continuity* of temporal development. There are, as Leibniz continually insisted, no gaps or jumps. But this also means that all acts and decisions
will carry on into effects often unintended. Any particular action, in a
sense, initiates a sequence that cannot be aborted. And so responsibility
demands that casual experiments with temporal sequences be viewed
with suspicion—for no action, no matter how innocent, can be without
repercussion; any action creates an irreversible sequence whose consequences will become part of whatever ensues. The better part of wisdom,
then, is prudential caution—and the more encompassing the conceivable outcome, the greater the prudential care to be exercised.

The fact of a decision presumes the reality of our freedom or ability to make it. But this freedom, while real, is intrinsically limited. It is
limited by the factuality of the situation in which we find ourselves, the
potentialities or capabilities we bring with us, the possibilities that are
discerned, and the limited knowledge we have of whatever else is transpiring. Our decisional freedom, in every instance, is thus bound by all
the constituents of the temporal context and the requirements of temporal continuity. The responsibility of freedom is to recognize these and
to stand ready to alter our procedures as unexpected developments
occur.

When we bring these various considerations together, what we find
commended is a genuinely pragmatic method of practical reasoning.
For what pragmatism insists upon is that decision and action are conducted in community with others while looking to temporally open but
historically formulated situations we seek to resolve. Dependent on the
condition of a decisional freedom-for-the-future in order to function,
the pragmatic method is pledged to keep the future open. And because
of our shared responsibility for what happens to others, it continually
tests itself by the way in which activities are working out.

The essence of the pragmatic method was voiced in Charles
Peirce's "pragmatic maxim": "Consider what effects that might conceivably have practical bearing you conceive the object of your conception
to have. Then your conception of those effects is the whole of your conception of the object."[17]

The *practical* meaning of a concept or proposal is not its logical
consistency, its internal coherence, or its emotive attraction. Its practical
meaning is not even to be seen in its responsiveness to the particular

problem that called it forth. For its function is not to address the past but to create, out of what is currently present, a new situation. The meaning of a concept or proposal is what *happens when it is put into practice*—not the goal it seeks to attain but what can actually be anticipated to transpire from its implementation—including the side-effects it may conceivably have on other concurrent events.

In journalistic use, pragmatism is often reduced to a kind of cheap opportunism or to a means-ends utilitarianism. It is neither.

To the reply of opportunism, one need merely point out that without guiding principles of actional maxims, we have no rational means of distinguishing what is important or unimportant in any situation, or for evaluating the success or failure of any action. Any new action is itself a difference in a dynamic stream of temporal change. One needs a clear set of valuational loyalties before a rational judgment can say that some conceivable outcome is important or unimportant to what is being attempted, or that some proposed course of action has worked out.

To the charge of utilitarianism, one must reply that its dichotomy of means and ends leads to endlessly abstract disputations as to whether the ends justify the means and if so how; such disputations cannot point to a lived concern with concrete reality. If time is itself a developmental continuity, then means and ends cannot be divorced as two separate objects of concern; in time as lived, all that is done forms a continuum; to segment them is as artificial as the segmenting of the continuity of time into minutes or hours or years or centuries, in whatever manner suits one's particular convenience; it violates the principle that every action is ontologically grounded in the nature of the continuity of time. Utilitarianism does this, as suggested, because it conceives of time not so much as what is to be fashioned, but as a landscape whose contours can be readily mapped out, just waiting to be traversed.

As Royce clearly pointed out, "space furnishes indeed the stage and the scenery of the universe, but the world's play occurs in time."[18] We are reminded of William James's continuing admonition that time is not space; the temporal is not spatial, even though we may pragmatically utilize spatial metaphors on occasion to mark out time.

The true artist finally realizes just what he was doing only when he finally views his newly completed masterpiece. The physician sees only at the end of his treatment what state of health has been *produced* by the procedures that have been followed from his original diagnosis. Both epitomize the essence of pragmatic thinking; each initiates a temporally ordered "procedure" because of a perceived negative condition—a vision still to be captured in its expression, an illness to be cured—because of what Aristotle had termed a "privation," Peirce, "a failure of habit,"

Heidegger, a "missing needed tool," and Dewey, a discerned valuational "lack to be fulfilled."

What is crucial to the physician as to any artist is not merely the final stage of the sequence of acts necessary to attain the final end, but the integrity of the entire procedural sequence itself. As Royce said, in defending the Peircean maxim, the animating purpose does not find its justification merely in its "final expression": it finds its justification in "its whole embodiment" of the entire sequence of all acts undertaken along the way.[19] The responsible moral agent and the responsible social reformer are like the conscientious doctor or the creative artist; they take time seriously as an ordered sequential prescription for the future, as a developmental process whose end-point does *not* already exist: it must first be produced by what we do in a *temporally ordered* way. And what we do—in all its ramifications—is inherently part of the conception or program which provoked its initiation.

The pragmatism of practical reason is then neither opportunism nor utilitarianism. It functions by being responsibly loyal to the temporal continuity of any given situation. It presumes that the ends we project are not predestined stages along a route to be traveled but valuational norms to be incarnated into a developing temporal reality. It invokes those aspects of past experience that seem germane in order to guide it in doing so. It sees the future, not as an ideal state to be attained, but as the increasing incarnation of sought-after values—as the patient's maximally possible state of restored health or the artist's completed painting. It proceeds with a diagnosis of the conditions offered in the immediate present, conceives itself as carrying a history forward by prescribing curative or creative procedures—modes of activity whose outcome can never be assured—while remaining alert to how particular prescribed procedures "work out" in the particular case at hand.

We are bound, as Dewey continually urged, to a continuum of means and ends, because every step of a process is the goal of an earlier act and every end is but a means to some later state of being. The continuity of time means the continuity of process. What we are *doing* to attain any future instantiation of values becomes part of the entire resultant situation we do in fact achieve. And what we achieve may well improve upon what we have received; but whether it does so or fails, it will produce the point of departure for those who come after.

Our heritage is that of past experiences—always facing problems to be solved, privations to be filled, lacks discerned—always looking to a future instantiation or incarnation of the normative judgmental value that is invoked. Our temporal experience, individually and socially, is structured largely in this way whenever we act, not on impulse, but on the careful assessment and remedial or transformational procedures by which practical reason guides its own activity in the world. The process of our organized societies, the process of any polity, is the social temporality of its citizens.

Its future will be what is actually produced by the corrective and creative procedures invoked because of needs discerned in the situations in which we find ourselves. What will be actually achieved will not be some particular spot already to be pointed out on a map—but rather the product of what is done by all who have some influence on the situation at every step along the way. What they do may well cure the particular social ills and ameliorate justifiable complaints incurred along the way by creating new situations that reach beyond the deficiencies and problems out of which they emerged. Into this continuing becoming, this continuing transformation of heritage into legacy, the process of a responsible polity continually looks toward what practically ensues as it seeks to achieve reformed institutionalizations of the values its members regard as the good they share together.

"Time," Machiavelli urged, "is the mother of truth."[20] It is certainly the mother of the social truths in which we are continually engaged, as Machiavelli, that masterfully dispassionate student of the dynamic of the life of the polis, spelled out in sometimes excruciating detail. Time is the form in which our social engagements find expression; our temporalized responses to its demands and the opportunities we see it as offering frame the varied ways in which we find ourselves carrying the heritage we acknowledge while creating the legacy we will effectively bequeath.

A constitutionally conceived polity conceives itself as a prescription for the future of the society it governs, as a temporal process of working out the problems that it finds given to it. The goods of free citizens are generally seen as degrees of temporal self-control to be attained by education, social contribution, and social deserts. Only in this ongoing process of the social temporality in which we all share are we able to find those responsibilities we are called upon to share, those goods we seek, and the fruits of our varied endeavors, which presume the harmonizing of our individuating temporalities in order to be realized.

"Time is the mother of truth" in every social endeavor in which we may engage. It delimits what has been offered, what potentialities and lessons have been provided, what possibilities can be discerned, and the parameters in which those possibilities may be seized. The "process of polity" is the process of a community that develops its members as individual citizens who, while pursuing their individuated futures, yet find that their time is contributing to the good of the whole. It is the process of encouraging its individual citizens, who are always socially bound, in their ultimate social obligation as individual selves who are continually contributing unique temporal perspectives into the social outlook to which they inherently belong. If each citizen is always engaged in forming the future, while bringing the past into the creation of that future, each free citizen is continually engaged in a temporal time-binding process. It is a continuing process that, at its best, is a common commitment to enhance the socially grounded freedom of its individuated members by using the strength of the whole to nurture themselves and then replenish by creating that future which it will proudly hand over as its legacy to those who come after.

Notes

Preface

1. On rethinking the *via negativa* and divine temporality, see Martin Heidegger, *Being and Time*, trans. John Macquarrie and Edward Robinson (New York: Harper and Row, 1962), 499, n. xiii; in German, *Sein und Zeit*, 8th ed. (Tübingen: Max Niemeyer Verlag, [1927] 1937), 427.

Essay 1. The Concept of Time in Western Thought

This essay is a slightly revised version of a lecture delivered at the Smithsonian Institution in Washington, D.C., on June 1, 1989.

1. Plotinus, "Time and Eternity," *Enneads* 3.7, trans. Stephen MacKenna, in *The Human Experience of Time: The Development of Its Philosophic Meaning*, ed. Charles M. Sherover (Evanston: Northwestern University Press, 2001), 78. (Hereafter cited as *HET.*)

2. Plotinus, "Time and Eternity," in Sherover, *HET,* 80

3. Saint Augustine, *Confessions*, Book 9, trans. Rex Warner, in Sherover, *HET,* 82–83.

4. Sir Isaac Newton, *Principia Mathematica*, "Scholium to Definition VIII," trans. Motte, in *The Leibniz–Clarke Correspondence, Together with Extracts from Newton's* Principia *and* Optiks, ed. H. G. Alexander (Manchester: Manchester University Press, 1956), 152. See also Sherover, *HET,* 100.

Essay 2. Talk of Time

This essay was originally published in *Centerpoint*, vol. 2, no. 3, issue 7 (Fall 1977), pp. 14–18.

Essay 3. The Question of Noumenal Time

This essay was originally published in *Man and World* 10, no. 4 (1977).

1. Immanuel Kant, *Critique of Pure Reason*, trans. N. K. Smith (New York: St. Martin's, 1929), A33=B49, p. 77–A35=B52, p. 78. (Hereafter cited as *CPR.*)

2. See Kant, *CPR,* A39=B56, p. 81 n. 3.

3. Ibid., A147=B186, p. 187.

4. Ibid., A46=B64, p. 85.

5. See Kant, *CPR*, B70, p. 89, and A293=B350, p. 297.

6. Ibid., Bxxvi–Bxxvii, p. 27.

7. See, for example, Kant, *CPR*, Bxxv, pp. 26–27, and Bxxviii–Bxxx, pp. 28–29.

8. Ibid., A62=B87, p. 100. See also Immanuel Kant, *Logic*, trans. R. Hartmann and W. Schwartz (Indianapolis and New York: Bobbs-Merrill, 1974), 44 n. 48.

9. Kant, *CPR*, B1, p. 41.

10. W. H. Walsh, *Kant's Criticism of Metaphysics* (Chicago: University of Chicago Press, 1975), 170 (italics mine).

11. Kant, *Logic*, 37.

12. Ibid., 44–45.

13. Ibid., 48–50.

14. René Descartes, "Fifth Meditation" and "Sixth Meditation," in *Meditations on First Philosophy*, in *The Philosophical Works of Descartes*, trans. E. S. Haldane and G. R. T. Ross, 2 vols. (Cambridge: Cambridge University Press, 1968), 1:191.

15. Descartes, "Fifth Meditation" and "Sixth Meditation," in *Meditations*, 1:185 (italics mine).

16. Descartes, "Sixth Meditation," in *Meditations*, 1:191 (italics mine).

17. Knowledge of the empirical self is no exception. For, Kant insisted, determination of the self and its "inner experience, depends upon . . . The reality of outer sense [which] is thus necessarily bound up with inner sense, if experience in general is to be possible at all" (Kant, *CPR*, Bxl–Bxli, pp. 35 n–36 n; compare B409, p. 370).

18. René Descartes, "Principle LVII," in *The Principles of Philosophy*, trans. J. Blom, from French version; see Sherover, *HET*, 582–83 (italics mine).

19. Immanuel Kant, *Kritik der praktischen Vernunft*, ed. J. Kopper (Stuttgart: Philipp Reclam, 1966), 210–11. (Hereafter cited as *KPrV*.)

20. Kant, *KPrV*, 217–18.

21. See Kant, *KPrV*, 196, 204, 226, and 197 n (italics mine).

22. Immanuel Kant, *Religion within the Limits of Reason Alone*, trans. T. M. Greene and H. H. Hudson (Chicago: Open Court, 1934), 63, 70.

23. Kant, *Logic*, 98.

24. Kant, *KPrV*, 193.

25. Kant, *Logic*, 94.

26. One might note the continuing import that Kant attached to temporal perdurance. In the "Inaugural Dissertation," for example, one finds him arguing that experiential *continuity*, as the principle of the possibility of change "resides in the concept of time [and] supposes the perdurability of the subject [*supponit perdurabilitatem subjecti*]" (IV, "Scholium").

27. This going beyond the phenomenal in terms of freedom is not only necessary but also appropriate; in the First *Critique* Kant maintained: "Reason has in respect of its *practical* employment the right to postulate what in the field of mere speculation it can have no right to assume without sufficient proof" (Kant, *CPR*, A776=B804, p. 617).

28. Kant, *CPR*, A177=B219, p. 209.

29. See Immanuel Kant, *Kritik der reinen Vernunft* (Hamburg: Felix Meiner), A182=B224, p. 235; compare *CPR*, p. 212. (*Kritik* hereafter cited as *KRV*.) The authority for "usual" translation is *Cassell's New German and English Dictionary* (New York: Funk and Wagnalls, 1936, 1939). The final quotation is from R. B. Farrell, *A Dictionary of German Synonyms* (Cambridge: Cambridge University Press, 1953), 384 n.

30. Compare H. J. Paton, *Kant's Metaphysic of Experience* (London: George Allen and Unwin, 1961), 2:163 n. 4.

31. Kant, *KRV*, A183=B226, p. 236 (see *CPR*, p. 214).

32. Kant, *KRV*, A183–84=B227, and A185=B228–29 (see *CPR*, pp. 214–15).

33. In this regard one might consider the divergent renderings of Kant's definition of *Realität*, in *KRV*, A143=B182, p. 201 nn. 2 and 3.

34. Kant, *KRV*, A200=B245, p. 250 (compare *CPR*, p. 226).

35. See Descartes, "Third Meditation," in *Meditations*, 1:168; René Descartes, *Objections and Replies*, in *Philosophical Works*, 2:56 and 219.

36. See Kant, *CPR*, A292=B348, p. 295, and note 37 below.

37. Ibid., A147=B185–87, pp. 186–87.

38. Charles M. Sherover, "Kant's Transcendental Object and Heidegger's *Nichts*," *Journal of the History of Philosophy* 7 (October 1969): 413–22.

39. See Kant, *CPR*, A249, p. 266; see also A251, p. 268, and A253, p. 271.

40. Paton, *Kant's Metaphysic*, 2:443.

41. See, for example, Immanuel Kant, "An Inquiry into the Distinctness of the Principles of Natural Theology and Morals," in Kant, *Critique of Practical Reason and Other Writings in Moral Philosophy*, ed. and trans. Lewis White Beck (Chicago: University of Chicago Press, 1949), 263, 266, 269–70. (Hereafter cited as *CPrR*.)

42. Immanuel Kant, *Anthropology from a Pragmatic Point of View*, trans. Mary J. Gregor (The Hague: Martinus Nijhoff, 1974), 59–60.

Essay 4. Time and Ethics: How Is Morality Possible?

This essay was originally published in *The Study of Time*, vol. 2, ed. J. T. Fraser and N. Lawrence (New York and Heidelberg: Springer, 1975).

1. See Kant, *CPR*, A147=B187, p. 187, together with the chapter entitled "System of All Principles of Pure Understanding." Taken together, it becomes quite clear that the Kantian categories are derived from or rooted in what Kant described as the four possible modes of temporal experience and that the Kantian principles of human knowledge are explicitly temporalized versions of those same categories.

2. Kant, *CPrR*, 224–25.

3. Ibid.

4. The "Typic" (to which N. Lawrence has kindly redirected my attention) hardly serves as the practical counterpart of the "Schematism" in the First *Critique*; in fact, Kant explicitly distinguished the two. Yet what is needed is a "moral

schematism" which would function as the fount of a temporal "procedure of the imagination" (compare *CPrR*, 177) for practical reason as the "Schematism" does for cognitive reason. For Kant's own explanations of his moral doctrines always involve a temporalizing imagination to bring and test possible imperatives *in concreto*. Yet apparently because the "Schematism" was tied, in the First *Critique*, to that notion of time which yields the determinism of the natural world, he eschewed its use and could not replace it in the realm of moral freedom.

5. Strangely enough, as Locke for one pointed out, Aristotle did not explicitly bring space into the discussion of time as measure. But it was certainly presupposed. His essay on time in the *Physics* was quite clearly concerned with time in terms of the measuring of the motion of physical entities; this seems especially clear from section 12 of that essay. It even seems true in his brief (and generally overlooked) discussion of psychological time (compare Aristotle, *On the Senses*, 448a–448b).

6. Compare Kant, *CPR*, A532–33=B560–61, p. 464.

7. G. W. Leibniz, "The Principles of Nature and of Grace, Based on Reason," in *Leibniz Selections*, ed. Philip P. Wiener (New York: Charles Scribner's Sons, 1951), 530.

8. Compare Immanuel Kant, *Groundwork of the Metaphysic of Morals*, trans. H. J. Paton (New York: Harper and Row), 115. (Hereafter cited as *GMM*.)

9. Compare Kant, *GMM*, 114, 126; Kant, *CPrR*, 165, 175, 200, 236: see also the discussion of the "Third Antinomy" in Kant, *CPR*.

10. Kant obviously could only have taken "prior" in a logical sense here; but if the capacity for free decision, and motivating action, is not also, in some sense, temporally as well as logically prior, it is not clear just what could be meant in any concrete instance. But, if there must be some temporal meaning somehow implicit, then the strict alleged nontemporality of moral reason collapses.

11. Kant, *GMM*, 119.

12. Compare Kant, *CPR*, A98–110. Kant never really pursued this, although, in view of the principle of the Copernican Revolution, he really was obligated to do so in the "Subjective Deduction," which was concerned with the dynamics of experiencing rather than with the "external world" as it is *already* structured in our interpretive knowledge of it. That he abandoned the "Subjective Deduction" in the Second Edition of the *Critique*, after but sketching it out in the First Edition, serves as a prime example of a great thinker who did not see the import of his own insight.

13. Compare Kant, *CPR*, A98–110.

14. For an indication of this temporal analysis of understanding generally, see Charles M. Sherover, *Heidegger, Kant, and Time* (Bloomington and London: Indiana University Press, 1971), esp. pp. 142–70.

15. See notes 2 and 3 above.

Essay 5. Experiential Time and the Religious Concern

This essay was originally presented at the Twenty-seventh Summer Conference ("Change, Aging, and the Passing of Time") of the Institute on Religion in an Age of Science, held at Star Island, New Hampshire, July 26–August 2, 1980. The author is indebted to both Jeannette Hopkins and Karl E. Peters for their helpful suggestions. The essay was originally published in *Zygon* 16, no. 4 (1981).

1. Saint Augustine, *The Confessions*, trans. Rex Warner (New York: New American Library, 1963), 267.

2. See, for example, Paul Tillich, *Dynamics of Faith* (New York: Harper and Row, 1958), esp. chap. 1.

3. Kant, *CPR*, A805=B833, p. 635.

4. William James, *A Pluralistic Universe* (New York: Longmans, Green, 1909), 254.

5. Alfred North Whitehead, *The Concept of Nature* (Ann Arbor: University of Michigan Press, 1957), 73.

6. Plotinus, *The Enneads*, 3.7.4.

7. This sketch is largely based on the analyses of temporal experience by Martin Heidegger in his *Kant and the Problem of Metaphysics*, trans. J. S. Churchill (Bloomington: Indiana University Press, 1962), and in his *Being and Time*. For a more detailed elucidation, see Sherover, *Heidegger, Kant, and Time*, esp. chaps. 7 and 8.

8. See Thomas S. Kuhn, *The Structure of Scientific Revolutions* (Chicago: University of Chicago Press, 1970).

9. From the standpoint of a phenomenological examination of human temporality, it is difficult to see how the notion of an eternally timeless present— with neither pastness nor futurity entering into it—can be rendered meaningful in any human sense. Its postulation seems to be an instance of negative theology: Heidegger, for instance, in *Kant and the Problem of Metaphysics*, argues that the Greek postulation of this idea can be explained as an inverse projection of a protest against temporality; see p. 249.

10. Saint Anselm, "Proslogium," in *Basic Writings*, trans. J. S. Deane (LaSalle, Ill.: Open Court, 1962), 7–8.

11. The classic statement of this view is that of Saint Thomas Aquinas: "Now because we cannot know what God is, but rather what He is not, we have no means for considering how God is, but rather how He is not" (*The Summa Theologica*, trans. A. C. Pegis [New York: Random House, 1945], 25 [pts. 1, 3]). The philosophic question, of course, is how we may be able to have knowledge of negative attributes if we are unable first to know of any commonality. To seek to do this by means of analogic reasoning does not appear to overcome the problem, for one cannot judge the validity or legitimacy of an analogy unless one already has separate knowledge of each of the entities that the analogy compares in terms of a presumably common, or similar, quality.

12. Aristotle, *Nicomachean Ethics*, 1139b. One might consult the *Metaphysics*, esp. 1074b–1075a, where it is plainly suggested that were God to have knowledge of change, this "would be change for the worse" and would destroy God's self-sufficient perfection. One could add one other temporal consideration to the attack on omniscience: if the future is constituted of genuinely open possibilities, it is thereby unresolved, and if in principle unresolved, then even divine foreknowledge cannot be complete.

13. The pragmatic force of Plato's famous dictum that time is but "the moving image of eternity" is to make sequential time the principle of order in the world of nature. See Sherover, *HET,* 15–20.

14. James, *A Pluralistic Universe,* 311.

15. See John Stuart Mill, *Theism* (Indianapolis: Bobbs-Merrill, 1957), esp. chaps. 1 and 2. This generally ignored essay presents an important analysis of the concept of deity. In many ways, it anticipates some of the issues developed in the writings of Charles Hartshorne, particularly in *Man's Vision of God and the Logic of Theism* (New York: Harper and Bros., 1941), which suggested several themes I touch on here.

16. Kant, *KPrV,* 217–18.

17. Martin Heidegger, *Sein und Zeit,* 7th ed. (Tübingen: Max Niemeyer, 1957), 427 n. 1; compare Heidegger, *Kant and the Problem of Metaphysics.*

18. See William Ellery Channing, "Likeness to God," in *The Works* (Boston: American Unitarian Association, 1888), 291–301. Channing's essay presents a cogent criticism of the *via negativa* of traditional theology and argues for the necessity of a concept of God commensurate with human predicates, a view which is very close to that expressed by Alfred North Whitehead in his King's Chapel lectures published under the title *Religion in the Making* (New York: Macmillan, 1926) and, from a quite different philosophic perspective, by the Russian religious existentialist Nicolas Berdyaev.

Essay 6. Are We *in* Time?

This essay was originally published in *International Philosophical Quarterly* 26, no. 1 (1986).

1. Isn't it the spatial metaphor that prompts the question "what is outside of time?" To various forms of this question, the tradition has responded with two different answers encapsulated in the one word "eternity." But is either really adequate?

If we accept the Platonic answer that eternity is timeless, we can neither give this notion any existential meaning nor can we explain how that which is immune to time itself engenders time and then how such "descended" time accords with its source; and, despite Augustine's disclaimer, we cannot really help asking about what was before it.

If we accept the amending assurance that eternity is but endless time, we face in temporal terms the infinite regress that had been foreclosed in logical terms, a problem only compounded by the contemporary penchant to reduce all explanation to that of efficient (mechanistic) causality, itself a reduction of the present to the past. In any case, a spatially conceived eternal time presents a picture that defies imaginative comprehension: a container without containing boundaries, a continuum without genesis or goal, a rationality devoid of any justificatory teleology.

2. See Descartes, *Meditations,* 1:168; and René Descartes, "Arguments Demonstrating the Existence of God" ("Addendum to Reply to Objection II"), in *Axiom II,* in *Philosophical Works,* 2:56.

3. R. G. Collingwood, "Some Perplexities about Time," in Sherover, *HET,* 561.

4. See John Locke, *Essay Concerning the Human Understanding,* ed. A. C. Fraser, 2 vols. (New York: Dover, 1894), 2.14, esp. sec. 14.

5. Alfred North Whitehead, *The Concept of Nature* (Cambridge: Cambridge University Press, 1920), 66.

6. See Aristotle, *On the Senses,* 448a.

7. Even Kant abandoned it; see, for example, *KPrV,* 193; and compare *CPrR,* 224–25: "But if pure reason of itself can be and really is practical, as the consciousness of the moral law shows it to be, it is only one and the same reason which judges a priori by principles, whether for theoretical or for practical purposes."

8. Josiah Royce, *The World and the Individual* (New York: Macmillan, 1904), 2:123.

9. Aristotle, *Nicomachean Ethics,* 1139b.

10. Royce, *World and the Individual,* 2:180.

11. Certainly the heliocentric picture of the solar system runs counter to naive common sense; so, also, does an electro-atomic theory of physical matter.

12. Prime examples being Martin Heidegger's *The Question Concerning Technology,* trans. William Lovitt (New York: Harper and Row, 1977); and William Barrett's *The Illusion of Technique* (Garden City: Doubleday, 1978).

13. See William James, *The Principles of Psychology* (New York: Henry Holt, 1890), 1:XV.

14. See, for example, "The Law of the Mind," esp. par. 127–32; "What Pragmatism Is," esp. par. 422 ff.; and "Issues of Pragmaticism," esp. par. 458 ff., in Charles Sanders Peirce, *Collected Papers of Charles Sanders Peirce,* ed. Charles Hartshorne and Paul Weiss (Cambridge: Harvard University Press, 1934), vols. 6 and 5.

15. Royce, *World and the Individual,* 2:218.

16. Compare Kant, *KPrV,* 217–18; Kant, *CPrR,* 219; and Heidegger, *Sein und Zeit,* 427 n. 1.

17. If we seek to trace current philosophic outlooks back to originating sources, we might perhaps consider the view expounded here (and especially in arguments by Peirce and Royce) as something of a development of the pre-Socratic doctrine of Empedocles and Anaxagoras that "like knows like"; i.e., if all our cognizing and acting are temporally constituted, then the only legitimate referential objects of our thinking must be conceived by us as somehow temporally constituted.

18. In its hard form, a theory of internal relations must insist (regarding formulations by means of symbolic logic) that, in the two propositions taken as true, "p and p" and "if p, then not q," the p cannot be the same p—just because its particular relation with q enters into it as part of its definition, i.e., its relations are not separable from but internal to it. Perhaps needless to add, whatever criticisms of the traditional logic one might have, on this score, its foundation in a theory of definition by genus-and-difference rather than arbitrary stipulation at least suggests something of a theory of internalized predicates in terms of its presumption of the hierarchy of being.

19. This kind of use seems suggested by Martin Heidegger in *What Is a Thing?* trans. Barton and Deutsch (Chicago: Henry Regnery, 1967), 232–42.

Essay 7. Perspectivity and the Principle of Continuity

This essay was originally published in *The Study of Time,* vol. 4, ed. J. T. Fraser and N. Lawrence (New York and Heidelberg: Springer, 1981).

1. Charles S. Peirce, "Issues of Pragmaticism," in *Values in a Universe of Chance: Selected Writings of Charles S. Peirce,* ed. P. Wiener (New York: Doubleday Anchor, 1958), 223; R. H. Lotze, *Metaphysic,* trans. and ed. Bernard Bosanquet, 2nd ed. (Oxford: Oxford University Press, 1887), sec. 149, in Sherover, *HET,* 203.

2. Aristotle, *Physics,* 219a–220a.

3. George Santayana, *Scepticism and Animal Faith* (New York: Dover, 1955), 230.

4. David Hume, *An Enquiry Concerning Human Understanding,* 12.3.

5. G. W. Leibniz, in Sherover, *HET,* 134.

6. Immanuel Kant, "Inaugural Dissertation," sec. 14.4, in Sherover, *HET,* 146.

7. Ibid., sec. 14.6, in Sherover, *HET,* 149.

8. Ibid., "Scholium," in Sherover, *HET,* 152. The original Latin reads: "supponit perdurabillitatem subjecti."

9. Sherover, *HET,* 351. Although James does not cite Kant, this thesis follows directly from the conjunction of two key sections of Kant's First *Critique,* namely, the "Schematism" and the "Highest Principle of all Synthetic Judgments"; see Kant, *CPR,* A137=B176–A147=B187, pp. 180–87; and A154=B193–A158=B197, pp. 191–94.

10. Since Aristotle, the concepts of "potentiality" and "possibility" have been generally confused. A current project of mine is an attempt to disengage their separate meanings. Briefly for the present purpose, one might take "potentiality" in the sense of defining capability (whether or not realized), for example, "An acorn has the potentiality of becoming an oak tree"; in contrast, a "possibility" would refer to a future set of conditions which must be met if that potentiality is to be realized, for example, "Because this acorn is being eaten by a squirrel, it does not have the possibility of growing into an oak tree." In these terms any present actuality would be seen as the merging of potentiality and possibility, in Leibnizian terms of the "necessary" and the "sufficient," in Heideggerian terms, of the "ontological" and the "ontic." But note that both within the standpoint of the present point to ways in which futurity is to be understood.

11. See, for example, Plato, *Theaetetus,* 183–86; Royce, *World and the Individual,* 2:II–VI; Martin Heidegger, *Being and Time,* trans. John Macquarrie and Edward Robinson (London: SCM, 1962), esp. sec. 41.

12. The "existential analytic," i.e., Division One of Heidegger's *Being and Time,* is a rigorous working-out of what this primordial future-orientedness involves in terms of an understanding of human activity; Division Two of this work seeks to explicate the temporal dimensions that are involved.

13. Descartes, *Meditations,* esp. the "Fourth Meditation."

Essay 8. *Res Cogitans:* The Time of Mind

This essay was originally published in *The Study of Time*, vol. 6, ed. J. T. Fraser (Madison, Conn.: International Universities Press, 1989).

1. This, I think, still stands even as we accept the thesis (implied by both Leibniz and Rousseau and explicitly developed by Royce and Heidegger) that the individuality of thought presupposes the sociality of human be-ing; that is, the "I" always and necessarily presupposes the "we." To demonstrate this thesis together with its basic compatibility with the Cartesian principle would, however, in the context of this essay, take us far afield.

2. Note Descartes's statement at the end of his "Fifth Meditation," together with the opening of the "Sixth," which limits our knowledge of "material things . . . [only] in so far as they are considered as the objects of pure mathematics" (Descartes, *Meditations*, 1:185) This proposal, that we can only understand the world of things to the extent that they meet (mathematical) ideas within our own minds which we necessarily use to think about them, does indeed foreshadow Kant's Copernican revolution: we can only come to know things insofar as they can appear to and meet the categorial structuring of our human modes of sensibility and understanding.

3. In view of Descartes's subsequent description of God as a transcendent mind beyond *our* understanding, we may well ask whether this is not but a secularization of the medieval doctrine of "negative theology."

4. Important to note is the comprehensive nature of thinking as encompassing virtually any act of consciousness as one that "doubts, affirms, denies, that knows a few things, that is ignorant of many, that wishes, that desires, that also imagines and perceives." See Descartes, *Meditations*, 1:157.

5. See Descartes, "Third Meditation," in *Meditations*, 1:168; Descartes, "Arguments Demonstrating the Existence of God (Addendum to Reply to Objection II)," in *Axiom II*, in *Philosophical Works*, 2:56; and Descartes, "Reply to Objections, V," in *Philosophical Works*, 2:219, par. 9.

6. Locke, *Essay Concerning the Human Understanding*, 2.14.3.

7. G. W. Leibniz, *The New Essays on the Human Understanding*, trans. A. G. Langley (LaSalle: Open Court, 1949), 4.7.7.

8. G. W. Leibniz, "Critical Remarks Concerning the General Part of Descartes' Principles" (1.7), in *Monadology and Other Philosophical Essays*, ed. P. Schrecker and A. Schrecker (Indianapolis: Bobbs-Merrill, 1965), 25.

9. Kant, *CPR*, A146–47=B186–87.

10. The term "transcendentally" is meant in a generally Kantian sense—as those interpretive categories which are employed, even when unexplicated but implicitly present while unwittingly presumed, in one's particular thinking—as founding the possibility of the particular thoughts one develops to understand one's own perceptions.

11. Hans-Georg Gadamer, *Truth and Method* (New York: Seabury, 1975), 107 ff.

12. This meaning will differ as it involves moral or prudential judgment—but such differentiations, important as they are intrinsically, are not germane to

the present discussion. For some further discussion of this, see essay 4 of this book. For a discussion of some of the sociopolitical inferences to be drawn from this phenomenological description, see essay 10.

13. The continuing allure of Platonism may well be, as Heidegger once suggested, a sign of a continuing attempt to escape from temporality. On any kind of Platonism, it is hard to see how one can explain why or how a completely atemporal realm of true "reality" could or should bring a temporal order into being. Even Plato could only do so by invoking a demiurgic myth.

14. Kant, *CPR*, A218=B265, A225=B273.

Essay 9. Toward Experiential Metaphysics: Radical Temporalism

This essay was originally published in *New Essays in Metaphysics,* ed. Robert Cummings Neville (Albany: SUNY Press, 1987).

1. Charles S. Peirce, "Letters to Lady Welby" (May 20, 1911), in *Values in a Universe of Chance: Selected Writings of Charles S. Peirce,* ed. P. Wiener (New York: Doubleday Anchor, 1958), 426.

2. Kant's word for "looking out" was *Anschauung,* usually translated as "intuition," and was argued by him to be the determinating frame of all the specific content of empirical knowledge.

3. See Jean-Paul Sartre, "Existentialism Is a Humanism," reprinted in many collections.

4. Leibniz, *New Essays on the Human Understanding,* 4.7.7; Leibniz, *Leibniz Selections,* 295.

5. Locke, *Essay Concerning the Human Understanding,* 2.14.4.16.

6. This would seem to be a prime point of Rousseau's *Of the Social Contract,* considered as a phenomenological description of the human condition even if expressed as the metaphysics of a justifiable democratic politics. See, for example, *Of the Social Contract,* ed. Charles M. Sherover (New York: Harper and Row, 1984), xxv and par. 55–57, 79–86.

7. See Royce, *World and the Individual,* 2:v.

8. See, for example, Donald R. Griffin, *Animal Thinking* (Cambridge: Harvard University Press, 1984).

9. Aristotle, in Book Delta (the "Lexicon" of the *Metaphysics*), offered what James had called "his most revolutionary stroke," the notion of potentiality; but Aristotle certainly left the distinction between potentiality and possibility anything but clear.

10. If the appearance of freedom is so radically discordant from the presumptive determinist reality, if our experiences of free decision are not real but discordantly illusionary, they are, by definition, cognitively irrelevant. If our own experience of free decision is hopelessly illusionary, how can we seriously attend to what appears within its outlook? A complete determinism poses an unbridgeable gulf between our own experience of intellectual freedom and an allegedly complete determinist world in which it claims to function. As such, any doctrine of complete denial of free thinking and decision can only yield a

cognitive skepticism that, in principle, cannot be transcended by free human thought.

11. G. W. Leibniz, "New System of Nature," 16, in Leibniz, *Leibniz Selections*, 116. This, indeed, seems to have been Kant's point in removing freedom from the realm of phenomenal appearance to that of the noumenally real. On this ground, all the standard determinist arguments are, in principle, illegitimate. Because of this sweeping claim, it would seem methodologically incumbent for the determinist to show that this separation should be ruled out before he asks us to attend seriously to his arguments, which only function within what the Kantian regards as the phenomenal realm in which efficacious causal explanation is but a necessary interpretive procedure.

12. See, for example, Kant, *CPrR*, 118, 153, and 224–25. For a crucial extension of this, see note 14 below.

13. Martin Heidegger, *The Metaphysical Foundations of Logic*, trans. Michael Heim (Bloomington: Indiana University Press, 1984), 19–20.

14. See Kant's *The Metaphysical Elements of Justice* (pt. 1 of *The Metaphysic of Morals*, trans. J. Ladd [Indianapolis: Bobbs-Merrill, 1965], 56) for a crucial statement about the concrete knowledge, out of freedom, of physical (proprietary) things not subject to the stringencies of the First *Critique:* " . . . if there is to be anything externally yours or mine [that is, any property], we must assume that intelligible possession (*possessio noumenon*) is possible. Thus, empirical possession is only possession in appearance (*possessio phaenomenon*), although in this connection the object that I possess is not regarded as an appearance, as it was in the Transcendental Analytic [of the *Critique of Pure Reason*], but as a thing-in-itself. That work was concerned with reason as it relates to theoretical knowledge of the nature of things and with how far it extends. Here, on the other hand, we are concerned with reason as it relates to the practical determination of the will in accordance with laws of freedom, and its object may be known either through the senses or merely through pure reason."

15. If we take modern physics seriously in its assertion that both light and sound "take time" to travel (i.e., manifest durational reality), we can only see and hear what is, in the most literal sense, already in the past by the time we are conscious of being aware of what these senses claim to tell us in the momentary present. Were classical English empiricism correct in its claim that our abstract or general ideas are only generalizations out of past sensory reports, then the ideas of which we are conscious could only be generalizations about the past, about what is over and done with—already reduced to historic actuality. Without some kind of—in the most literal sense—a priori knowledge, we then have no rational basis for projecting such generalizations into the immediate present, much less the future. As such they may indeed provide grounds for historical understanding but no ground whatsoever for deliberation or decision. It is for this reason that the "empirical" tradition so easily comes to terms with a determinist metaphysic, whether on an efficaciously causal or logical plane: its epistemology, being entirely genetic, can do no more than trace the present as an extension of the determinate past by efficacious sequence; and its methodology, bound by

what is already given, can do no more than trace the logical implications of its accepted premises; on neither level can it transcend the actual given and face within its own terms, contingency, chance, or real possibility—which is to say, futurity—with any philosophic seriousness.

16. Immanuel Kant, *Critique of Judgment,* trans. Meredith (Oxford: Clarendon, 1928), 141, 149.

17. Kant, *Critique of Judgment,* 99.

18. In this regard, Peirce may well have been true to the underlying spirit (if not all the letters) of the Critical philosophy by merging Kant's distinction between the pragmatic and the practical into the pragmatical. (See Kant, *CPR,* A800=B828.)

19. One has merely to consider what human industry has already done to the enveloping atmosphere of the Earth. While it has transformed the level of human living upon the Earth, it has orbited a "junkyard in the sky," consisting of the debris of investigatory projectiles. The changes in the human organism (so far) result less from deliberate intrusions onto genetic inheritance than from the effects of man-made environmental changes intruding upon us as environmental inhabitants.

20. In contrast to a naive pragmatism, workability, then, is not the nature of truth; but workability is surely, as Royce had urged, at least one essential criterion of truth: for any statement about workability implicitly says not only that any truth must harmonize with the world but also that "the world is such that within it this procedure works to produce that result."

21. See, for example, Heraclitus, frag. 67.

22. As but one of Kant's intimations of this, see the closing passage of *Critique of Judgment,* 149: "Freedom is the one and only conception of the supersensible which (owing to the causality implied in it) proves its objective reality in nature. . . . Consequently the conception of freedom, as the root-conception of all unconditionally-practical laws, can extend reason beyond the bounds to which every natural, or theoretical, conception must remain hopelessly restricted."

23. See Heraclitus, frag. 54; compare Aristotle, *Ethica Eudemia,* 125a, 25.

24. Because human experience cannot attain to any insight into eternity, whether it be construed with Aristotle as "all unending time" or with Plato as literally devoid of the temporal—we have no way of knowing what such "principles," or their ontological ground, might be beyond the horizon of possible temporally formed human experience. To say that they are "trans-temporal" is a more limited claim, i.e., that they appear to function in any temporal juncture, at any "moment" of our experiential time.

25. Is this not at least the implicit meaning of Kant's "Highest Principle of Synthetic Judgments"? Its key sentence reads: "The conditions of the *possibility of experience* in general are at the same time the conditions of the *possibility of the objects of experience*" (Kant, *CPR,* A158=B197).

26. The ultimate object of that speculative thought in what I term a philosophical "cosmology" that seeks rational insight into transcendent beings is, of course, God. That such belief can only properly emerge from a "moral teleology" was argued by Kant (see *Critique of Judgment,* 144 ff.); but Kant argued that

our conception of God must necessarily accord with the temporality of the human outlook, even though that *conception can not* be taken as truly descriptive (see Kant, *KPrV*, 217–18). Quite independently, Heidegger urges a similar outlook: "If God's eternity may be 'construed' philosophically, then it only can be understood as a primal and unending temporality" (with the explicit consequent that the tradition of negative theology is thereby reopened). See Heidegger, *Sein und Zeit*, 427 n. 1.

Essay 10. The Temporality of the Common Good: Futurity and Freedom

This essay was originally published in *The Review of Metaphysics* 37, no. 3 (March 1984).

1. Niccolò Machiavelli, *Discourses on the First Ten Books of Titus Livius*, in *The Prince and Discourses* (New York: Modern Library, 1940), 3.1, p. 297.

2. All citations from Aristotle in this essay are from the Ross translation published by Oxford University Press.

3. Josiah Royce, *The Problem of Christianity* (New York: Macmillan, 1913), 2:37.

4. Josiah Royce, *Studies of Good and Evil* (New York: D. Appleton, 1908), 208.

5. Royce, *The Problem of Christianity*, 2:64.

6. Paul Ricoeur, "The Political Paradox," in *History and Truth*, trans. C. A. Kelbley (Evanston: Northwestern University Press, 1965), 250. In this same essay, Ricoeur defends the thesis (which I implicitly invoke) that "Rousseau is at bottom Aristotle . . . in voluntarist language"; compare 253.

7. Notably, it was ancient practice (in Greece as in China) to divide day and night into twelve hours between sunrise and sunset, their "durations" thus varying with the season. It was only in the 1550s, coincidentally with the rise of the mechanical clock, that there arose our present presumption that the twenty-four-hour cycle is divided into 1,440 evenly paced minutes. This comparatively recent turn to a completely quantifiable common time (which again augments the priority of the social in our individual outlooks) may be a root of the existentialist protest against technology (as also of the recent arrival of the concept of alienation), for the mechanistic time of a worker tending a machine contrasts radically in his everyday life with the qualitative flow of his leisure. Compare, for example, Georges Gurvitch, *The Spectrum of Social Time* (Dordrecht: D. Reidel, 1964), esp. xxii–xxv.

8. Kant, *Anthropology*, 59.

9. I am using the two often confused terms "freedom" and "liberty" in the sense of "positive freedom (i.e., opportunity)" and "negative liberty (i.e., absence of restraints)" as explicated by T. H. Green: "what I call freedom in the positive sense: . . . the liberation of the powers of all men equally for contributions to a common good" (*Liberal Legislation and Freedom of Contract*, in T. H. Green, *Works* [London: Longmans Green, 1911], 3:372); compare "On the Different Senses of 'Freedom' as Applied to the Will and to the Moral Progress of

Man," in *Works*, 2:308-33. For a rather different analysis of these two concepts in opposition to much of my argument here, see Isaiah Berlin, "Two Concepts of Liberty," in *Four Essays on Liberty* (London: Oxford University Press, 1969), 118-72.

10. Josiah Royce, *Outlines of Psychology* (New York: Macmillan, 1903), 302, compare 325.

11. Martin Heidegger, *Vom Wesen des Grundes*, 5th ed. (Frankfurt: Vittorio Klostermann, 1965), 53.

12. Plotinus, *The Enneads*, trans. S. MacKenna, 4th rev. ed. (New York: Pantheon Books, 1969), 3.7, p. 225.

13. G. W. Leibniz, *The Political Writings of Leibniz*, trans. and ed. P. Riley (Cambridge: Cambridge University Press, 1972), 26, 29, 23, 24 n, 24 n, 25.

14. Alexander Hamilton, "The Report on the Subject of Manufactures," in *The Papers of Alexander Hamilton*, ed. H. C. Syrett and J. E. Cooke (New York: Columbia University Press, 1966), 10:267, 340, 275; compare Jacob E. Cooke, *Alexander Hamilton* (New York: Charles Scribner's Sons, 1982), esp. 99-102.

15. Machiavelli, *Discourses*, 1.4.

Essay 11. The Process of Polity

This essay was originally published in *The Study of Time*, vol. 7, ed. J. T. Fraser (Madison, Conn.: International Universities Press, 1992).

1. Montesquieu, *The Spirit of the Laws: A Compendium of the First English Edition*, ed. D. W. Carrithers (Berkeley: University of California Press, 1977), 15.1-3, pp. 257-60; Rousseau, *Of the Social Contract*, 1.4, pp. 8-12.

2. All quotes in this essay from Aristotle's *Nicomachean Ethics* and *Politics* are from *The Complete Works of Aristotle*, vol. 2., ed. Jonathan Barnes (Princeton: Princeton University Press, 1984).

3. As the Italian political theorist Gaetano Mosca noted, it was Rousseau who is "the real parent of the doctrine of popular sovereignty and hence of modern representative democracy" (Mosca, *The Ruling Class*, trans. H. D. Kahn [New York: McGraw-Hill, 1939], 254). With regard to the American experience, there are passages in *The Federalist* that suggest Rousseau's influence; but more to the point, perhaps, is that Montesquieu's principles, which provided the structure of the American Constitution, were compromised on the issue of slavery, a compromise which led de Tocqueville in the 1830s to predict the inevitability of the American Civil War.

4. Kant, *CPR*, A316=B373, p. 312.

5. Alexander Hamilton, James Madison, and John Jay, *The Federalist*, ed. J. E. Cooke (Middletown, Conn.: Wesleyan University Press, 1961), No. 62, p. 421.

6. For a fuller presentation of the historical development of this concept of polity, its crucial concept of a *temporalized* constitutionalism, and the ensuing repercussions and implications for all social theory as well as correlation with other themes touched on in this essay, see Charles M. Sherover, *Time, Freedom, and the Common Good* (Albany: SUNY Press, 1989).

7. Paul Ricoeur, *Political and Social Essays*, ed. D. Stewart and J. Bien (Athens: Ohio University Press, 1974), 268.

8. Edmund Burke, "Speech on the Representation of the Commons in Parliament," in *Selected Writings and Speeches*, ed. P. J. Stanlis (Chicago: Henry Regnery, 1963), 330 (italics mine).

9. Thucydides, *History of the Peloponnesian War*, trans. R. Warner (London: Penguin Books, 1954), 144.

10. Madison, *The Federalist*, No. 14, p. 84; in Sherover, *Time, Freedom*, 156 ff.

11. As one student of mine phrased the problem in very contemporary terms, who has the time, much less the dedication, to do nothing else but watch C-Span all day long?

12. Rousseau, *Of the Social Contract*, 3.4, par. 197, p. 164.

13. Ibid., par. 201–4, p. 65.

14. See *The Federalist*, especially Nos. 1, 9, 10, 14, 31, 37, 39, 51, 63, 71.

15. Hamilton, *The Federalist*, No. 78, p. 523.

16. Peirce, *Collected Papers*, 5:184.

17. Ibid., 281–82.

18. Royce, *World and the Individual*, 2:125.

19. Ibid., 136.

20. Machiavelli, *Discourses*, 1.3, p. 117.

Works Cited

Anselm, Saint. *Proslogium*. In *Basic Writings*. Trans. J. S. Deane. LaSalle, Ill.: Open Court, 1962.

Aquinas, Saint Thomas. *Basic Writings of Saint Thomas Aquinas*. 2 vols. Trans. Anton C. Pegis. New York: Random House, 1945.

Aristotle. *The Complete Works of Aristotle*. Ed. Jonathan Barnes. 2 vols. Princeton: Princeton University Press, 1984.

Augustine, Saint. *Confessions*. Trans. Rex Warner. New York: New American Library, 1963.

Barrett, William. *The Illusion of Technique*. Garden City, N.Y.: Doubleday, 1978.

Berlin, Isaiah. *Four Essays on Liberty*. London: Oxford University Press, 1969.

Burke, Edmund. *Selected Writings and Speeches*. Ed. Peter J. Stanlis. Chicago: Regnery, 1963.

Cassell's New German and English Dictionary. New York: Funk and Wagnalls, 1936, 1939.

Channing, William Ellery. *The Works*. Boston: American Unitarian Association, 1888.

Collingwood, R. G. "Some Perplexities About Time." In *The Human Experience of Time; The Development of Its Philosophical Meaning*. Ed. Charles Sherover. Evanston, Ill.: Northwestern University Press, 2001.

Cooke, Jacob E. *Alexander Hamilton*. New York: Charles Scribner's Sons, 1982.

Descartes, René. *Meditations on First Philosophy*. In *The Philosophical Works of Descartes*. Trans. E. S. Haldane and G. R. T. Ross. 2 vols. Cambridge: Cambridge University Press, 1968.

———. *Objections and Replies*. In *The Philosophical Works of Descartes*. Trans. E. S. Haldane and G. R. T. Ross. 2 vols. Cambridge: Cambridge University Press, 1967.

———. *The Principles of Philosophy*. In *The Philosophical Works of Descartes*. Trans. E. S. Haldane and G. R. T. Ross. 2 vols. Cambridge: Cambridge University Press, 1967.

Farrell, R. B. *A Dictionary of German Syntax*. Cambridge: Cambridge University Press, 1953.

Freeman, Kathleen. *Ancilla to the Pre-Socratic Philosophers: A Complete Translation of the Fragments in Diels, Fragmente Der Vorsokratiker*. Cambridge: Harvard University Press, 1957.

Gadamer, Hans-Georg. *Truth and Method*. New York: Seabury, 1975.

Green, Thomas Hill. *Works of Thomas Hill Green*. 3 vols. London: Longmans, Green, 1911.

Griffin, Donald R. *Animal Thinking*. Cambridge: Harvard University Press, 1984.

Gurvitch, Georges. *The Spectrum of Social Time*. Dordrecht: D. Reidel, 1964.

Hamilton, Alexander. "The Report on the Subject of Manufactures." In vol. 10, *The Papers of Alexander Hamilton*. Ed. H. C. Syrett and J. E. Cooke. New York: Columbia University Press, 1972.

Hamilton, Alexander, James Madison, and John Jay. *The Federalist*. Ed. J. E. Cooke. Middletown, Conn.: Wesleyan University Press, 1961.

Hartshorne, Charles. *Man's Vision of God and the Logic of Theism*. New York: Harper and Bros., 1941.

Heidegger, *Being and Time*. Trans. John Macquarrie and Edward Robinson. New York: Harper and Row, 1962.

———. *Kant and the Problem of Metaphysics*. Trans. J. S. Churchill. Bloomington: Indiana University Press, 1962.

———. *The Metaphysical Foundations of Logic*. Trans. Michael Heim. Bloomington: Indiana University Press, 1984.

———. *The Question Concerning Technology*. Trans. William Lovitt. New York: Harper and Row, 1977.

———. *Sein und Zeit*. 7th ed. Tübingen: Max Niemeyer, 1957.

———. *Vom Wesen des Grundes*. 5th ed. Frankfurt: Vittorio Klostermann, 1965.

———. *What Is a Thing?* Trans. W. B. Barton Jr. and Vera Deutsch. Chicago: Henry Regnery, 1967.

Hume, David. *An Enquiry Concerning Human Understanding*. Ed. L. A. Selby-Bigge. 2d ed., rev. P. H. Nidditch. Oxford: Clarendon, 1978.

James, William. *A Pluralistic Universe*. New York: Longmans, Green, 1909.

———. *Principles of Psychology*. 2 vols. New York: Henry Holt, 1890.

Kant, *Anthropology From a Pragmatic Point of View*. Trans. Mary J. Gregor. The Hague: Martinus Nijhoff, 1974.

———. *Critique of Judgement*. Trans. James Creed Meredith. Oxford: Clarendon, 1928.

———. *Critique of Practical Reason and Other Writings in Moral Philosophy*. Ed. and trans. Lewis White Beck. Chicago: University of Chicago Press, 1949.

———. *Critique of Pure Reason*. Trans. Norman Kemp Smith. New York: St. Martin's Press, 1929.

———. *Groundwork of the Metaphysics of Morals*. Trans. H. J. Paton. New York: Harper and Row, 1964.

———. *Logic*. Trans. R. Hartmann and W. Schwartz. Indianapolis: Bobbs-Merrill, 1974.

———. *Metaphysical Elements of Justice*. Trans. J. Ladd. Indianapolis: Bobbs-Merrill, 1965.

———. *Religion Within the Limits of Reason Alone*. Trans. T. M. Greene and H. H. Hudson. Chicago: Open Court, 1934.

Kuhn, Thomas S. *The Structure of Scientific Revolutions*. Chicago: University of Chicago Press, 1970.

Leibniz, Gottfried Wilhelm. *Leibniz Selections.* Ed. Philip P. Weiner. New York: Charles Scribner's Sons, 1951.

———. *The Leibniz-Clarke Correspondence, Together with Extracts from Newton's Principia and Opticks.* Ed. H. G. Alexander. Manchester: Manchester University Press, 1956.

———. *Monadology and Other Philosophical Essays.* Ed. P. Schrecker and A. Schrecker. Indianapolis: Bobbs-Merrill, 1965.

———. *New Essays Concerning Human Understanding.* Trans. A. G. Langley. LaSalle, Ill.: Open Court, 1949.

———. *The Political Writings of Leibniz.* Trans. and ed. Patrick Riley. Cambridge: Cambridge University Press, 1972.

Locke, John. *Essay Concerning Human Understanding.* Ed. A. C. Fraser. 2 vols. New York: Dover, 1894.

Lotze, Rudolf Hermann. *Metaphysic.* Trans. and ed. Bernard Bosanquet. 2d ed. Oxford: Oxford University Press, 1887.

Machiavelli, Niccolò. *Discourses on the First Ten Books of Titus Livius.* In *The Prince and The Discourses.* Trans. Mark Musa. New York: Modern Library, 1950.

Mill, John Stuart. *Theism.* Indianapolis: Bobbs-Merrill, 1957.

Montesquieu, Charles-Louis de Secondat, Baron de. *The Spirit of the Laws: A Compendium of the First English Edition.* Berkeley: University of California Press, 1977.

Mosca, Gaetano. *The Ruling Class.* Trans. H. D. Kahn. New York: McGraw Hill, 1939.

Paton, H. J., *Kant's Metaphysic of Experience.* London: George Allen and Unwin, 1961.

Peirce, Charles Sanders. *Collected Papers of Charles Sanders Peirce.* 6 vols. Ed. Charles Hartshorne and Paul Weiss. Cambridge: Harvard University Press, 1934.

———. *Values in a Universe of Chance: Selected Writings of Charles S. Peirce.* Ed. Philip P. Weiner. New York: Doubleday, 1958.

Plato. *Theaetetus.*

Plotinus. *Enneads.* Trans. Stephen MacKenna. 4th ed., rev. New York: Pantheon, 1969.

Ricoeur, Paul. *History and Truth.* Trans. C. A. Kelbley. Evanston, Ill.: Northwestern University Press, 1965.

———. *Political and Social Essays.* Ed. D. Stewart and J. Bien. Athens: Ohio University Press, 1974.

Rousseau, Jean-Jacques. *Of the Social Contract.* Trans. and ed. Charles M. Sherover. New York: Harper and Row, 1984.

Royce, Josiah. *Outlines of Psychology.* New York: Macmillan, 1903.

———. *The Problem of Christianity.* New York: Macmillan, 1913.

———. *Studies of Good and Evil.* New York: D. Appleton, 1908.

———. *The World and the Individual.* 2 vols. New York: Macmillan, 1904.

Santayana, George. *Skepticism and Animal Faith.* New York: Dover, 1955.

Sartre, Jean-Paul. "Existentialism is a Humanism." In *Existentialism from Dosto-evsky to Sartre*. Ed. Walter Kaufmann. Rev. ed. New York: New American Library, 1975.

Sherover, Charles M. *Heidegger, Kant, and Time*. Bloomington: Indiana University Press, 1971.

————. "Kant's Transcendental Object and Heidegger's *Nichts*," *Journal of the History of Philosophy* 7 (October 1969): 413–22.

————. *Time, Freedom, and the Common Good*. Albany: State University of New York Press, 1989.

————, ed. *The Human Experience of Time: The Development of Its Philosophic Meaning*. Evanston, Ill.: Northwestern University Press, 2001.

Thucydides. *History of the Peloponnesian War*. Trans. Rex Warner. London: Penguin Books, 1954.

Tillich, Paul. *Dynamics of Faith*. New York: Harper and Row, 1958.

Tocqueville, Alexis de. *Democracy in America*. Ed. P. Bradley. New York: Knopf, 1980.

Walsh, W. H., *Kant's Criticism of Metaphysics*. Chicago: University of Chicago Press, 1975.

Whitehead, Alfred North. *The Concept of Nature*. Ann Arbor: University of Michigan Press, 1957.

————. *Religion in the Making*. New York: Macmillan, 1926.

Index of Names

Acton, John Emerich Edward
  Dalberg-Acton, Baron, 175
Anaxagoras, 8, 158, 211n. 17
Anselm, 85, 87
Aquinas, Thomas, 76, 209n. 11
Aristotle, xvi, 4, 6, 7, 8–9, 14, 26, 38, 54,
  86, 98, 100, 108, 128, 142, 155,
  163–65, 166, 168, 170, 173, 175, 180,
  184, 187, 188, 208n. 5, 209n. 12,
  212n. 10, 214n. 9, 216n. 24, 217n. 6
Augustine, Saint, xii, 10–13, 20, 69, 77,
  150, 210n. 1

Berdyaev, Nicolas, 18, 210n. 18
Bergson, Henri, xi, xiv, 17–18, 24, 98, 126
Berkeley, George, 35
Berlin, Isaiah, 217–18n. 9
Burke, Edmund, 191

Channing, William Ellery, 88, 210n. 18
Cicero, Marcus Tullius, 173
Collingwood, R. G., 95
Copernicus, Nicolaus, 76

Darwin, Charles, 75
Descartes, René, xiv-xv, 15, 24, 37–40, 42,
  45, 46, 47, 77, 87, 95, 120, 123–25,
  134–35, 136–37, 138, 140, 143–44,
  150–51, 169, 213nn. 1–3
Dewey, John, 13, 24, 103, 126, 133, 159,
  173, 202
Duns Scotus, John, 108

Emerson, Ralph Waldo, 19, 159
Empedocles, 158, 211n. 17

Fagg, Lawrence, xix
Fichte, Gottlob, 16–17
Fraser, J. T., xix

Galileo, 75, 76, 123–25
Green, T. H., 217n. 9
Griffin, Donald R., 214n. 8

Hamilton, Alexander, 172, 180, 193
Hartshorne, Charles, xi, 19, 210n. 15
Hegel, Georg Wilhelm Friedrich, 16–17,
  103, 170, 172
Heidegger, Martin, xi, xiii, 18, 24, 67, 82,
  84, 99, 103, 106, 108, 117, 126, 147,
  151, 157, 167, 169–70, 173, 202, 205,
  209nn. 7, 9, 212n. 12, 213n. 1, 214n.
  13, 216–17n. 26
Heraclitus, xi, 4, 5, 6, 7, 156, 158
Hobbes, Thomas, 172, 176, 177
Hopkins, Jeannette, 209
Hume, David, 113, 140
Husserl, Edmund, 18, 24, 98, 126

James, William, xiv, 13, 19, 23, 24, 72, 84,
  87, 98, 106, 107, 116, 126, 147, 198,
  201, 212n. 9

Kant, Immanuel, xi, xii–xiii, xiv, xv,
  16–17, 24, 25, 31–51, 52–68, 70, 77,
  84, 87, 88, 98, 100–1, 103, 105, 106,
  107, 116, 117, 125–26, 137, 138, 140,
  144, 148, 151, 154, 157, 167–68, 171,
  173, 188, 206nn. 17, 26, 27, 207n. 4,
  208nn. 10, 12, 211n. 7, 212n. 9,
  213nn. 2, 10, 214n. 2, 215nn. 11, 14,
  216nn. 18, 22, 26
Kepler, Johannes, 76
Kuhn, Thomas S., 77

Lawrence, N., 207n. 4
Leibniz, Gottfried Wilhelm, xi, xiv,
  15–16, 38, 43, 45, 46, 50, 55, 67, 77,
  87, 98, 101–2, 103, 107, 116, 117,

225